TARGET
FCE

STUDENT'S BOOK

Bess Bradfield

www.richmondelt.com/exams

Contents

 # Introduction

About *FCE*

FCE (First Certificate in English) is an exam set by the University of Cambridge ESOL examinations. If you pass, you will get a qualification which shows that you have an upper-intermediate level of English and that you can:

- use English in a range of situations with native or non-native speakers
- understand written texts such as letters, newspaper articles and fiction
- understand spoken English in a range of situations such as extracts from the radio, and talks and interviews
- pick out factual detail and identify opinion and attitudes from longer reading and listening texts
- follow instructions and ask and answer questions appropriately
- express opinions and offer advice
- take part in a conversation on a wide range of topics
- make notes in English while somebody is talking in English.

About *Target FCE*

Target FCE will help you improve your English, practise the question types used in *FCE*, and develop the skills you need to pass the exam. Each of the 12 units in the book looks at one of the topics that could appear in the exam, and contains sections on grammar, vocabulary and word building, as well as realistic exam practice on all five papers.

Exam practice

Each unit includes work on all five exam papers, so there are plenty of opportunities to practise every part of the exam. The exam tasks are supported by *Exam tips*, which give you helpful hints on how to do that task. The *Workbook* contains lots more exam practice questions.

Language focus and Vocabulary

Each unit introduces and re-uses important topic vocabulary. The *Grammar* and *Word building* sections systematically practise the key language areas you could need for the exam. There is also a *Language summary* section at the back of the book (pages 156 to 167), which looks at the language points covered in the lessons in more detail. You can get further practice of the language points and vocabulary in the *Workbook* and in the *On target?* review units.

The CD-ROM Exam Trainer

There are two ways you can use the CD-ROM. You can do a normal practice test under exam conditions, or you can use the *Exam trainer* to get extra tips and advice about how to do each question. You can also print out your scores to see how you improve while you are studying.

The format of the exam

Paper	Part	Number of questions / timing	Task type
1 Reading *1 hour*	Part 1	8	Multiple choice
	Part 2	7	Gapped text
	Part 3	15	Multiple matching
2 Writing *1 hour 20 minutes*	Part 1	1	Compulsory task
	Part 2	1	Choice of five tasks
3 Use of English *45 minutes*	Part 1	12	Multiple-choice cloze
	Part 2	12	Open cloze
	Part 3	10	Word formation
	Part 4	8	Key word transformation
4 Listening *approx. 45 minutes*	Part 1	8	Multiple choice (discrete items)
	Part 2	10	Sentence completion
	Part 3	5	Multiple matching
	Part 4	7	Multiple choice (long text)
5 Speaking *14 minutes*	Part 1	3 minutes	Interview
	Part 2	3 minutes	Long turn
	Part 3	3 minutes	Collaborative task
	Part 4	4 minutes	Discussion

1

ur life

UNIT TARGETS

Topic vocabulary: family and friends ● home life ● free time
Grammar: present tense review ● past simple ● *used to* and *would*
Word building: adjective suffixes ● verb patterns (1) ● *-ed* and *-ing* adjectives
Writing: an informal email ● linkers (1)
Exam preparation: Reading Part 1 ● Use of English Parts 2 and 3 ● Listening Part 1 ● Speaking Part 1 ● Writing Part 1

Family and friends

1 In pairs, discuss photos A–C and say why you think people might keep these photos.

> **Useful language**
> As far as I can tell, the photo shows ...
> One possibility is that ...
> It looks as if / though they're ...
> People may / might / could / would keep this because ...

2 What do you think the relationship is between the people in each photo?

I think that this woman is the bride's new mother-in-law.

3 Think about the people in your life. Write down the name of a person you associate with each of the illustrations. Don't spend too long thinking!

1  2

3  4

4 🔊 1.1 Listen to someone explain what the illustrations mean, then tell your partner whether you *agree* or *disagree* with the explanations and why.

5 🔊 1.1 Listen again and complete phrases 1–8.

1 someone you **get on** _____ with
2 you **enjoy** _____ other's company
3 you might not **have a lot** _____ **common with** them
4 someone who **drives** you _____
5 this is someone you **look** _____ **to**
6 someone you **take** _____ in your family
7 a person you've **fallen** _____ **love with**
8 someone you **feel really close** _____

Word boost ▶ Family and friends ▶ Workbook p. 4

Over to you!

6 Choose **five** expressions from Activity 5 and match them to different people in your life. In pairs, take it in turns to describe each person, giving details.

7 How good a listener were you? Write one sentence about each of your partner's 'important people'. Then compare sentences. Did you remember correctly?

1 Describe the photos and answer the questions.

  1 What kind of people do you think live in these homes?

  2 Which home would you prefer to live in? Why?

3 For questions 1–8, choose the answer (**A**, **B**, **C** or **D**) which you think fits best according to the text. Question one has been given as an example.

1 What advantage did Bill's parents have?

  A They came from wealthy families.

  Ⓑ Their income was higher than the average.

  C They lived close to the people they worked with.

  D Their house was the largest in Des Moines.

2 As a boy, what did Bill think of his brother and sister?

  A They did not enjoy his company.

  B They did not seem like children to him.

  C They preferred to spend time with adults.

  D They did not want to get to know him fully.

3 What do we learn about Michael in paragraph 2?

  A He had some very untidy habits at home.

  B He found sharing a room inconvenient.

  C He was proud of his collection of handkerchiefs.

  D Bill was very sympathetic about Michael's illnesses.

4 What does 'was not her strong suit' mean in line 25?

  A was not something she did often

  B was something she complained about

  C was not something she did well

  D was her least favourite thing

5 Bill suggests that dinner was usually late because his mother

  A got caught up in other tasks.

  B never finished all the housework.

  C often forgot to prepare any food.

  D spent too long shopping after work.

6 How did Mrs Bryson feel about the food she prepared?

  A She was extremely embarrassed about it.

  B She did not expect her family to eat it.

  C She had a worse opinion of it than her son did.

  D She did not think it was too badly burned to eat.

7 Why does Bill think that his parents got on so well?

  A Mr Bryson enjoyed eating over cooked food.

  B Mrs Bryson did not notice that her husband hated the food.

  C Mr Bryson forgave his wife for her terrible cooking.

  D Mr and Mrs Bryson both enjoyed food with strong flavours.

8 Bill was interested in his mother's magazines because

  A he didn't have very much to do at home.

  B he was keen to learn more about his mother's work.

  C they showed him a very different way of life.

  D he wanted to learn how to look after a house properly.

Exam practice

Reading Part 1: *checking context*   **Exam tip**

When you have to read a long text for a Part 1 task, don't panic!

➤ Read the text first and try to work out the gist (general meaning) of each paragraph. You do NOT need to understand every single word in the text.

➤ Read the questions, but not the options. Then read the text again carefully and underline the answers as you find them.

➤ For each question, go back and read the options. Choose the one which best matches the evidence in the text.

2 Read the extract from an autobiography quickly for gist and find **two** similarities or differences between the writer's home and your own. Tell your partner about them.

Life and Times of the Thunderbolt Kid

.... by Bill Bryson

Because my parents both worked we were better off than most people of our socio-economic background (which in Des Moines in the 1950s was most people). We – that is to say, my parents, my brother Michael, my sister Mary Elizabeth (or Betty) and I – had a bigger house on a larger lot than most of my parents' colleagues. It was a white clapboard house with black shutters and a big screened porch atop a shady hill on the best side of town.

My sister and brother were considerably older than I – my sister by six years, my brother by nine – and so were effectively adults from my perspective. They were big enough to be seldom around for most of my childhood. For the first few years of my life, I shared a small bedroom with my brother. We got along fine. My brother had constant colds and allergies, and owned at least four hundred cotton handkerchiefs, which he devotedly filled with great honks and then pushed into any convenient resting place – under the mattress, between sofa cushions, behind the curtains. When I was nine he left for college and a life as a journalist in New York City, never to return permanently, and I had the room to myself after that. But I was still finding his handkerchiefs when I was in high school.

The only downside of my mother's working was that it put a little pressure on her with regard to running the home and particularly with regard to dinner, which frankly was not her strong suit anyway. My mother always ran late and was dangerously forgetful into the bargain. You soon learned to stand aside at about ten to six every evening, for it was then that she would fly in the back door, throw something in the oven, and disappear into some other quarter of the house to embark on the thousand other household tasks that greeted her each evening. In consequence she nearly always forgot about dinner until a point slightly beyond way too late. As a rule you knew it was time to eat when you could hear potatoes exploding in the oven.

We didn't call it the kitchen in our house. We called it the Burns Unit.

'It's a bit burned,' my mother would say apologetically at every meal, presenting you with a piece of meat that looked like something – a much-loved pet perhaps – salvaged from a tragic house fire. 'But I think I scraped off most of the burned part,' she would add, overlooking that this included every bit of it that had once been flesh.

Happily, all this suited my father. His palate only responded to two tastes – burned and ice cream – so everything was fine by him so long as it was sufficiently dark and not too startlingly flavourful. Theirs truly was a marriage made in heaven, for no one could burn food like my mother or eat it like my dad.

As part of her job at the Des Moines Register (the local newspaper) my mother bought stacks of housekeeping magazines – *House Beautiful, House and Garden, Better Homes and Gardens, Good Housekeeping* – and I read these with a certain avidity, partly because they were always lying around and in our house all idle moments were spent reading something, and partly because they depicted lives so absorbingly at variance with our own. The housewives depicted in my mother's magazines were so collected, so organized, so calmly on top of things, and their food was perfect – their lives were perfect. They dressed up to take their food out of the oven! There were no black circles on the ceiling above their stoves, no mutating goo climbing over the sides of their forgotten saucepans. Children didn't have to be ordered to stand back every time they opened their oven doors.

(margin: ne 25)

Vocabulary in context: *home life*

4 In pairs, find words in the text which refer to a) parts of a house, b) household appliances or furniture. How many other words can you think of?

a) shutters (paragraph 1)

5 Write a definition or an example sentence for the following words and expressions in the text:

1 had the room to myself (paragraph 2)
2 always ran late (paragraph 3)
3 overlooking (paragraph 4)
4 into the bargain (paragraph 3)
5 a marriage made in heaven (paragraph 5)

Word boost ▶ Home life ▶ Workbook p. 4

Over to you!

6 What's life like in *your* house? Write 50 words on one of the topics below on a piece of paper. Be as interesting or as funny as possible.

housework mornings mealtime evenings Sundays

Mornings in my house are always a stressful time ...

7 When you've finished, give your description to the teacher. *Don't* write your name.

8 Read the descriptions from the rest of the class and try to match one to each of your classmates.

1 Mrs Bryson wants her family to help her make dinner, but everyone has an excuse! In pairs, decide which is the best / worst excuse. Do you ever help out at home?

1 Don't ask me - I **help** with dinner nearly every evening!
2 **Have** you ever **tried** my cooking? It's terrible!
3 **I'm doing** my homework at the moment.
4 **I've been working** since 7:00. I need a rest!
5 **I've** already **had** a sandwich, so I'm not hungry.
6 I **don't live** here - I'm just visiting!

2 Complete gaps 1-4 in the table with the tenses in the box. Then match uses A-F to examples 1-6 in Activity 1.

present continuous   present simple   present perfect

Present tense review

1	A	unchanging or permanent present situations
	B	regular or repeated actions
2	C	changing or temporary present situations
3	D	past actions or situations that don't specify a time
	E	past actions with a present result
4	F	actions that started in the past and continue into the present

Watch out! stative verbs

We don't usually use a continuous form with certain verbs used to describe states (*be*, *like*, etc.).

I hate cooking. **NOT** ~~I am hating cooking.~~

Language summary ▶ p. 156

3 Work in pairs and write the correct present form of the verbs. Have you ever used excuses like these?

1 **A:** At last, you (**arrive**)! I (**wait**) here all morning!
   B: Sorry I (**be**) late. I overslept.
2 **A:** (**you / do**) anything at the moment? Can you help me tidy up?
   B: Er … we (**do**) a project for school. Sorry, it (**be**) really important.
3 **A:** Carla, hurry up! You (**get**) ready for hours!
   B: I (**come**)! It (**take**) effort to look this good, you know.
4 **A:** Listen! They (**play**) my favourite song! (**you / want**) to dance?
   B: So sorry, but I (**hurt**) my leg, so I can't dance. Otherwise I'd love to!

4 In pairs, look at the sentences and label the timelines with the correct tenses. Explain the difference in meaning between sentences A and B.

A I **lived** there last summer.
B I**'ve been** living there for years.

Present perfect vs past simple

tense	past	present
1	▼	
2	∿∿∿∿	→

Language summary ▶ p. 156

5 Work in pairs. Write excuses for people in the following situations! Include at least four of the words in the list.

ago   already   for   since   last   then

1 you don't want to go out with your friends tonight
   *Sorry but I've **already** got plans. I promised to babysit ages **ago**.*
2 you were late home last night
3 you missed your last English lesson
4 you forgot it was your friend's birthday yesterday

Over to you!

6 Imagine you are going to interview someone for a programme called *Your Home, Your Life*. Prepare six interesting questions to ask, including a range of tenses.

Student A: You will interview the person in photo A.
Student B: You will interview the person in photo B.

7 Take turns to interview each other. Answer the questions as if you were the person in the photo. Then decide which person you would most like to meet and why.

Get ready: *used to* and *would*

1 Read the quotations. Has Liz and Danny's relationship got better or worse?

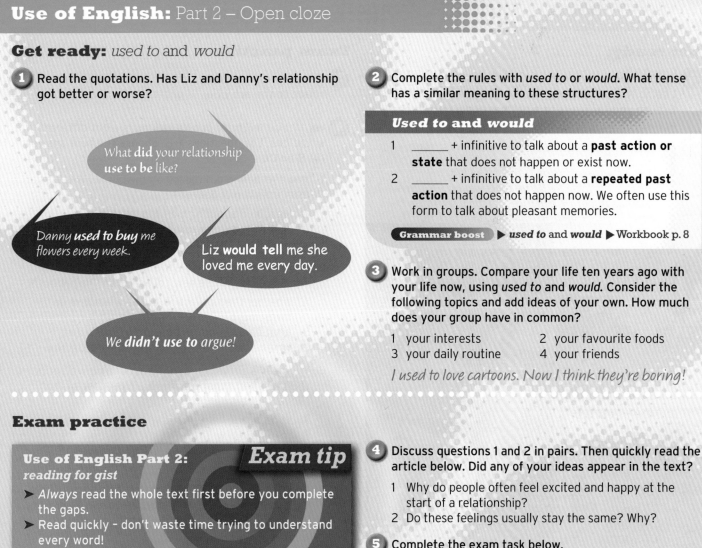

What **did** your relationship **use to be** like?

Danny **used to buy** me flowers every week.

Liz **would tell** me she loved me every day.

We **didn't use to** argue!

2 Complete the rules with *used to* or *would*. What tense has a similar meaning to these structures?

Used to and would

1 _____ + infinitive to talk about a **past action or state** that does not happen or exist now.

2 _____ + infinitive to talk about a **repeated past action** that does not happen now. We often use this form to talk about pleasant memories.

Grammar boost ▶ *used to* and *would* ▶ Workbook p. 8

3 Work in groups. Compare your life ten years ago with your life now, using *used to* and *would*. Consider the following topics and add ideas of your own. How much does your group have in common?

1 your interests   2 your favourite foods
3 your daily routine   4 your friends

I used to love cartoons. Now I think they're boring!

Exam practice

Use of English Part 2: reading for gist

Exam tip

➤ *Always* read the whole text first before you complete the gaps.
➤ Read quickly – don't waste time trying to understand every word!
➤ Think about the general meaning of the text when you choose your answers.

4 Discuss questions 1 and 2 in pairs. Then quickly read the article below. Did any of your ideas appear in the text?

1 Why do people often feel excited and happy at the start of a relationship?
2 Do these feelings usually stay the same? Why?

5 Complete the exam task below.

For questions **1–12**, read the text below and think of the word which best fits each gap. Use only **one** word in each gap. There is an example at the beginning **(0)**.

Write your answers IN CAPITAL LETTERS.

Love and relationships

In the past, the first stages **(0)** ......*OF*...... love were often described as 'lovesickness', and many people **(1)** .... to believe that love was a kind of madness! However, **(2)** .... could be a rational, scientific explanation for the intense feelings we experience when we fall **(3)** .... love. Studies suggest that, when we are beginning a relationship, our brains produce a hormone called dopamine which causes us to feel great joy and excitement. But watch out: this doesn't last! **(4)** .... about a year, levels of the hormone recede, and we return to our usual emotional levels.

So **(5)** .... don't all relationships fall apart at that point? Luckily, it seems that a year is just enough time for couples to find out how well they get **(6)** .... with their partners, and how much they enjoy **(7)** .... other's company. As a result, new bonds of love, affection and friendship are created which can last a lifetime. According to May Wilks, who **(8)** .... been happily married to Jack **(9)** .... seventy-eight years, 'true love takes work. When we were first dating, Jack used **(10)** .... buy me flowers every week, and he **(11)** .... walk me home every evening after work. He's just as kind and loving today. Now I'm 106, Jack still tells me every day **(12)** .... beautiful I am! I couldn't be any happier.'

Get ready: *free time*

1 Look at the photos and rank the activities from 1–4, with 1 being the activity you would enjoy doing the most. Explain your answers to a partner and agree on one activity to do together tomorrow.

Useful language

I can't stand ... / I (don't) fancy (+ -ing) ...
I absolutely love ... / I'd be really up for (+ -ing) ...
I'd much rather (+ infinitive) ... than ... because ...

2 In pairs, complete the table. Can you add any more expressions? Find three people in the room who share one of your interests.

a bike ride   computer games   a concert   ~~a crossword~~
a (youth) club   dancing   a drive   the guitar
a puzzle   a quiet night in   a walk   the beach
some friends round   shopping   swimming   yoga

staying in		going out	
do	*a crossword*	go	
have		go for	
play		go to	

Word boost ▶ Free time ▶ Workbook p. 4

Exam tip

Listening Part 1:
preparing to listen
You will hear different speakers talking on a range of topics. Before you listen:
➤ read each question and option carefully and try to predict the topics you will hear.
➤ underline any key words in the question.

Exam practice

3 Read the exam task in Activity 4. Find questions which relate to the activities in photos A–D.

4 🔊 1.2 You will hear people talking in eight different situations. For questions **1–8, c**hoose the best answer (**A, B** or **C**).

1 You overhear a girl talking on the phone. What is her main criticism of Steve?

   A He talked about himself too much.
   B He told too many jokes.
   C He did not share her interests.

2 You hear a man talking about starting a collection. What does he advise new collectors to think about?

   A whether their collection will be a worthwhile investment
   B what kind of objects they are interested in
   C whether it will be easy to start their collection

3 You hear a girl telling a friend about a conversation she's just had. What was the main purpose of the conversation?

   A to persuade her parents to allow her to have a party
   B to explain how tired and stressed she'd been feeling
   C to suggest that the family spend more time together

4 You hear a student talking on the radio about a type of puzzle called sudoku. Why does he advise people not to try it?

   A It is very addictive.
   B It is less interesting than other hobbies.
   C It does not require any special skills.

5 You hear a woman talking about her hobby of bird watching. What is the most important thing people can do for birds?

   A grow special trees and plants
   B keep cats out of the garden
   C put out water for them

6 On the radio, you hear a man talking about music. What is he doing?

   A talking about his family's musical interests
   B explaining how difficult it is to make money from music
   C describing the background to his career in music

7 You overhear a couple talking about their free time. What do they agree about?

   A They watch too much television.
   B They need to do something different.
   C They are going to go cycling.

8 You hear a woman talking about her hobby. Why did she start riding?

   A She wanted to take up a sport.
   B She was passionate about horses.
   C She wanted to help her friend.

A

B

C

D

1 Look at the photos. Which activities do you do? Who do you usually do them with? Are there any activities you *never* do? Why?

2 Work in pairs. Match the pairs of questions 1–3 with the headings in the list. Then write **one** more question for each category.

Home life   Leisure time   Likes and dislikes

1 _____
   a   Do you prefer spending time alone or with other people? (Why?)
   b   What is your favourite part of the day? (Why?)

2 _____
   c   How much time do you usually spend at home? (What do you usually do?)
   d   Could you tell me something about your family?

3 _____
   e   Do you play any sports or games? (What do you play?)
   f   Do any of your friends have an interesting hobby? (What does she / he do?)

3 🔊 1.3 Listen to six people answering the questions in Activity 2. Which questions are they responding to? Match speakers 1–6 to questions a–f.

Exam practice

> **Speaking Part 1:**
> *personal preferences*
>
> ### Exam tip
>
> In Part 1 you will answer questions about yourself. Try to make your answers as interesting as possible!
> ➤ Use a variety of expressions to talk about your likes, dislikes and interests: don't just say *I like* or *I don't like*.
> ➤ Expand your ideas by giving reasons for your opinions, or by giving examples.
>
> *I can't get enough of … , because it's …*
> *I've always had a passion for … , Last year, I …*

4 🔊 1.3 Listen again and complete the phrases for talking about likes and dislikes. Write the name or speaker number of the person who gives these opinions.

Person	Opinion
1	I absolutely _____ sailing
2	I'm _____ graphic novels (=comics)
3	is really interested _____ spiders
4	I'm not keen _____ sport
5	I'd probably _____ be with friends

5 Work in pairs. How many more useful expressions can you think of for talking about likes, dislikes and preferences?

6 Ask and answer the questions in Activity 2 with your partner.

Adjective suffixes

1 We can add suffixes (=*endings*) to some nouns and verbs to change them into adjectives. In groups, add one more example for each suffix. Can you think of any more adjective suffixes?

suffix	example
-able	rely → reliable
-al	music → musical
-ent	excel → excellent
-ful	hope → hopeful (*full of hope*)
-ic	artist → artistic
-ish	child → childish
-ive	act → active
-less	hope → hopeless (*without hope*)
-ous	glamour → glamorous
-y	sport → sporty

2 In pairs, write the correct adjective form of the words in **bold**.

The Simpsons
family profile

MATT GROENING

The Simpsons are one of the world's most (**1** _____ fame) families! As well as baby Maggie, they consist of:

Marge (the mother) – the most (**2** _____ depend) person in the household, Marge is a (**3** _____ help) and loving Mum. She's always very (**4** _____ protect) of her family – even when they get into trouble!

Homer (the dad) – (**5** _____ greed), lazy and (**6** _____ care) at work, Homer isn't a great role model as a dad! He is often (**7** _____ self), but, in the end, his love for his family always wins out.

Bart (the son) – the star of the show for many people, Bart is loud, rude and (**8** _____ mischief). A (**9** _____ nature) comedian, he's fortunately also very (**10** _____ like) and funny too!

Lisa (the daughter) – completely (**11** _____ differ) from Bart, Lisa is very clever and (**12** _____ knowledge). Highly (**13** _____ success) at school, Lisa is the brains of the family! She's (**14** _____ hero) in defending her moral and (**15** _____ politics) beliefs, although she can be self-righteous at times.

Verb patterns (1): *verbs + infinitive / gerund*

3 Read the profiles from the website *Friends Online*. Which person would you most like to reply to? Why?

◁ ▷

Basia, 16, Poland

I'm a creative, artistic person who <u>likes reading</u> and drawing, and loves playing the guitar. I want to study music at university – if I manage to pass my exams! This year I've decided to learn more about music, art and literature from other countries, so please get in touch if you share any of these interests. I look forward to hearing from you – I promise to reply to every email.

. . . .

Diego, 18, Argentina

I'm a very sporty, active person. I love to play football and go surfing. I also really enjoy skateboarding, although I'm not very good. I've given up doing tricks – I keep falling off! What else? Oh yes, I'm interested in lots of other things, like computer games and TV, but I can't stand shopping! I'd really like to hear from people who are into the same stuff. I hope to hear from you soon.

4 <u>Underline</u> all the examples of verb/expression + *to* infinitive OR verb/expression + gerund (*-ing* form).

5 In pairs, complete the table with expressions from Activity 4 and the list below. Can you add any more?

agree   can't help   don't mind   give up   hate
practise   prefer   pretend   seem   start

+ *to* infinitive	+ gerund	+ gerund OR *to* infinitive
		like

Over to you!

6 Write a short profile of yourself for the *Friends Online* website. Use at least **two** adjectives formed with the suffixes in Activity 1 and at least **five** verbs or expressions followed by *to* + infinitive or a gerund.

7 Read the other students' profiles and decide which **three** people you have the most in common with!

Word boost ▶ Workbook p. 76

Get ready: *-ed* and *-ing* adjectives

1 In sentences 1 and 2, which adjective is used to talk about a) how we feel, b) how something makes us feel?

1 My family is boring! 2 I'm bored by my family.

2 Complete the sentences with the correct *-ing* or *-ed* form of *embarrass-*, *excit-* or *tir-*.

1 When my mum turned up at the party, I was really _____ . Everyone laughed.
2 We were all really _____ when our sister married the pop star. We hoped we'd become famous too!
3 I felt so _____ after looking after my nieces all day, I went to bed early.
4 Going shopping with my mum is quite _____ . She never stops!
5 Dad, please stop dancing! It's so _____ . You look ridiculous.
6 Having a famous parent would be really _____ . Life would certainly be out of the ordinary!

3 In pairs, talk about how you would feel in the following situations. Use *-ed* and *-ing* adjectives.

1 Your dad wants you to help him do some gardening.

*"I'd be really **annoyed**. Gardening is **boring**!"*

2 Your elderly relatives are coming to stay with you for a week.
3 You're doing your homework when a friend phones you for a chat.
4 Your mum buys you some computer games for your birthday.
5 You're home alone when you hear a strange noise.

Word boost ▶ *-ed* and *-ing* adjectives ▶ Workbook p. 5

Exam practice

4 Read the exam task, ignoring the gaps. What are the disadvantages of having a celebrity parent?

5 Complete the exam task.

> **Use of English Part 3:** *the stem word* **Exam tip**
>
> When you complete a gap, remember that:
> ➤ you must *always* change the stem word.
> ➤ you may need to add a suffix, a prefix or both to the stem word, or make internal changes to the spelling.

For questions **1–10**, read the text below. Use the word given in capitals at the end of some of the lines to form a word that fits in the gap **in the same line**. There is an example at the beginning **(0)**.
Write your answers IN CAPITAL LETTERS.

Celebrity parents

For many people, having a **(0)** ....*FAMOUS*.... parent would be a dream come true. Imagine introducing Ronaldinho or Keira Knightley to your friends! Think about the glamorous lifestyle you'd lead, and all the wild, **(1)** .... parties you'd go to! — **FAME**

— **EXCITE**

But celebrity families aren't **(2)** .... fun. For a start, stars don't make the most **(3)** .... parents. For some, their career will always come first. Then, there's all the **(4)** .... from the press. Growing up is often hard: but think about how **(5)** .... you'd feel if you had to read about your mistakes in the news! And last but not least, celebrity children come under huge pressure to — **NECESSARY** **DEPEND** **ATTEND** **EMBARRASS**

— **FASCINATE** **CONTINUAL**

be beautiful, **(6)** .... and talented. After all, they know that people are **(7)** .... comparing them to their mums or dads!

When you read the latest gossip about Jack Osbourne or Paris Hilton (son of a heavy metal singer and daughter of a highly **(8)** .... businessman, respectively), you get the **(9)** .... that life as a celebrity's child brings a lot of problems too. So, maybe the press is being **(10)** .... when it mocks famous offspring. Maybe we should show them more sympathy! — **SUCCESS** **IMPRESS** **KIND**

Prepare

1 In pairs, discuss the questions.
1 How often do you email your friends and family?
2 What kind of things do you usually write about?

Analyse the task

2 Read the task below, then read Mark's email. Which of these things should you do in your reply?

☐ use linkers to connect ideas
☐ organise your work into paragraphs
☐ write about all the notes
☐ copy language from Mark's email
☐ use formal language
☐ use contractions (*I'm*, *it's*)

> Your English-speaking friend, Mark, has written you an email. Read Mark's email and the notes you have made. Then write an email to Mark, using **all** your notes. Write **120–150** words in an appropriate style.

3 Read the example task and model answer in the Writing reference on pages 168-9 and check your answers to Activity 2.

Mark
8th September
Re: Hello!

Sorry I haven't replied sooner! I went to visit my cousins at the weekend (the ones who live on the coast). What did you get up to?

1 Tell him

You'll have to meet my cousins some time, because I think you'd like them! They're both really energetic, fun people, and they're always having crazy adventures. They're coming to visit next month. Maybe you could visit then too?

2 Apologise and say why not

My cousins gave me a few surfing lessons at the beach, but as you can see, I wasn't very good! Have you ever been surfing? I love it, it's really exciting! What kinds of things are you into?

3 No, because ...

4 Give examples

Anyway, I'd better go. I need to get ready for college, so I'll call you later!

Mark

Improve your writing:

linkers (1): basic linkers

When you are writing it is important to link your ideas in a clear and logical way. Some of the most basic linkers are *and, or, so, but* and *because* but many more are possible!

4 Which linkers can you find in Mark's email? How many other linkers can you think of?

5 Work in pairs and join the sentences in 1–6 in as many different ways as possible. Use the linkers above or your own ideas. Does the meaning change when you use different linkers?

1 My brothers and I fell out. We'd had a huge argument.

My brothers and I fell out as a result of a huge argument.

2 I get on like a house on fire with my mum. My dad never listens to me.
3 My best friend is my next-door neighbour. This means I see him every day.
4 Do you take after your dad? Do you resemble your mum?
5 The door of my house is blue. The shutters are also painted blue.
6 I don't talk to my ex-girlfriend often. She drives me mad.

6 Read the mini-profile below. What do the linkers *and, also, as well* and *too* have in common? Where do we usually put these linkers in a sentence?

I'm obsessed with surfing and swimming and I'm really into skateboarding as well. My sister is also pretty keen on skateboarding. She's mad about football too.

7 Think of at least two interesting things to say about topics 1–4. Write three sentences, connecting your ideas with different linkers. When you've finished, explain your sentences to a partner. Which topic would they like to learn more about? Give them more details.

1 a person who's sometimes annoying

My brother's sometimes annoying. He's really mischievous, and he often gets me into trouble too! I wish he would calm down, because sometimes he gets on my nerves!

2 a place where I feel relaxed
3 an activity I can't stand doing
4 something I wouldn't want to live without

Ready to write!

8 You are going to do the task in Activity 2. Read Mark's email and the notes again. Which note or notes ask(s) you to:

1 give a reason?
2 talk about your interests?
3 say sorry?
4 give a description?

9 Read the *Exam tip* and brainstorm ideas for each note. Look at the ideas in the table to help you.

Exam tip

Writing Part 1:
understanding the task

Always read the prompt material and all the notes carefully *before* you start writing. Think about:
➤ who is writing to you: a friend or a stranger? Should your reply be formal or informal?
➤ what type of answer you need to write for each note. Do you need to give information, apologise, or make a request?
➤ how you can complete the task as fully as possible. Brainstorm ideas for each note before you write.

Writing reference ➤ p. 168

Notes	Example ideas	Your own ideas
1	my brother came to stay went to the cinema	
2	away on holiday revising for exams	
3	can't swim hate sport	
4	going for bike rides watching films	

10 Write your email, using ideas from Activity 9. Remember to respond to all of the notes.

11 Look at the checklist on page 169. Check your email and make any corrections.

Unit 1

1 Complete the text. Write the correct form of the verbs.

Our best friends?

Many people's idea of 'family' (**0** _includes_ **include**) a small four-legged pet – usually a cat or a dog. At the moment, there (**1** _____ **be / already**) more dogs and cats than people on the planet, and the number (**2** _____ **grow**). Today, the USA, China and Brazil (**3** _____ **have**) the biggest dog and cat populations in the world. Since 1998, the number of dogs and cats in Brazil (**4** _____ **rise**) by over 30%!

Our attitudes to animals have changed. People (**5** _____ **not / used to / think**) of dogs and cats as 'pets'. In the past, people (**6** _____ **keep**) cats because they (**7** _____ **catch**) mice, and dogs were useful because they guarded the house. Today, cats and dogs more closely (**8** _____ **resemble**) family members or friends. The heiress Paris Hilton, who (**9** _____ **buy**) her little dog Tinkerbell to cheer herself up when she felt depressed, (**10** _____ **carry**) her pet everywhere, often dressed in matching outfits and jewels!

2 Write suitable questions for the answers. More than one correct question may be possible.

0 He's got two brothers and a step-sister.

How many brothers and sisters does he have?

1 No, I've never been in love.
2 We've been staying at my mother-in-law's house for three weeks.
3 My grandmother came from Columbia.
4 No, we didn't use to get on at all when we were young!
5 My dad is a very dependable, reliable person.
6 We live in a large white house with a black front porch.

3 Think of a famous person you know well. Complete these sentences as if they were true for this person.

1 At the moment, I'm working ...
2 I often ...
3 I've never ...
4 Before I was famous, I didn't use to ...

4 Choose the correct alternatives.

0 I'm really close **to** / **with** my sister.
1 I don't get on **good** / **well** with my cousin.
2 I can't stand **to do** / **doing** housework.
3 We decided **to get** / **getting** married last year.
4 Can you **do** / **play** this crossword?
5 Granddad's stories are always long and **bored** / **boring**.
6 He really looks **up** / **out** to his mum.
7 We usually **go** / **go for** a walk on Sundays.
8 They had a marriage **done** / **made** in heaven.

5 Choose the correct suffix to form the adjective. For each adjective, write a sentence about someone you know.

0 protect **-al** / **-ive** / **-ous**

My dad is very protective of his family, and he tries to make sure that nothing bad ever happens to us.

1 depend **-able** / **-ed** / **-ful**
2 hero **-al** / **-ic** / **-less**
3 success **-less** / **-ful** / **-able**
4 greed **-ful** / **-y** / **-ous**
5 self **-ish** / **-ive** / **-y**

6 Work in pairs. Write definitions for **six** words or expressions from this unit.

7 Find another pair. Take it in turns to read out your definitions. The other pair has ten seconds to guess the word or phrase. Which pair gets the most correct answers?

UNIT TARGETS

Topic vocabulary: appearance ● personality
● fashion
Grammar: relative clauses ● articles
Word building: compound adjectives ● phrasal verbs (1)
● extreme adjectives
Writing: an article ● punctuation and spelling
Exam preparation: Reading Part 2 ● Use of English
Parts 1 and 4 ● Listening Part 2 ● Speaking Part 2
● Writing Part 2

Appearance

1 Do you recognise any of the people in photos A–D? Why are they famous?

2 In groups, complete the table with the adjectives. Try to add as many extra ideas as you can to each category.

bald   curvy   clean-shaven   dyed   freckled
glamorous   gorgeous   hideous   pale   plump
skinny   slim   stubbly   stunning   tanned   wavy
well-built   wrinkled

hair/ beard	build / size	skin / complexion	general appearance
bald			

3 Take turns to describe people in the photos. After each description, decide as a group how attractive the person is on a scale of 1 to 10. Give reasons for your score.

4 🔊 2.1 You are going to hear a 'face reader' explain what people's faces can reveal about their personality. In pairs, match physical features 1–6 to the people in photos A–D. Then listen and check.

Face reading	what does your face say about you?	
Physical feature	**Person**	**Personal quality**
1 round face	A	lively, extrovert
2 square chin		
3 curly hair		
4 thick eyebrows		
5 wide mouth		
6 large forehead		

5 🔊 2.1 Listen again and complete the third column in the table in Activity 4. Do you agree that people's appearance can tell you about their personality?

Word boost ▶ Appearance ▶ Workbook p. 10

Over to you!

6 Work in pairs. Student A turn to page 149. Student B turn to page 151.

A   B

C   D

1 Look at the photos and discuss the questions in groups.

1 What do you think these people are doing? Why?
2 Do you ever watch shows like these? Why? / Why not?
3 Which show would you most like to appear on? Why?

2 Read the introductory sentence to the article opposite. In groups, discuss what kind of warnings or advice you think Saskia will give.

3 Quickly read the whole article. Were you right?

Exam practice

> ### Reading Part 2:
> *understanding text flow*
>
> **Exam tip**
>
> Try to understand how the text is organised before you complete the gaps.
> ➤ Read the whole text first for gist and work out what the main ideas are in each paragraph.
> ➤ Look at the extracted sentences. Do any of them have similar topics to the paragraphs in the text?
> ➤ Look for links between the grammar and vocabulary in the extracted sentences and in the text. Think carefully about any pronouns (*he, it, this*) or linkers (*however, although*, etc.).

4 Read the article again carefully. In pairs, write one sentence about each paragraph, summarising the main ideas.

Paragraph 1: TV can help people to become successful very quickly.

5 Choose from the sentences A–H the one which fits each gap (1-7). There is one extra sentence which you do not need to use.

A Show business is probably the most competitive industry in the world.

B You could say they're just trying to teach wannabes how to be more realistic about themselves and their abilities.

C They take from them a message that becoming famous is quick and easy.

D Just because someone hasn't got the celebrity factor, it doesn't mean that they haven't got other, more impressive qualities.

E Shows like these mislead people about the reality of fame.

F However, most of them are pretty clueless about how we're meant to achieve this.

G These distinctive personality traits are what keep the media interested.

H In order for us to promote someone effectively, we have to be convinced that they genuinely have something original and exciting to offer.

Vocabulary in context:
personality

6 Find words in the article which mean the opposite of the following adjectives:

Paragraphs 2-5

1 talented
2 hard-working
3 calm
4 sociable
5 ordinary, conventional

Paragraphs 6-7

6 serious
7 modest
8 polite
9 kind
10 sensible

7 In pairs, discuss who your favourite and least favourite celebrities are, giving reasons. Write sentences describing how your partner feels about *two* celebrities.

Word boost ▶ Personality
▶ Workbook p. 10

Whn will I b famous?

So you want to be a star?

Saskia Young, the co-founder of *The Raw Talent Agency*, talks about the dream and the reality of the fame game.

Television can turn yesterday's nobody into a millionaire overnight. Think about Leona Lewis. Before *The X-Factor* she was just another pretty singer. After her win, she released a best-selling debut album and became an international celebrity.

Young people watch reality shows like these and think, 'that could be me'. **[1]** And it certainly seems that way, when even talentless *Big Brother* stars can become rich and famous, apparently overnight. Slogging your way through a long degree or dealing with the stress of job applications lack the appeal of becoming an 'instant' celebrity.

Since founding *The Raw Talent Agency* in 2004, we've seen the number of applicants rocket from a few hundred a year to almost fifty times that. Each young hopeful expects us to transform their lives. **[2]** A depressingly large number of would-be stars don't seem to have any real skills, apart from their own amazing powers of self-deception. One boy, who told us 'I want to be as famous as Brad Pitt', later confessed he hated acting. What's more, he quite cheerfully admitted to being lazy, refusing to take on any job which involved getting up before midday!

As a talent agency, we're not looking for 'wannabes', i.e. people who just want to copy their favourite celebrities. **[3]** And you don't necessarily need to be good-looking to catch our eye. In fact, we often prefer to take on people who aren't conventionally attractive, because they're more likely to stand out and be remembered.

If you look carefully, you'll see that many A-list stars are striking rather than stunning. They're often slightly eccentric too. For example, Angelina Jolie has the reputation for being rather fiery, while Michael Jackson was notoriously

shy. **[4]** Bland people eventually just fade away.

Unfortunately, we do have to reject the majority of applicants. Of course, this can be devastating for some, and I can't say that I enjoy this part of my job. But I always try to offer positive feedback too. **[5]** They might be a very funny or smart person, or maybe they're really creative. It would be a shame to waste these skills on reality TV.

One thing that's a bit different about my agency is that we consider each applicant very carefully on their own unique merits. We try not to be arrogant like the judges on *Pop Idol* or *The X-Factor*! **[6]** However, I can't stand watching people like Simon Cowell being rude to contestants. It's cruel to mock someone for their dreams, however silly they might seem.

The sad truth though, is that not everyone can be 'the next big thing'. For every success story, there are tens of thousands who never become stars. **[7]** To make it to the top, you've usually got to have exceptional talent, work extremely hard, and stay utterly focused. But most of all, you've got to be very, very lucky!

Over to you!

8 Would you like to be famous? Why? / Why not? Tell your partner.

9 Work in groups. You are going to plan your own reality TV show! Decide together:

1 what the show is called.
2 what the people on the show will do.
3 what kind of contestants will take part.
4 what the prize will be.

10 Present your idea to the rest of the class. When all the groups have finished, the class should vote for the idea they would most like to watch on TV!

1 Choose the colour that appeals to you the most. Then read the analysis. Tell your partner whether you agree, explaining why / why not.

A If you picked orange, you're an active, energetic person, **whose** interests include sports and nature.

B White, **which** is a pure colour, appeals to people who like order and logic.

C 'Purples' are deeply spiritual and are fiercely loyal to the people **that** they care about.

D In classrooms and offices, **where** others struggle, bright and ambitious 'yellows' excel.

E A 'red' person, **who** usually has strong emotions, is energetic and dynamic.

F 'Blues' are thoughtful, quiet people, and they're often happiest at peaceful moments **when** they're alone.

G The reason **why** some prefer black is because it's dark and mysterious. These people are often unconventional thinkers.

H Helping others is something **that** kind and sympathetic 'greens' really care about.

2 Put the relative pronouns in **bold** in Activity 1 into the correct categories below.

people   places   possession   reasons   things   times

Relative clauses

- **Defining relative clauses** give essential information about the word they refer to.
  We can omit the relative pronoun if it is the object of the clause.
- **Non-defining relative clauses** give non-essential ('extra') information.
  We use commas to separate non-defining relative clauses from the rest of the sentence.
- **Relative pronouns + prepositions.** In formal English, we put a preposition before *whom* or *which*. In informal English we use *who* or *which* and put the preposition at the end of the clause.

Language summary ▶ p. 157

3 Read the rules and, in pairs, answer the questions below.

1 How many brothers have 'I' got in each sentence? Are the relative clauses defining or non-defining?

　A My brother **who's a doctor** has green eyes.
　B My brother, **who's a doctor,** has green eyes.

2 Which sentence is more formal? In which sentence can you omit the relative pronoun?

　A That is the actor **who** everyone is talking **about**.
　B That is the actor **about whom** everyone is talking.

3 Do the sentences in Activity 1 contain defining or non-defining relative clauses?

Watch out! what

We can also use *what* to mean 'the thing(s) that'.
What I read in the colour quiz was very accurate.

We don't use *what* in relative clauses.
There was a part of the analysis which what I didn't agree with.

4 Complete the gaps with a relative pronoun, *what* or Ø (no relative pronoun). If there is more than one possible answer, write both options. Remember to add any missing commas.

Rebel, rebel!

1 Adolescence is a time _____ most of us seek to become more independent, a change _____ parents often find shocking.

2 There are some teenagers _____ want to go out every night, and others _____ retreat to their bedrooms _____ they listen to loud music.

3 And then there are the teenagers about _____ everyone complains – the ones _____ behaviour seems to get completely out of control.

4 But neuroscientists _____ have studied the brain argue that teenage rebellion is perfectly natural.

5 _____ is interesting is that they have discovered the brain is still growing _____ we are teenagers.

6 This may be the reason _____ teenagers can get moody and emotional!

5 Are there any situations in which it's good to be a rebel? Discuss the question with your partner, giving examples and reasons.

Over to you!

6 Work in groups. Divide your group into two teams, A and B. Team A follow the instructions on page 149. Team B follow the instructions on page 151.

Get ready: *articles*

1 Complete the table with *a / an*, *the* or Ø (no article).

Articles	
article	**use for …**
1	• nouns which have been previously mentioned • specifying a particular item
2	• singular countable nouns used for the first time • someone's job
3	• plural and uncountable nouns • to talk about things in a general sense

2 Complete the quotations in pairs. Write *a / an*, *the* or Ø. Which two quotations do you find most interesting?

1 It is only _____ shallow people who do not judge by _____ appearances. *Oscar Wilde*
2 Regardless of how you feel inside, always try to look like _____ winner. *Arthur Ashe*
3 I never saw _____ ugly thing in my life. *John Constable*
4 She got her looks from her father. He's _____ plastic surgeon. *Groucho Marx*
5 _____ world is governed more by _____ appearances than _____ realities. *Daniel Webster*

Grammar boost ▸ Articles ▸ Workbook p. 13

Exam practice

3 Complete the exam task. When you have finished, check your answers carefully.

> **Use of English Part 4:**
> *following instructions*
>
> ➤ Count the number of words you write carefully. Contractions count as two words, e.g. *I'm* = *I am*.
> ➤ The key word must stay exactly the same, so never add verb endings or plurals.
>
> *Exam tip*

For questions **1–8**, complete the second sentence so that it has a similar meaning to the first sentence, using the word given. **Do not change the word given.** You must use between **two** and **five** words, including the word given.

Write **only** the missing words IN CAPITAL LETTERS.

0 This is the first time I've been on reality TV.   **NEVER**

I *HAVE NEVER BEEN* on reality TV before.

---

1 There wasn't a close resemblance between the star and her daughter.   **TAKE**

The daughter of the star .... her mother.

2 My brother dances professionally, and he wants to become famous.   **PROFESSIONAL**

My brother, ..., wants to become famous.

3 The last time the band performed was a year ago.   **FOR**

The band .... a year.

4 Whenever I meet a new person, I get very shy.   **PEOPLE**

Meeting .... feel shy.

5 She is internationally famous.   **AROUND**

She .... world.

6 Being followed everywhere is the part of being famous that I enjoy the least.   **DISLIKE**

What I .... famous is being followed everywhere.

7 Sara plays the guitar and her brother sings in the band.   **SINGER**

Sara, ... in the band, plays the guitar.

8 I prefer doing homework to watching boring reality TV shows!   **RATHER**

I'd .... boring reality TV shows!

Get ready: *fashion*

1 Imagine you are going on a long train journey and have to sit next to one of the people in the photos. Who would you choose and why?

2 In pairs, complete the table with the words in the list. Add as many other words as you can.

baggy   bangle   casual   colourful   conservative
denim   designer label   fitted   flip-flops   high heels
leather   earrings   hippyish   hoodie   patterned
pendant   piercing   ring   trendy   unconventional
sandals   scruffy   smart   suit   woollen

Clothes	*baseball cap, logo,*
Footwear	*(ankle / knee-high) boots,*
Jewellery	*necklace, bracelet,*
Fit / Design / Material adjectives	*plain, tight, cotton,*
General style / appearance adjectives	*smart, elegant,*

3 In pairs, describe the people in the photos and answer the questions.

1 What do you like / dislike about their style?
2 What do you think the people's clothes tell you about their lives and personalities?

Useful expressions

This ... really suits / doesn't suit him.
Her ... matches / doesn't match her ...
His clothes fit / don't fit him well.
I think her image is a bit like / nothing like mine!
I imagine he's /she's ...

Word boost ▶ Fashion ▶ Workbook p. 10

Exam practice

Listening Part 2: *approaching the task*

Exam tip

Read the sentences carefully before you listen. They will give you clues about the topics you are going to hear.
➤ Predict the kind of information you need to listen for. For example, *a number, a place, a job.*
➤ If you find a recording difficult, don't panic! Stay calm and keep listening. Remember, you don't need to understand every word to answer the questions.

4 Read the *Exam tip* and the sentences in the exam task below. Which of the following are **definitely** going to be discussed on the programme?

Sylvie's life now ☐
Sylvie's opinion of someone ☐
Sylvie's love of reality TV shows ☐
Sylvie's clothes ☐
Sylvie's emotions ☐

5 🔊 2.2 You will hear an interview with a woman called Sylvie Brand, who appeared on the television show *Fashion Fix*. For questions **1–10**, complete the sentences.

A Reality TV Makeover

1 Sylvie is wearing a .... for the interview.

2 Sylvie usually prefers to wear jeans, ... and a smart top.

3 Kenji worked as the .... on *Fashion Fix*.

4 Sylvie now considers Kenji to be one of her ....

5 Kenji contacted Sylvie approximately .... weeks after the show.

6 Kenji and Sylvie have met each other at concerts and ....

7 The show's counsellor arranged for Sylvie to investigate a pretend ....

8 During the 'mystery evening', Sylvie played the role of a ....

9 On her first day on the show, Sylvie visited a make-up artist, a style consultant, and a ....

10 Sylvie is currently teaching at a ....

Over to you!

6 How do you think that shows like *Fashion Fix* change people's lives? Do they always change them for the better? Discuss your ideas in pairs.

How important do you think personal appearance is to these people?

1 Look at photos A and B. Discuss questions 1–3 in pairs.

1 Why do you think the people are dressed like this?
2 Are there any situations in which you would change your usual style?
3 Do you think that the clothes you wear can affect the way people think about you? How?

2 You are going to hear a student comparing photos A and B and saying how important he thinks personal appearance is to these people. Before you listen, look at the ideas below and complete the diagram in pairs. Can you add any more ideas?

Photo A	Both photos	Photo B
having fun		

> having fun   smartly dressed
> making an effort   rebellious
> on a date   wants to make an impression
> unconventional style   looks nervous
> image is important

3 2.3 Listen to a student talking about the photos. Does he include any of your ideas?

Exam practice

Speaking Part 2:
preparing to speak

Exam tip

➤ There are two parts to a Part 2 task: you must compare the photos *and* answer the question.
➤ Don't just describe one photo then the other – try to talk about both photos together right from the start.
➤ If you don't know a word for something in the photo, don't panic! Think of another way of describing it, or move onto something else.

4 Work in pairs. Student A look at the photos on page 149. Student B look at the photos on page 151.

1 Draw a diagram like the one in Activity 2. Spend a minute trying to write as many similarities and differences as possible.
2 When you have finished, look at your notes and underline the best ideas.

5 2.4 Listen to the instructions and take it in turns to describe your photos. Listen to your partner and write down the main *similarities* you hear. How many did your partner include?

Compound adjectives

1 In groups, read the TV show titles and decide what you think the shows will be about. Which show would you most / least like to watch? Why?
1 The world's most self-obsessed celebrities
2 Exposed: the two-faced liar who deceived us all
3 How to be world-famous in six months
4 Cold-blooded murder in Hollywood

2 Read the explanation and <u>underline</u> the compound adjectives in Activity 1.

Compound adjectives

A compound adjective is formed from two or more words, often connected with a hyphen (-). For example, *old* + *fashioned* = *old-fashioned*.

3 Match 1–5 with A–E. Which compound adjectives describe **appearance** and which describe **personality**? What are the opposites of these words?
1 A prejudiced person is often **narrow**
2 He's a very **well**
3 Many Mediterranean people are **dark**
4 I'm quite **thick**
5 She's a very caring and **warm**

A -**hearted** person.
B -**haired** with brown or black eyes.
C -**skinned**. I rarely get offended.
D -**dressed** man. He always looks smart.
E -**minded** and intolerant.

4 Imagine that Rosa and Matteo are a famous celebrity couple. Write a paragraph about who they are, what they are like, and why they are in the news. Include at least five compound adjectives.

Rosa and Matteo are both famous for being ...

Phrasal verbs (1): *relationships*

5 Look at the story of Rosa and Matteo's relationship. Then form two phrasal verbs to go with each picture.

1	get ...	away
2	go ...	on
		out

3	fall ...	out
4	split ...	for
		up

5	make ...	back together
6	get ...	up
		out

7	settle ...	down
8	bring ...	up
		for

6 Which phrasal verbs can go before *with* + someone?

7 Write the story from Activity 5. Use phrasal verbs 1–8.
1 *Rosa and Matteo got on really well together.*

Over to you!

8 Rosa and Matteo are in the news again! In groups, decide whether they are a) getting divorced or b) having another baby. Divide into two teams:

Reporters: think of five questions to ask Rosa and Matteo. Include at least five different items of vocabulary from this page.
Rosa and Matteo: Decide what to tell the Press. What happened? How are you feeling? What do you think about each other? What are you going to do next?

9 Act out your role plays. When you have finished, write a short summary to publish on *Celebrity!* website.

Word boost ▶ Workbook p. 77

Get ready: *extreme adjectives*

1 Read sentences A and B. Then answer the questions.

A I was **surprised** that the celebrities had split up!

B I was **astonished** that the celebrities had split up!

1 Which adjective is more 'extreme'? (= *strong*)
2 Which adjective(s) could follow the adverbs
   a) absolutely, b) very, or c) really?

2 Work with a partner and make pairs of normal and extreme adjectives. Can you think of any other pairs?

amazing   angry   attractive   bad   big   crowded
devastated   dirty   exhausted   filthy   funny   furious
good   gorgeous   hideous   hilarious   huge   packed
scared   terrible   terrified   tired   ugly   upset

normal	extreme
big	huge

3 Imagine you are a celebrity. Choose a memorable event. Make notes about what happened and how you felt.

the premiere of your film   your biggest-ever concert
your first TV appearance   a celebrity wedding

4 Work in pairs. Talk about your memorable event for **one** minute, using as many extreme adjectives as possible. Listen to your partner and count the adjectives you hear. Whose description was the most 'extreme'?

Word boost ▶ extreme adjectives ▶ Workbook p. 11

Exam practice

Use of English Part 1:
reading for gist

> Read the text first to understand the main topics.
> For each gap, look at *all* of the options and think about each word in context. Don't just pick the first word which seems to fit!

Exam tip

5 Read the text in the exam task quickly, ignoring the gaps. What are the author's main criticisms of celebrity gossip? Do you agree?

6 Complete the exam task.

For questions **1–12**, read the text below and decide which answer (**A**, **B**, **C** or **D**) best fits each gap.

Celebrity gossip

(0) *WHETHER* you like it or loathe it, celebrity gossip is hard to avoid. Newspapers, magazines and websites are absolutely **(1)** .... with photos of the stars – often unflattering ones of them in embarrassing situations, or looking **(2)** .... after a long night out. Celebrities, **(3)** .... the badly-behaved ones, regularly get more media coverage than many politicians. It seems we're **(4)** .... by scandal, eager to know who is going **(5)** .... with whom, whose marriage has just fallen apart, and who's been having problems. Thanks to the public's **(6)** .... for gossip, 'exclusive' shots of stars like Britney Spears and Cristiano Ronaldo can fetch a paparazzo $500,000 each!

Celebrities **(7)** .... that money-hungry reporters and photographers follow them everywhere they go, often **(8)** .... great personal distress. In response, celebrity hunters argue that famous people shouldn't be so **(9)** .... and sensitive. Instead, they should accept their loss of privacy as the **(10)** .... of wealth and success. But have things gone too far? Do we really have a 'right' to read about stars having a mental breakdown, or to see pictures of them looking **(11)** .... devastated after they've **(12)** .... up with their husband or wife? There seems to be a fine line between curiosity and cruelty.

0	**A**	If	**B**	Whereas	**C**	Whether	**D**	Regardless
1	**A**	tight	**B**	crowded	**C**	busy	**D**	packed
2	**A**	terrific	**B**	terrified	**C**	terrible	**D**	terrorised
3	**A**	peculiarly	**B**	especially	**C**	remarkably	**D**	occasionally
4	**A**	interested	**B**	keen	**C**	fascinated	**D**	fond
5	**A**	out	**B**	on	**C**	together	**D**	over
6	**A**	hunger	**B**	wish	**C**	love	**D**	want
7	**A**	disagree	**B**	accuse	**C**	deny	**D**	complain
8	**A**	making	**B**	causing	**C**	beginning	**D**	resulting
9	**A**	hard-working	**B**	badly-behaved	**C**	cold-hearted	**D**	thin-skinned
10	**A**	value	**B**	price	**C**	worth	**D**	charge
11	**A**	greatly	**B**	completely	**C**	very	**D**	considerably
12	**A**	divided	**B**	cut	**C**	torn	**D**	split

Prepare

1 Discuss photos A, B and C in pairs.

1 How could these people inspire others?
2 Which person do you find the most inspiring? Why?

Analyse the task

2 Quickly read the article on the right, which a student wrote for Part 2 of the Writing Paper.

1 Why did the student write about the woman in the photo?
2 What has the woman inspired the student to do?

3 How does the writer make the article more interesting? Tick the ideas which he / she uses (one is incorrect), and find an example of each.

uses a mixture of formal and informal
    language ☐
includes questions ☐
gives reasons for opinions ☐
uses linkers to connect ideas ☐
gives examples ☐
includes a range of adjectives ☐

My inspiration: J. K. Rowling

When I was younger I used to hate reading, but one person changed my attitude completely. That person was J.K. Rowling, whose amazing Harry Potter novels are loved by millions.

Why is J. K. Rowling such an inspiration for me? I find her personal history almost as impressive as her fascinating stories. When she started writing, she was a single mother, struggling to bring up a baby daughter alone. Many publishers rejected her first novel, but she didn't give up. Thanks to her hard work and determination, J.K. Rowling is now a best-selling author.

Today, J.K. Rowling continues to provide a positive role model for her fans. Even though she's a celebrity, she's never vain or arrogant. In fact, she's a very caring person who does a lot of charity work.

She has definitely made a big impact on me. Not only do I now love reading, but I've been inspired to study literature at university. Maybe one day I'll even write my own books, instead of just reading them!

Improve your writing:
punctuation and spelling

4 It is important to use correct punctuation in a writing task. Write sentences 1–6 with the correct punctuation. With a partner, discuss why you had to make each change.

1 in my opinion this actors best role was captain jack sparrow
2 its true that hes the only footballer to have won three world cup medals
3 what was the name of the director who made jurassic park and jaws
4 shes a colombian singer whose most famous song is whenever wherever
5 i think he writes the simpsons cartoons doesnt he
6 this actress has got beautiful long blonde hair and used to be married to tom cruise

5 Discuss *who* you think the people in Activity 4 are and *how* they might inspire people. Check your answers on page 149.

6 Always check your work! Look at these sentences from three students' work and correct the mistakes.

1 I'm inspired by George Clooney ~~beeuse~~ *because* he campaigns ~~extremily~~ hard to protect the environment.

Check your spelling!

2 At the ~~begining~~ of the ~~jorney~~, this ~~exploror~~ stayed in some ~~accomodation~~ ~~wich~~ was ~~realy~~ ~~unconfortable~~.

Use a dictionary!

3 I'm ~~writting~~ about someone ~~whose~~ my ~~bigest~~ inspiration – my teacher! I look forward to her lessons, as ~~their~~ always ~~interested~~.

Correct this!

Ready to write!

You have seen this advertisement in an international magazine.

INSPIRING PEOPLE

Tell us about a person you admire and why they inspire you.
We will publish the most interesting articles next month.

Write your article in **120–180** words.

7 Read the task above then choose a person to describe. Choose one of the following:

1 a celebrity, hero, or other famous person.
2 someone you know well, for example a teacher or a relative.

8 Brainstorm as many ideas as you can about your person, using these headings to help you.

personality   achievements   your opinion

9 Discuss your ideas with a partner and decide on the **six** most important ideas to include in your article.

Writing Part 2: *an article*   **Exam tip**

➤ Write a title that gives the main idea.
➤ Try to involve the reader. You can address him / her directly (*I'm sure you'll agree that* ...) or ask one or two questions (*Have you heard* ...?).
➤ Make your article more interesting by including a range of language, e.g. adjectives and adverbs, phrasal verbs, collocations, relative clauses, linkers, one or two idioms.
➤ Give personal opinions and give reasons or examples to support your views.
➤ Think of a suitable start and finish for your article – don't just stop writing!

Writing reference ▶ page 170

10 Read the *Exam tip* and look again at the article on page 26. Decide how you are going to organize your ideas into paragraphs.

Paragraph 1: introduce the person ...

11 Write your article, making it as interesting as possible.

12 Swap your article with your partner. Look at the checklist on page 170 and suggest any corrections you think would be useful.

Unit 2

1 Join the sentences using a relative clause. You may need to change the order of the sentences or place one sentence inside another.

0 *Elle* is the world's best-selling fashion magazine. It was founded in France.

Elle, which was founded in France, is the world's best-selling fashion magazine.

1 Salma Hayek wore a gorgeous dress. It was made of silk.
2 Gabriela Mistral is a poet from Chile. She was the first Latin-American to win the Nobel Prize.
3 I met my hero Pelé. I'll never forget that time.
4 Liv Tyler is an actress. Her father is the Aerosmith singer, Steve Tyler.
5 Roman Polanski directed the film *The Ninth Gate*. His wife also starred in it.
6 Pablo Picasso was born in Málaga. It is also the birthplace of Antonio Banderas.
7 The Prada fashion label began in Milan. An annual Fashion Week is now held in the city.
8 Graceland used to be Elvis's home. It's now a museum.
9 Bob Marley died in 1981. He's a famous reggae songwriter.

2 Complete the text. Use words from the unit.

Jean-Paul Gaultier is not a conventional fashion designer– in fact, he's quite **(0)** e_c_c_e_n_t_r_i_c. He likes to shock people at his shows, for example by using elderly male models with **(1)** b_ _d heads and **(2)** w_ _ _ _ _ _d skin. He thinks that you don't need to be conventionally **(3)** g_ _ _ -l_ _ _ _ _g to be a good fashion model, and he thinks that fashion-lovers should be **(4)** b_ _ _ _-m_ _ _ _ d, not prejudiced. His own appearance is unusual – he often wears items of women's clothing, especially **(5)** sk_ _ _ s, and he often wears jewellery, like **(6)** e_ _ _ _ _ _s! Gaultier is a very confident, outspoken designer who dares to be **(7)** d_ _ _ _ _ _ _t. In the past, he has **(8)** f_ _ _ _ _ o_ _ with other, more **(9)** co_ _ _ _ _ _ _ _ _e designers who have criticised his deliberately controversial style. Nonetheless, he remains hugely popular. His catwalk shows are always absolutely **(10)** p_ _ _ _d with fans, who include the celebrities Madonna, Pedro Almódovar and Marilyn Manson!

Units 1–2

3 Write the correct form of the verbs.

0 I've always wanted (**meet**) Nelson Mandela.
to meet
1 At the moment, the stars (**wear**) Versace.
2 You're just in time! *The X Factor* (**not begin**) yet.
3 My sister (**rarely / buy**) designer labels.
4 The singer kept (**try**) to become famous.
5 Leonardo da Vinci once (**draw**) plans for a helicopter.
6 Models need to practise (**walk**) confidently down the catwalk.

4 Complete the text with the correct words.

DENIM has **(0)** *been* around for **(1)** _____ long time. Invented in seventeenth-century Italy, it was designed as **(2)** _____ strong, tough material to be worn by sailors! Levi Strauss, **(3)** _____ lived and worked in **(4)** _____ USA, made the first modern-style jeans. The 1950s was the time **(5)** _____ blue jeans first became really popular. For young people, they were **(6)** _____ symbol of rebellion, like leather jackets and long hair. They **(7)** _____ now one of the most popular fashion items in **(8)** _____ world.

5 Complete the sentences. Use the adjective form of the words in the list.

> arrogance   greed   like
> protect   ~~style~~   tire

0 I think Nicole Kidman's very ___*stylish*___. She always looks good.
1 He's very _____, so he finds it easy to make friends.
2 Simon Cowell's so _____. He always thinks he's right!
3 My dad's very _____. He wants to keep us safe.
4 Fashion Week is very _____. There's so much to see and do!
5 She's so _____ - she's eaten all of the chocolates!

6 Prepare a one-minute talk about a friend or member of your family. Describe their appearance, style and personality, and say how you feel about him / her. Then give your talks in pairs. What are the **three** most interesting things your partner tells you?

3

Topic vocabulary: travel ● geography and climate
● accident and emergency
Grammar: narrative tenses ● comparative linkers
Word building: comparatives and superlatives
● verb patterns (2) ● easily-confused nouns
Writing: a story ● linkers (2)
Exam preparation: Reading Part 3 ● Use of English
Parts 1 and 2 ● Listening Part 3 ● Speaking Part 3
● Writing Part 2

A

B

C

D

E

Travel

1 In pairs, discuss photos A–E. What might people enjoy about these holidays? Which kind of holiday would you prefer? Why?

2 🔊 **3.1** Listen to three speakers talking about holidays. For each speaker, decide which of the activities in photos A–E they would probably like to do:

1 the most 2 the least

3 🔊 **3.1** Complete these sentences from the recording. Then listen again and check your answers.

1 When I do get a couple of **days** _____, I want to **make the** _____ **of** them.
2 I don't mind **saving** _____ **for** something special.
3 I usually **go** _____ sporty **holidays**.
4 If you **set** _____ **early**, you can often get a really good place.
5 I don't think we're really **missing** _____.
6 Holidays are all about **leaving** my worries _____.
7 They're always desperate to **fit** _____ as much as possible before they **head** _____ to the airport.

Word boost ▶ Travel ▶ Workbook p. 16

Over to you!

4 Imagine that one half of the class are **travel agents** and the other half are **tourists**. Follow the instructions.

Travel agents: Work in pairs to design a new holiday package that will appeal to students in your class. Consider the following ideas:
● **location** (e.g. beach / city / countryside)
● **accommodation** (e.g. campsite / villa / hotel)
● **activities** (e.g. day trips / evening entertainment)

Tourists: Work in pairs and decide what your ideal holiday would be. Think about location, accommodation, and activities.

5 Now follow these instructions.

Tourists: visit each pair of travel agents and find out about the holidays. Choose one of the holidays to go on.
Travel agents: try to sell your holiday.

6 Which holiday package was the most popular? Why?

1 Look at the photos. How dangerous do you think these activities are? In pairs, order the activities from the most to the least dangerous.

2 What's the most adventurous thing you've ever done? Tell your partner.

3 Quickly read the reviews on page 31 and match the people to the photos. Who felt generally positive about their experience? Who felt less positive?

Exam practice

Reading Part 3: *Exam tip*
reading for specific information

After you have read through the text or texts for gist:
➤ read the questions and <u>underline</u> the key words.
➤ read the text again carefully to find information that relates to each question.
➤ think about synonyms and paraphrases – the words in the question will not match the text exactly.

4 Read the exam task questions in Activity 5 carefully and <u>underline</u> the key words.

5 You are going to read a webpage on which four people have reviewed their holiday experiences. For questions 1–15, choose from the reviewers (A–D). The reviewers may be chosen more than once.

Which reviewer mentions

1 planning to go back to the place they visited?
2 doing something they had been wanting to try for a while?
3 not being allowed to do something?
4 wishing they'd been able to do other things on the trip?
5 feeling concerned about an aspect of someone's leadership?
6 that their review is incomplete?
7 that they will never forget this trip?
8 not having been adequately advised on what to expect on the trip?
9 having a positive experience of their holiday accommodation?
10 not having sufficient skills to do something?
11 travelling a very long way on the trip?
12 being impressed by someone's expertise?
13 becoming unwell on holiday?
14 reading about the trip before travelling?
15 travelling through a variety of landscapes?

Vocabulary in context:
geography and climate

6 Read the reviews again and find words which mean:

1 thick wood in a hot part of the world (review A)
2 small hills of sand (review B)
3 valley with steep sides and a river running through it (review B)
4 the sides of a hill or mountain; inclines (review C)
5 large mass of ice (review C)
6 top of a mountain (review C)

7 In groups, look at the weather words in **bold** in the reviews. For each word, decide whether it:

1 is a *noun*, *verb* or *adjective*.
2 relates most closely to a) temperature, b) wet weather, c) windy weather or d) icy weather.

8 Work in groups. You are going to appear on a travel programme talking about your country. Consider:

1 what you are going to say about your country's a) geography and b) climate.
2 what kind of information tourists would be most interested in.

9 Present your ideas to the class. Whose programme do you think would be most useful for tourists?

Word boost ▶ Geography and climate ▶ Workbook p. 16

Extreme Travel!

Jacek   **Costa Rica Wildlife Expedition**

Puerto Rico Wildlife Expedition

Never again! In the whole three months I was there, it must have **poured** every single day. It isn't much fun wearing **soaking** wet clothes all day, and especially not when you're trying to get to sleep. I know that the word 'rainforest' should have given me a clue, but I felt that the holiday literature did not give an adequate warning of what to expect. As a result, many of us (including me!) arrived without all the right gear or equipment for a jungle expedition, and the attitude of the tour leader was pretty unsympathetic. What's more, her rather relaxed attitude to safety did little for my peace of mind. Much of the wildlife there is deadly poisonous, but we were given very little advice on how to protect ourselves. I used to lie awake in my tiny tent all night, petrified of spiders and convinced I'd got all kinds of infectious diseases! All in all, I would rate the trip as two stars – the forests were beautiful, but the organisation was poor.

B   **Lucy**   **Moroccan Off-road Safari**

MOROCCAN OFF-ROAD SAFARI

The Safari is more than a holiday – it's an experience that will stay with me for a lifetime. The tour began in Marrakech, where my family and I met our guide, Azef, and were given the keys to our specially-built off-road vehicle. We travelled across dunes and rocks from dawn to dusk, enjoying some very generous local hospitality at night. The desert was simply breathtaking, although the contrast between the **scorching** daytime temperatures and night-time **frost** did take some getting used to. After a few days, we were glad to feel a light **breeze** in the mountains, although we did have a bit of a hiccup on the second day when Dad managed to get us completely stuck in a gorge! Fortunately, as well as being a wonderfully informative guide, Azef turned out to be a brilliant mechanic too, and – much to our astonishment – soon had us out of the river. Despite our little accident, we all enjoyed ourselves hugely. The ever-changing scenery was spectacular, and the local expertise was invaluable. I would wholeheartedly recommend this trip to anyone looking for something a bit 'different'.

C   **Yara**   **Trek Kilimanjaro**

TREK KILIMANJARO

Like many amateurs, I'd heard the descriptions of 'gentle slopes' and '**mild** climate' on the travel programmes and romantically assumed that climbing Kilimanjaro would be all about the great views. I soon found out that it would also require higher levels of strength and ability than I possessed. Kilimanjaro may have **temperate** weather at its base, but as we got closer to the top of the volcano we encountered huge, forbidding **glaciers**, and my breath **froze** on my face. Disappointingly for me, I never made it to the summit. I suffered dizziness as a result of climbing at such high altitudes, and my expedition leader refused to let me climb any further. At the time, I was extremely upset and even angry about this, and felt like I'd wasted my money. But the tour company offered me half price off a return climb next year, which is pretty generous of them. So watch this space – I'll let you know how it goes!

D   **Andrea**   **Storm Chasers USA**

Storm CHASERS

I'd been saving for this holiday for the last five years, and it didn't disappoint. We saw giant **hailstones**, almost the size of golf balls, and stood in the **downpour** of three big **thunderstorms**. But the best experience came on the last day, actually when we were heading back to the airport. I'd seen tornadoes on TV before, but nothing really compares to the sheer thrill – and terror – you experience when you feel one **blow** past, ripping up fences and buildings just metres away from you. I'd rate this holiday as four stars –the tour guides were great, and the extreme weather itself was beyond brilliant. But I did get a bit fed up with the mini-van, especially when it was hot and **humid** outside. It would have been nice to get out more, instead of just going from one uncomfortable motel to another. We covered huge stretches of country every day, with no chance to fit in any 'normal' holiday activities, like sightseeing or shopping.

 11 Work in groups. Agree on one of the holidays above to go on together. Explain your decision to the rest of the class. Which holiday was the most popular? Why?

10 The website has a 'rate this review' feature. Readers can vote on whether they found a particular review *very helpful*, *quite helpful*, or *not helpful*. In pairs, agree a rating for each review. Give reasons for your opinions.

Useful expressions

I've always dreamed about + -ing …
… would be a holiday of a lifetime.
I couldn't put up with the … weather.
… sounds / doesn't sound like fun to me.

1 Read the first lines from some English novels. In pairs, decide which line you find the most interesting and why.

A It was a bright cold day in April, and the clocks **were striking** thirteen.

(George Orwell, 1984)

B Dr Iannis **had enjoyed** a satisfactory day in which none of his patients **had died** or got worse.

(Louis de Bernières, Captain Corelli's Mandolin)

C I **had been making** the rounds of the Sacrifice Poles the day we heard my brother had escaped.

(Iain Banks, The Wasp Factory)

D James Bond, with two double bourbons inside him, **sat** in the final departure lounge of Miami Airport and **thought** about life and death.

(Ian Fleming, Goldfinger)

2 Work in pairs. Complete the rules with the correct tenses. Then decide what the tenses in **bold** in Activity 1 are, and why the writer used them.

Narrative tenses

Tense	Used for
1	the main events in a story; descriptions. *It all began a year ago, on a dark and stormy night.*
2	background events in a story; actions which happened before another past action. (NOW) *When the hero **had left**, the villain **stole** the jewels.*
3	actions which were happening before or which were interrupted by another past action. (NOW) *We'd **been walking** for hours before we **found** water.*
4	setting the scene in a story; temporary situations. *The sun **was shining**. It was a beautiful day for an adventure.* actions which were interrupted by another past action. (NOW) *While we **were sleeping**, something terrible **happened**.*

Language summary ▶ p. 158

3 Complete the text with the correct form of the verbs. Sometimes more than one answer is possible.

The name's Fleming ... Ian Fleming

Before Ian Fleming *wrote* (**0** write) his famous James Bond novels, he (**1** already / lead) quite an exciting life. After he (**2** finish) school, he (**3** travel) round the world and (**4** make) a living as a journalist and banker. While he (**5** work) as an intelligence officer during World War II, he (**6** meet) many real-life spies! He (**7** invent) the James character while he (**8** live) in a villa in Jamaica, inspired by his wife, Anne, who (**9** encourage) him to write novels for years. Fleming (**10** name) his hero after the author of one of the books he (**11** read) at the time – *Birds of the West Indies* by James Bond! Sales of the Bond novels (**12** leap) when the American president, J. F. Kennedy (**13** recommend) them in 1961. Unfortunately, Ian Fleming, who (**14** drink) heavily for many years, (**15** die) of a heart attack in 1964, but not before he (**16** write) twelve James Bond novels and two collections of short stories – and created one of the most famous characters in fiction.

4 Write your own first line of a novel! Complete the sentences. Use each narrative tense at least once.

1 When James Bond arrived at the party, he ...
2 An amazing thing happened while I ...
3 The day before she robbed the bank, Rosa ...
4 All night long, the detective ...
5 As soon as he saw her, he ...
6 For three whole weeks, the spy, Felipe ...

Over to you!

5 Work in groups. Choose **one** of the first lines you wrote in Activity 4 and write it on a piece of paper. Then follow the instructions.

1 Give your story to the person on your left.
2 Read the line you've been given and write the next sentence in the story.
3 Continue steps 1 and 2 until each story is six sentences long.
4 Read your story to the rest of the group. Vote for the best one.

Get ready: *so, such, too, enough*

1 Read visitors' comments on a new go-karting track. Who liked the experience? Does go-karting appeal to you? Why? / Why not?

1	so / such / such a	I was **so** excited that I went round twenty times! We had **such** fun we recommended it to our friends. We had **such a** good time I didn't want it to end.
2	too	The track was **too** dangerous. I felt very unsafe.
3	enough	There were **enough** thrills to keep everyone happy. My kids loved it, but one ride was enough for me!
4	not ... enough	The karts were**n't** fast **enough** for adults. There was**n't enough** information about what to do.

2 Match the words in the table with the definitions in the list. Which of the expressions in **bold** do we use to express a criticism?

> not as much as is necessary   describing cause and effect
> more than is necessary   as much as is necessary

3 Look at the table again. Then work in groups and answer the questions.

1 What's the difference between the way we use *so*, *such*, and *such a*?
2 Where can we put the word *enough* in a sentence?

Exam practice

5 Read the exam task quickly, ignoring the gaps. What can you do in Darwin? Which dangerous animals are mentioned in the text?

6 Complete the exam task.

4 Imagine that you have just stayed at the Ice Hotel in the photo. Write six comments on your experience, including these words.

> enough   not enough   so   such
> such a(n)   too

Grammar boost ▶ *so, such, too, enough*
▶ Workbook p. 19

Use of English **Exam tip**
Part 2: *part of speech*

➤ Think about what kind of word is missing from the gap, e.g. *verb form, noun, article, preposition, linker.*
➤ If you add a verb form, make sure that it agrees with its subject, e.g. *he has been.*

For questions **1–12**, read the text below and think of the word which best fits each gap. Use only **one** word in each gap. There is an example at the beginning **(0)**.

Write your answers IN CAPITAL LETTERS.

Croc shock!

(0) ....*IF*........ theme parks and action films aren't exciting **(1)** .... for you, why not try something a little more extreme? Since 2008, thrill-seekers **(2)** .... been travelling down to 'Crocasaurus Cove' in Darwin, Australia, where they can try the latest craze – swimming with crocodiles! Getting in a pen with crocodiles is far **(3)** .... dangerous to attempt without protection, so visitors are lowered under water in a see-through cage. Crocodiles are **(4)** .... strong that the walls of the cage had to be made 145 millimetres thick! This experience is not for the faint-hearted – crocodiles have attacked the cage several **(5)** ...., and you can see their teeth marks on the sides. But for many people, it's an adventure of a lifetime. According to Elisa Delgado, 18, 'I've **(6)** .... been so terrified in my life! But it was **(7)** .... a thrill that I'm going to come back again **(8)** .... year.'

Adrenalin junkies who want to get close **(9)** .... dangerous wild animals can also try diving with sharks, petting poisonous snakes, or going **(10)** .... safari with lions and rhinos. But even the least brave **(11)** .... us have probably already met a far more dangerous predator, without even travelling abroad. The common mosquito is officially **(12)** .... deadliest animal on the planet, being responsible for more deaths than sharks, lions and crocodiles together!

Get ready: *accident and emergency*

1 Look at illustrations A–D. Which person or people do you think is facing the most serious problem? Why?

A

B

C

D

2 Work in groups. Match eight of the verb phrases in the list to pictures A–D. Write sentences to describe what's happening in each illustration.

> attack   bite   break down   catch fire
> crash into something   feel sick   get lost   get stuck
> hurt oneself   run a temperature   slip on something
> sting   run out of something important

Watch out! *get + past participle*

In some English expressions we use *get* + past participle instead of a reflexive verb to talk about something we do to ourselves.

*"Why are you late?" "We **got lost**!"* (NOT *"We lost ourselves!"*)

3 What do you think happened to the people in pictures A–D? In pairs, think of suitable endings to each story.

4 Compare your stories with another pair. Which of their stories had the most exciting ending?

Word boost ▶ Accident and emergency ▶ Workbook p. 16

Exam practice

Listening Part 3: *listening twice*

Exam tip

➤ If you can't answer a question the first time you listen, don't panic! Leave it blank and come back to it later. Don't stop listening, or you'll miss the answers to other questions.
➤ Listen again carefully. This time, make sure you write an answer for all of the questions.

5 🔊 3.2 You will hear five people talking about a time when something went wrong. For questions 1–5, choose from the list (A–F) the reason each speaker gives. Use the letters only once. There is one extra letter which you do not need to use.

Speaker 1 ☐   Speaker 2 ☐   Speaker 3 ☐
Speaker 4 ☐   Speaker 5 ☐

A being over confident
B not listening to someone's advice
C not doing enough research
D losing something
E taking the wrong equipment
F not staying calm

Over to you!

6 Imagine you had a similar experience to one of the speakers in the recording! Choose a story and make notes about the following:

• background (place, people, etc.)
• the main actions (what happened?)
• feelings (at the time / afterwards)

7 In pairs, follow the instructions for Students A and B. Then swap roles.

Student A: You are telling your story on the radio. Make it as interesting as possible by using a range of language, including extreme adjectives.

Student B: You're a radio presenter who finds Student A's story absolutely fascinating! Respond using ideas from the box.

Useful expressions

Really? I don't believe it! No! Wow!
That's absolutely terrible / quite incredible!
How scary / amazing (How + adjective)
What fun / a nightmare! (What + noun)
That's the most ... story I've ever heard.

1 Read the advertisement for Adventure Park.
Which attraction would you want to visit the most / least? Why?

Come to Adventure Park

and let our thrilling rides and activities bring adventure to your life!

Here are just some of the attractions we offer:

climbing wall
reptile house
paintballing centre
rollercoaster
big-screen cinema
wave pool

2 3.3 Listen to two students talking about the park. In what order do they discuss the attractions? Which **two** attractions do they agree to visit?

3 3.3 In pairs, complete the table with the expressions for organising a discussion. Can you add any more ideas? Listen and tick (✓) the expressions you hear.

Let's start with …   Me neither.
Let's talk about … first.   Me too.   Neither do I.
OK, have we decided which … ?   So do I.
Sounds good to me!   We need to make a decision.
First of all, let's …   To sum up, …

Starting a discussion	
Agreeing or disagreeing	
Trying to reach a conclusion	

Exam practice

4 Work in groups of four (two pairs). Take it in turns to do the exam task opposite.

Speaking pair: Do the task, using expressions from Activity 3.

Listening pair: Imagine you are examiners. Time the students who are speaking and stop them after three minutes. Afterwards, report back to the speaking students on how well you think they did. Did they answer both questions? Did they talk to each other?

Speaking Part 3: *Exam tip*
understanding the task

➤ Spend most of your time discussing the first question. Talk about *all* of the photos or pictures before you decide on an answer to the second question.
➤ Take it in turns to speak. Ask for your partner's opinion and respond to what he /she says.
➤ Remember, there is no 'right' answer to the questions. You will get marks for the way you answer the task, not for your opinions.

• What risks do people take in these jobs?
• Which job is the most dangerous?

Comparatives and superlatives

1 In pairs, guess the correct answers to the quiz. Check your ~~.~~

What is it?

1 This is **the largest desert of all**, covering 9,100,000 km^2.

2 This very common insect is **almost as deadly as** the mosquito, causing millions of fatalities. It can jump **much higher than** most other insects!

3 The second-longest river is **not quite as long** as the Nile, but it's **twice as long as** the Rio Grande.

4 Many sports are **just as enjoyable as** this, but this is **by far the most popular** sport in the world!

2 Add the expressions in **bold** in Activity 1 to the table.

The same

• exactly as + *adjective / adverb* + as

Small difference

• nearly + *adjective / adverb* + as

• a bit / a little / slightly + *comparative* + than

Big difference

• far / a lot + *comparative* + than

• easily + *superlative*

3 Complete the second sentence so it has a similar meaning to the first sentence, using the word given.

1 All other mountains are much smaller than Everest.

   Everest _____ in the world. **EASILY**

2 The villa and the chalet are exactly the same size.

   The chalet _____ the villa. **AS**

3 I'd never been on such a bad holiday before.

   It was the _____ been on. **EVER**

4 Karachi is less crowded than the beach.

   Karachi _____ the beach. **NOT**

4 Read the sentence below. Which part tells us about the *cause* of something, and which part tells us about the *result*?

The further we walked, **the** more tired we became.

5 Complete the sentences, then add one sentence of your own. Explain your ideas to your partner.

1 The older I become, …

2 The more mistakes I make, …

3 …, the more frightened I get!

Verb patterns (2):
gerund or infinitive with a change in meaning

6 Some verbs can be followed by a gerund *or* an infinitive. The gerund or infinitive changes the meaning of the verb. What does *remember* mean in these sentences?

1 I will always remember **visiting** my friend in the USA.

2 I must remember **to write** and thank her.

A remember something that needs done in the future

B remember a past action

7 In pairs, write the correct form of the verbs in **bold**. Try to explain the difference in meaning between *red verb* + *gerund* and *red verb* + *infinitive*.

1 We stopped (**drive**) when we realised we were lost. We stopped (**ask**) directions at a petrol station.

2 The crew tried (**sail**) the Pacific, but it was too hard. Next year, they're going to try (**use**) a bigger boat.

3 I'll never forget (**see**) the rare tree frog in the forest. I wish I hadn't forgotten (**bring**) my camera!

4 Even though she was tired, she went on (**climb**). She went on (**become**) a world-famous climber.

Over to you!

8 You are going to interview your partner about some of their most memorable experiences. Write five questions, including the prompts.

   the most   forgotten (+ infinitive)
   tried (+ gerund)   better   furthest

What's the most disgusting thing you've ever eaten?

9 Ask and answer your questions in pairs. Which answer did you find the most surprising?

Word boost ▶ Workbook p. 78

Get ready: *easily confused nouns*

1 Some nouns have very similar meanings. Complete the sentences with the words in the lists.

| nature   scenery   view |
| beach   coast   shores |
| journey   travel   trip   way |

1 We enjoyed the varied mountain
   _____.
2 I like getting close to _____
   on long walks.
3 There's a wonderful _____ of
   the sea from here.

4 They live on the east _____
   of America.
5 She liked to fish on the _____
   of the lake.
6 I love sunbathing on the
   _____.

7 We're going on a long _____
   next week.
8 Air _____ can be expensive.
9 What's the quickest _____ to
   London from here?
10 We're going on a weekend
   _____ to the beach.

Word boost ▶ Easily confused nouns ▶ Workbook p. 17

Exam Practice

2 Read the exam task, ignoring the gaps.
What does the text tell us about:

1 a town called Busan?   2 pizza?

3 Complete the exam task.

Use of English Part 1: *eliminating options*   **Exam tip**

For each gap, eliminate the options you know are wrong in the context.
➤ Some words belong with other words, e.g. *interested in; go on a trip.*
➤ Some words have similar but not identical meanings. For example, *forest* and *wood* both refer to areas where trees grow, but a *forest* is bigger than a *wood.*

For questions **1–12**, read the text below and decide which answer (**A**, **B**, **C** or **D**) best fits each gap.

It's a record!

In 1955, the first ever **(0)** *EDITION* of *The Guinness Book of Records* was published. Enthralled readers learned about the world's **(1)** .... ocean (the Pacific – approximately 4,300 metres to the bottom), or the biggest birds on **(2)** .... (ostriches). The book, which **(3)** .... became known as *Guinness World Records*, **(4)** .... on to become a huge success. In modern editions, more space is devoted to human **(5)** .... , some of which seem quite bizarre! For example, in 2008, people in the Korean seaside town of Busan set a record for opening the greatest number of parasols on a sandy **(6)** .... !

All Guinness records have to be provable. You might think the top of a **(7)** .... mountain gives the most spectacular **(8)** .... in the world, but this is opinion, not fact, and would not be permitted as a record. The Guinness team take their roles as judges very **(9)** .... Every year, employees make long **(10)** .... around the world to observe and assess record-breaking attempts so that only accurate information is recorded – from the **(11)** .... of the longest ride on a lawn mower (260 days), to the width of the biggest pizza (over 37 metres in diameter!).

This remarkable archive of trivia has even **(12)** .... a record of its own – as the world's biggest-selling copyright series!

0	A	copy	B	story	C	edition	D	number
1	A	deepest	B	tallest	C	lowest	D	farthest
2	A	planet	B	globe	C	earth	D	world
3	A	after	B	since	C	later	D	next
4	A	moved	B	carried	C	kept	D	went
5	A	results	B	awards	C	merits	D	achievements
6	A	beach	B	shore	C	bay	D	coast
7	A	peculiar	B	different	C	particular	D	distinct
8	A	scenery	B	sight	C	landscape	D	view
9	A	importantly	B	strongly	C	seriously	D	heavily
10	A	travels	B	ways	C	routes	D	journeys
11	A	period	B	duration	C	age	D	progression
12	A	done	B	set	C	put	D	laid

A

B

C

Prepare

1 Discuss photos A, B and C in pairs.

1 What are the people doing?
2 Why do you think they are doing it?
3 How do you think they are feeling?

Analyse the task

2 Quickly read the story opposite and match it to one of the photos A–C. Were your answers to the questions in Activity 1 correct?

3 Read the story again and answer the questions in pairs.

1 What tenses does the writer use? Why doesn't the writer use only the past simple?
2 What adjectives and adverbs can you find? Why do you think the writer uses so many?

Extreme housework!

Alice looked at the clock in horror. She had overslept! After grabbing her mum's ironing board and a bag of washing, she ran for the beach. Unfortunately, thanks to the ironing board, she couldn't move as quickly as usual! By the time she arrived, her friends had been waiting impatiently for nearly thirty minutes.

Alice and her friends were about to attempt something quite remarkable. They wanted to break a world record for the largest number of people to iron underwater!

As soon as Alice arrived, everyone walked into the sea. To begin with, Alice found it difficult to sink while she was still holding her equipment! But eventually, she reached the bottom. First, she set up her board, then she started ironing. She felt very silly!

A short while later, Alice headed back to shore. As she was pulling her soaking wet board onto the sand, the waiting crowds cheered loudly. Alice was absolutely delighted to learn they'd broken the record, but her dad was less pleased. She had just ruined his favourite shirt!

Improve your writing: *linkers (2): time*

4 When you are writing a story, it is a good idea to use a range of time linkers.

1 Work in pairs and find examples in the story on page 38.

Paragraph A: after; by the time

2 How many more time linkers can you think of in 30 seconds?

5 Time linkers often help us to understand the order of events. Look at these sentences from the story on page 38 and answer the questions.

- **By the time** she arrived, her friends had been waiting for nearly thirty minutes.
- Her dad was less pleased. She had **just** ruined his favourite shirt!
- **As** she was pulling her board onto the sand, the waiting crowds cheered.

1 Which tense do we usually use to talk about
 a) a finished event?
 b) an event which happened before another event?
 c) something which was interrupted by another action?
2 Which time linkers can we use with these tenses?
3 What do the linkers in the three sentences mean? Why are they used here?

6 Complete sentences 1–6 with some of the time expressions in the list. Look carefully at the tenses.

| ago as soon as during finally for since while |

1 A few years _____ , we stayed in a really terrible hotel!
2 _____ we'd arrived, the problems started.
3 After we'd been waiting _____ half an hour in the hall, a grumpy receptionist appeared.
4 By the time we _____ checked in, the kitchen had stopped serving dinner.
5 The bar staff played music all night _____ we were trying to sleep.
6 We have never been back _____ then!

7 Imagine you are the person in either photo B or C. Complete the sentences using your own ideas.

1 **Before** ...

Before the show started, I was absolutely terrified.

2 **At first,** I ...
3 **Then,** I ...
4 **When** I was ... , I felt ...
5 **In the end,** I ...
6 **Afterwards,** I ...
7 I'd **never** ...

Ready to write!

You have decided to enter a short story competition in an international magazine. The story must **begin** with the following words:
As soon as we set off, things started to go wrong.
Write your story in **120–180** words.

8 Read the task above and brainstorm some ideas for your story. Think about the following questions:

1 Who are the main characters in your story?
2 Where are they going? Why?
3 What things could go wrong on this type of journey?
4 How might that make people feel?
5 Will your story end happily or unhappily? Why?

9 Look at the table below and write a paragraph plan. Decide which information you are going to include in each paragraph, and in what order.

First paragraph	• Begin with the words given. • Introduce the characters and set the scene.
Middle paragraph(s)	• Develop the main part of the story. • Remember to use descriptive language.
Final paragraph	• Bring the story to a definite conclusion. Try to think of an interesting or humorous last line.

10 In pairs, take turns to tell your story. Listen to your partner and suggest ways they could improve their story.

add more detail at the beginning
give a clear ending

Writing Part 2: *a story* — Exam tip

➤ Write a plan before you write! Your story should have a clear beginning, middle and end.
➤ Use paragraphs and linkers to organise your ideas.
➤ Include a range of narrative tenses and time and sequencing expressions.
➤ Make your writing more interesting by using a range of language, especially adjectives and adverbs.
➤ Think about why you're writing. Is your story for a competition? If so, why would it win? Is it for a website / magazine? If so, why would people want to read it?

Writing reference ▶ p. 171

11 Write your story. Remember to start with the words given in the task! When you have finished, look at the checklist on page 171. Check your story and make any corrections.

Unit 3

1 Complete the sentences. Use the correct form of the verbs in the lists.

> cook   go on   miss   never / experience   save up
> sink   start   already / trek   wait   watch

0 After Alice had jumped into the sea, she ___sank___ to the bottom.

1 We _____ through the jungle for days by the time Phil joined us.

2 While he _____ the nature documentary, he noticed an unusual bird.

3 When the coach finally arrived, we _____ for hours!

4 The car broke down on the motorway, so we _____ our flight.

5 At this time yesterday, I _____ lunch on the campfire.

6 By the time we got to the festival, the headline band _____ playing.

7 We _____ a fantastic package tour to Greece three years ago.

8 She _____ all year, and she had nearly got enough money for a holiday.

9 Until last winter, I _____ freezing cold temperatures.

2 Complete the sentences with words from the list. For questions 4–6, write the correct form of the verb.

Comparisons

> easily   just   nearly   slightly

0 My week in France was ___just___ as much fun as the week in the UK.

1 This is _____ the greatest distance that I've ever travelled.

2 This campsite is _____ as good as the hotel. All it needs is a pool!

3 The train takes _____ longer than the bus.

Verbs + gerund / infinitive

> bring   warn   go

4 Oh no! I've forgotten _____ my camera!

5 I tried _____ her about the danger, but she didn't listen.

6 We've stopped _____ on holiday abroad – it's too expensive.

3 Choose the correct alternatives, and complete the sentences with your ideas.

0 I usually **go** / **set** off for this class at ... *7.00, straight after breakfast.*

1 If I could have a day **away** / **off** next week, I would...

2 If your car **stops** / **runs** out of fuel, you should ...

3 I'll never forget **seeing** / **to see** ...

4 You can really hurt **you** / **yourself** if you ...

Units 1–3

4 Choose the correct alternatives to complete the proverbs and sayings.

0 When a single hair has fallen from your head, you are not yet **bald** / **pale** / **smooth**. *(Sierra Leone)*

1 There are plenty of **acquaintances** / **colleagues** / **mates** in the world, but very few real friends. *(China)*

2 Make sure to get on **best** / **good** / **well** with your equals if you are going to fall **apart** / **away** / **out** with your superiors. *(Germany)*

3 **Journey** / **Travel** / **Trip** broadens the mind. *(Britain)*

4 You never meet your mother-**by** / **in** / **with**-law on the day that you are **good** / **fair** / **well**-dressed. *(America)*

5 A woman gets 30 percent of her beauty from **view** / **scenery** / **nature** and 70 percent from make-**on** / **out** / **up**. *(China)*

5 Complete the text with the correct form of the words in **bold**.

6 What do you think the main challenges would be of living alone in the wilderness? How well do you think you would cope?

4

aving the planet

UNIT TARGETS

Topic vocabulary: environment ● time ● animals
Grammar: future forms ● other uses of the gerund and infinitive
Word building: determiners ● phrasal verbs (2) ● noun suffixes
Writing: a formal email ● linkers (3)
  Exam preparation: Reading Part 2 ● Use of English Parts 3 and 4 ● Listening Part 4 ● Speaking Part 2 ● Writing Part 1

A

Baby Mei Mei born in captivity

B

The hottest summer on record!

C

WHAT A WASTE!

Environment

1 Work in pairs. Match these extracts from news stories to the headlines A–C. Then complete the gaps.

> dumps   litter   recycle   throw

1 The government is facing a crisis as **rubbish (1)** _____ reach the limit of their capacity. Local authorities may soon be unable to collect household waste or clear up **(2)** _____ from the streets as there will be nowhere to store it. Experts warn that we must reuse and **(3)** _____ more of the materials we **(4)** _____ **away** as a matter of urgent priority.

> change   emissions   fumes   heatwave   warming

2 Millions are suffering in the worst **(5)** _____ ever recorded. Scientists argue that this is direct evidence of **global (6)** _____. Unless we do more to reduce **carbon (7)** _____ and other pollution from industry and car **exhaust (8)** _____, **climate (9)** _____ looks set to worsen.

> conservation   endangered   extinction   habitat   wild

3 A Chinese zoo celebrated the new arrival yesterday of a Giant Panda, one of the world's most **(10)** _____ **species**. In the **(11)** _____, the panda is in danger of **(12)** _____. More money needs to be spent on **(13)** _____ to prevent its natural **(14)** _____ from being destroyed by farming and housing development.

2 Work in groups. Imagine you are the editors of a national newspaper. Discuss stories A–C and choose one to put on the front page.

> **Useful language**
>
> *.... would be my first choice, because ...*
> *To me, ... is more dramatic / shocking.*
> *This photo will make more of an impact.*

3 🔊 4.1 How green are you? For each statement, do you agree (✓), or disagree (✗)? Listen to Fabio and note down his opinions. How do you compare?

1 I recycle glass and paper ☐
2 I always switch off the lights when I leave a room. ☐
3 I walk, cycle, or use public transport whenever I can. ☐
4 I only buy things which are essential. ☐

Word boost ▶ Environment ▶ Workbook p. 22

Over to you!

4 In pairs, discuss this statement:

'It's our planet – we should all take care of it.'

 Discuss photos A and B in pairs.

1 To what extent do you think that photos A and B are connected?

2 Why do you think the problem in photo B is so big? How can we prevent it from getting worse?

Useful expressions

This happens because of ...
One of the effects of ... is ...
This leads to ...
Another factor is ...

---

2 What do you think the man is doing in the photo on page 43? Why do you think he is doing this? Quickly read the article and check your answer.

Exam practice

Reading Part 2: *finding clues*

Exam tip

Look for clues in the extracted sentences to help you decide how to complete the text. Think about:

► pronouns like *which, this, he* or *it* which might refer to a person, idea or thing in the text just before a gap.
► synonyms (words with the same meaning to those in the text), e.g. *solution = answer.*
► words with a topic connection, e.g. if a sentence includes the word *marine*, it might be useful to look for words like *ocean* or *sea* in the text.

3 Seven sentences have been removed from the article. Choose from the sentences A–H the one which fits each gap (1–7). There is one extra sentence which you do not need to use.

A From 1991 until its closure in 2001, the record was held by the Fresh Kills Landfill, near New York City!

B There is still no real solution to the problem.

C Even this small gesture could help save wildlife.

D Every year, we create more than 1.5 billion tonnes of waste.

E In the past, most manufactured goods were biodegradable, so waste eventually disappeared.

F If that happens, the consequences for marine ecosystems could be devastating.

G You don't need to be a scientist to help.

H This is because around 90% of the waste is plastic, which is a highly toxic material.

Vocabulary in context: *time*

4 We use different verbs to talk about *time*. In pairs match definitions a–d to the verbs in **bold** in the text. Then complete sentences 1–4 with these verbs.

a go by   b continue
c use time   d need an amount of time

1 The writer is going to _____ a few weeks at sea.

2 The smell of rubbish can _____ for weeks!

3 Several years have _____ since the European Space Agency began working in Tenerife.

4 It may _____ many years for us to clear up the Great Pacific Garbage Patch.

5 Read the article again and underline five expressions which include the word *time*. Which expressions mean:

1 for the present?   4 having a break?
2 a useless activity?   5 it is necessary to wait to
3 occasionally?   find out something?

Word boost ▶ Time ▶ Workbook p. 22

Throwing our future away?

Keith James is a leading researcher for 'What a Waste', an international study of waste and its global impact.

My family often teases me for having such a 'rubbish' job (get it?), and at times, I almost agree. As part of my research, I have **spent** days wading through rotting food and other deeply unpleasant items. Once, I had to visit an overflowing underground sewer. Several days **passed** before I could wash the stench out of my hair!

So why do I do what I do? Well, I strongly believe that waste is one of the greatest environmental problems facing us today. It might surprise you to learn that the largest man-made structure ever built is *not* the Great Wall of China. **1** [ ] This rubbish dump grew to be 12 kilometres wide, and 25 metres higher than the Statue of Liberty. Shockingly, this is only the biggest collection of rubbish ever to be established *on land*.

Next month, I'm taking some time out from my studies in order to go sailing in the Pacific Ocean. But don't feel jealous – I'm going there to fish for litter! Between Hawaii and California there floats an island of rubbish which is bigger than Spain. For the time being, this 'island' is held together by swirling ocean currents, but scientists are concerned that it may eventually spread throughout the Pacific. **2** [ ]

By the end of my month at sea I'll have transported several boatloads of this disgusting mess back to shore. Afterwards, I'll be working with a team of other scientists to sort through it, before disposing of it more safely. It will be a depressing task, but not, I hope, a waste of time. **3** [ ]

According to the UN Environment Programme, ocean refuse kills more than a million seabirds and 100,000 animals annually, and poisons many more. **4** [ ] Only time will tell what the long-term effects of this pollution might be. However, all meat and fish eaters are potentially at risk, as the poisons in the refuse will eventually be passed along the food chain.

The problem of waste is undoubtedly very serious, but changing people's attitudes is proving difficult. We are living today in a throwaway society. **5** [ ] Depressingly, this figure is still growing. We've covered the planet in rubbish dumps, and we've even managed to pollute the rest of the solar system! According to the European Space Agency in Tenerife, there are currently more than 600,000 pieces of rubbish orbiting the globe. Many are fragments of old satellites, but ESA researchers have also found tools, pens and even CDs, all discarded by untidy astronauts. If aliens ever do decide to visit planet Earth, they'll have to navigate through a lot of litter to get here!

Whether on land, in the oceans or in space, the problem of rubbish has developed into a crisis in recent years. **6** [ ] But many modern items will not break down. Plastic objects may **take** thousands of years to degrade, and electrical goods can **last** for thousands more.

However, this dim state of affairs could have a rosier future. If we all work together, we can make a real difference. **7** [ ] Only buy what you need, reuse and recycle when you can, and think carefully before you throw anything away. You might just save the planet!

Over to you!

6 Work in pairs. Write a 50-100 word dialogue between a researcher at the ESA and a reporter interested in the ESA's work (see paragraph 6 in the article). Include at least three *time* expressions from Activity 5.

7 Find another pair and take it in turns to perform your dialogues. The pair who is listening should decide:

1 which of the time expressions they hear.
2 whether they think they were used correctly.

1 Imagining the future is difficult! Read predictions A–G. Why do you think people said or published these statements? Which mistake do you think is the worst?

A By 1985, … air pollution **will have reduced** the … sunlight reaching the Earth by one half. (*Life* magazine, 1970)

B *Titanic* **sails** from New York April 20. (1912 advertisement. The *Titanic* sank on April 15)

C It doesn't matter what he does, he **will** never **amount** to anything. (Albert Einstein's teacher, 1895)

D We**'re getting** married on September 14th. (Announcement of Jennifer Lopez's and Ben Affleck's wedding, 2003. Days later the wedding was called off.)

E Computers in the future **may weigh** no more than 1.5 tons. (*Popular Mechanics* magazine, 1949)

F By 2000, … machines **will be producing** so much that everyone in the US will … be independently wealthy. (*Time* magazine, 1966)

G The sky looks clear. It seems it**'s going to be** fine tomorrow. (Local radio, May 22, 1999. The next day, a record-breaking tornado blew across Oklahoma, USA.)

2 Match the verbs in bold in Activity 1 to the future forms in the list. Then complete the rules with the future forms.

future continuous ⬜	present continuous ⬜
future perfect ⬜ *A*	present simple ⬜
going to future ⬜	*will* future ⬜
may / might / could ⬜	

Future forms

1 _present simple_ for timetabled events.

2 _____ for general predictions and facts, and decisions made at the moment of speaking

3 _____ for planned future actions and predictions based on evidence

4 _____ for fixed future arrangements

5 _____ for future actions in progress at a particular time or over a period of time

6 _____ for actions completed before a particular time in the future

7 _____ when we are not sure about the future

Language summary ▶ p. 159

Watch out! time linkers

We often use present tenses, especially the present simple, to talk about the future in clauses after a time linker (e.g. *after, as soon as, when, until*).

The situation **won't** *improve until we stop* (NOT ~~will stop~~) *polluting the planet.*

3 Complete the opinions of what life will be like in the next millennium by choosing the correct alternatives. Then write your own posting, using three different future forms.

◀▶ lish.com/discussion/future

Instead of train stations, we **(1)** **'ll be having** / **'ll have** rocket stations! The timetables **(2)** **will say** / **will have said** things like "the next rocket to Mars **(3)** **leaves** / **might leave** at 7:00." By the way, cool website – I **(4)**'m **having** / **'ll have** some friends round tonight so we can add more ideas together! *Selena*

Because of global warming, the climate **(5)** **is going to be** / **is being** scorching hot. After the water **(6)** **will dry** / **has dried** up, we'll have big problems. A thousand years from now, I think we **(7)** **experience** / **will be experiencing** a worldwide drought. ☹ *Jacek*

I think that by the year 3000 scientists **(8)** **will have invented** / **will invent** cures for many of today's diseases. It's impossible to be certain, but there **(9)** **will** / **may** not even be any illnesses at all! By the time that **(10)** **will happen** / **happens**, maybe we'll have found a way of avoiding old age too! ☺ *Danny*

4 Compare your postings in groups. Is each person mainly optimistic or pessimistic about the future?

Over to you!

5 Read this first line from a story. What do you think 'something' could be? Brainstorm ideas in groups.

'Tomorrow, something happens that will change our lives forever.'

IDEAS
environmental crisis (pollution? no more electricity?)
scientists announce an amazing invention (what?)
hero saves the planet! (who? how?)
natural disaster (heatwave? flood? earthquake?)

6 In your group, choose your best idea from Activity 5 and write the rest of the story. Write 80–120 words, using a variety of future forms.

7 Tell your stories to the class. Then vote on which story was a) the most imaginative, b) the most believable!

Get ready: *other uses of the gerund and the infinitive*

1 Read the text. Do you believe it is ever possible to predict the future? Why? / Why not?

2 Look at the verb forms in **bold** in Activity 1. In pairs, complete the table with the ideas in the list. Can you add any other ideas?

- after an adjective
- after a preposition
- after make + object
- after *let* + object
- ~~after *would rather*~~
- after model verbs
- as a noun
- to express purpose

<u>Would you rather know</u> what is going to happen to you, or simply wait and <u>let destiny take</u> its course? Many people are <u>desperate to learn</u> what the future holds. Unfortunately, <u>predicting the future</u> is notoriously difficult! It usually takes a lot of research – and luck – <u>to predict</u> the future correctly. Nevertheless, fortune tellers and astrologists want to <u>make us believe</u> that they <u>can see</u> things which are hidden to the rest of us. However, if these 'mystics' were really as <u>good at predicting</u> the future as they claim, surely they would all have won the lottery by now?!

gerund (-*ing* form)	infinitive with *to*	infinitive without *to*
		after 'would rather'

Grammar boost ▶ Other uses of the gerund and the infinitive ▶ Workbook p. 25

Exam practice

3 Complete the exam task.

Exam tip

Use of English Part 4: *thinking about language*

➤ This paper tests all kinds of language, but common areas include: *verb tenses, gerunds and infinitives, phrasal verbs, linkers, collocations* and key grammatical structures such as *modal verbs, conditionals, passive, reported speech.*
➤ Remember, you may need to change both the grammar *and* the vocabulary.

For questions **1–8**, complete the second sentence so that it has a similar meaning to the first sentence, using the word given. **Do not change the word given.** You must use between **two** and **five** words, including the word given. Write **only** the missing words in **CAPITAL LETTERS**.

0 After we've prepared our equipment, we'll begin our trip to the Great Pacific Garbage Patch.   **SETTING**
We'll prepare our equipment *BEFORE SETTING OFF* for the Great Pacific Garbage Patch.

---

1 Reaching the Great Pacific Garbage Patch involves a four-hour journey.   **TAKES**
It .... the Great Pacific Garbage Patch.

2 I want to study Environmental Science.   **INTERESTED**
I .... Environmental Science.

3 The protest march will be starting shortly, so you need to hurry.   **ABOUT**
The protest march ...., so you need to hurry.

4 There's no point in trying to clean up the ocean, as the task is too big.   **WASTE**
Trying to clean up the ocean ...., as the task is too big.

5 The Greenpeace activist had the respect of all the other campaigners.   **UP**
All the other campaigners .... the Greenpeace campaigner.

6 Looking after the environment is everyone's responsibility.   **CARE**
It is everyone's responsibility .... the environment.

7 We expect temperatures to increase every year.   **GO**
We think that .... every year.

8 I don't know why the government closed the rubbish dump.   **MADE**
I don't know .... the rubbish dump.

Get ready: *animals*

1 Work in pairs and try to complete the quiz. Then check your answers on page 150. How well did you do? Did you learn anything new?

Easy *(1 point each)*

1 This animal has got eight legs and **catches** its **prey** in a web.

2 This strange **mammal carries** its **young** in a pouch and is very good at jumping.

Harder *(2 points each)*

3 This pretty flying **insect** usually **feeds on** flowers and can taste with its feet.

4 This **rare** animal has become endangered **in the wild**, where it lives on a **diet** consisting of 95% bamboo plants.

5 This huge bird can run at speeds of up to 70 k to **escape** from **predators**, but only has a tiny brain. Its brain is smaller than one of its own eyes.

Very hard *(3 points each)*

6 This large and highly dangerous snake **breeds** underwater. Unusually for a **reptile**, it **gives birth** to live offspring instead of **laying** eggs.

7 This grey animal became Australia's biggest **pest** after it was **set free** there by settlers in the 1800s. It destroyed the habitats of many **native** species, which became **extinct** as a result.

8 This **common** but very **unpopular** insect can **survive** for up to nine days without its head!

2 Choose four of the words and expressions in **bold** from Activity 1 and write definitions. Then swap your answers with a partner and correct each other's work.

A rare animal is one which is not very common.

3 In groups, write six more animal quiz questions (include easy, harder and very hard questions). Include at least six of the words in **bold** from Activity 1.

4 Find another group and take turns to ask and answer questions. Which team are the 'animal experts'?

Word boost ▶ Animals ▶ Workbook p. 22

Exam practice

Listening Part 4: *listening to a long text*

Exam tip

Listening to a long text can be difficult. To make it easier:
➤ read the rubric and the questions carefully *before* you listen and underline any key words.
➤ listen and choose the best options. Don't waste time writing long notes.
➤ don't panic if you can't answer a question immediately. Keep listening and move on to the next question.
➤ when you've heard the recording twice, choose an answer for every question, even if you still aren't sure.

5 4.2 You will hear an interview with a conservationist, Eddie Scherbaum, who talks about his work with animals. For questions 1-7, choose the best answer (A, B or C).

1 What concern does Eddie have about conservation?
  A He thinks it is a depressing field to work in.
  B He wishes progress would happen more quickly.
  C He feels bad because he can only save a few animals.

2 What does Eddie think is currently the biggest reason for animal extinctions?
  A loss of habitat
  B illegal hunting
  C climate change

3 What does Eddie say about famous people?
  A They recognise that animals are good for their image.
  B They should do more to help environmental issues.
  C Many of them are genuinely interested in conservation.

4 How does Eddie feel about working with animals?
  A He would prefer to work indoors.
  B He enjoys every moment he is at work.
  C He admits they can be difficult to work with.

5 Why doesn't Eddie have a favourite animal?
  A He does not wish to be unfair in any way.
  B He does not feel fond of any particular species.
  C He believes that all of them are equally appealing.

6 What does Eddie think of the waldrapp ibis?
  A It isn't very likeable.
  B It's really unattractive.
  C It lacks intelligence.

7 Which kind of animal is Eddie going to work with for his next project?
  A a worm
  B a frog
  C a gorilla

Over to you!

6 Should we try to save all endangered animals, or should we allow some species to become extinct? Why?

Why are these people doing these things?

1 Look at the photos above. In pairs, discuss the question above the photos. Think of as many ideas as you can.

2 🔊 4.3 Listen to the instructions and to a student's response. Did Akiko use any of your ideas?
Do you think she did the task well or badly? Why?

Exam practice

4 🔊 4.4 Work in pairs. Student A look at the photos below. Student B look at the photos on page 151.

1 Listen to the instructions and complete the task.
2 Listen carefully while your partner is speaking. You will need to answer a question about their photographs!

5 Tell your partner:

1 how well you think they did and why.
2 which comparative expressions you heard them use.

3 Look at these expressions from Akiko's task. In pairs, decide which describe things that are the same (S) and which describe things that are *not* the same (D). Can you think of any other expressions like these?

1 Both pictures are connected to the theme of …
2 Both of them show …
3 The main difference between the pictures is that …
4 … are completely different.
5 In the first picture … but in the second picture …
6 Another similarity is that …
7 … just as (+ *adjective*) as …
8 … but they look much (+ *comparative*) …
9 In contrast, …
10 … is probably less (+ *comparative*) …

> **Speaking Part 2:** *comparison* **Exam tip**
>
> ➤ DON'T waste time describing every detail in each photo!
> ➤ Answer both parts of the question.
> ➤ Always talk about both photos together. You will not get high marks if you talk about each photo separately.
> ➤ Use a variety of expressions for making comparisons.
> ➤ Give reasons for your opinions and explain your ideas.

Student A

What might people enjoy about keeping these animals?

Determiners: *countable and uncountable nouns*

1 Read the quotation below. In your opinion, what are the **three** biggest issues facing the world today? Compare your ideas with your partner. Do you share any of the same concerns?

> Humanity is facing a <u>huge number of problems</u> for the future. We'll need to put in <u>a great deal of work</u> to sort things out!

2 Look at the <u>underlined</u> expressions in the quotation above. Then answer the questions in pairs.

   1 Which of the nouns in blue is *countable* and which is *uncountable*?
   2 When can we use the expressions in red?

3 Which of these words or expressions can we use with countable nouns, uncountable nouns, or both? Can you add any more?

> a few   a/an   all of   a little   a lot of   any   each   enough   every   a large amount of   few   many   much   no   none of   some of   the

Countable nouns		Uncountable nouns
	a lot of	

4 Which sentence in each pair is more positive? What is the difference in meaning between the words in **bold**?

   1 A We've got **a little** time to save the planet, so we needn't panic.
       B We've got **little** time to save the planet, so we need to hurry.

   2 A I have **few** worries about the environment. We're doing OK.
       B I have **a few** worries about the environment. We need to do more.

Phrasal verbs (2): *solving problems*

5 Are you good at solving problems? Work in teams of four and try to complete the quiz in two minutes! Then check your answers on page 150. Which questions did you find the most difficult? Why?

Two minute quiz!

Take this two minute quiz and **find out** how good you are at solving problems! If you **come across** a question you can't answer, don't worry. **Carry on** with the rest of the quiz and **come back** to it afterwards!

A Someone has mixed the letters of these 'environment' words up! Can you **sort** them **out**?

   TPLONUOLI
   HDTUGRO
   NONCETIXTI

B You are working in a conservation team which is **looking after** some rare and very hungry frogs. Your boss has asked you to **look into** the problem of how to feed them all.

If 6 people can feed 6 frogs in 6 minutes, how many people will you need to feed 60 frogs in 60 seconds?

C Can you **work out** how to complete this series?

   A B D G K P ?

D Can you **fill in** the gaps? Write a letter which will complete the red verb and start the blue verb.

   BREE_IE
   CATC_IDE
   HUN_RACK

6 Work in pairs. Match definitions 1–6 to six of the phrasal verbs in **bold** in Activity 5. Then write definitions or example sentences for the other four phrasal verbs.

   1 complete
   2 investigate
   3 discover
   4 continue
   5 take care of
   6 return

Over to you!

7 Write your own quiz! In pairs, write six questions about vocabulary or grammar from Units 1–4. Include at least **three** determiners and **three** phrasal verbs.

8 Find another pair and take turns asking questions. The pair with the most correct answers wins!

Word boost ▶ Workbook p. 79

Get ready: *noun suffixes*

1 Work in groups.
1 Complete the table with the noun form of the words in the list.
2 Add at least **three** more examples of your own to each column.
3 Can you think of any more noun suffixes?

achieve   creative   criticise   cruel   depress   excite   free   friend   ~~happy~~
ill   independent   please   pollute   race   relax   stupid   violent

-ation	-dom	-ence	-ion	-ism	-ity	-ment	-ness	-ship	-ty	-ure
							happiness			

2 Choose **one** of the nouns above. Write notes about what it means to you.

To me, happiness means spending time with friends and family.

3 Work in pairs and take it in turns to talk for **one** minute about your topic. Listen carefully to your partner and find one thing that you agree with.

Word boost ▶ noun suffixes ▶ Workbook p. 23

Exam practice

4 Read the exam task, ignoring the gaps. Why does the author mention these films: *Blindness, Independence Day, Batman*?

5 Complete the exam task.

Exam tip

Use of English Part 3: *suffixes*
To change the part of speech of a word, you often need to add a suffix.
➤ Revise common suffixes before your exam.
➤ Look carefully at each gap and decide which part of speech is missing.
➤ Choose an appropriate ending for the word.
➤ Don't forget to think about prefixes and any other spelling changes too!

For questions **1–10**, read the text below. Use the word given in capitals at the end of some lines to form a word that fits in the gap **in the same line**. There is an example at the beginning **(0)**.
Write your answers **IN CAPITAL LETTERS**.

The end of the world?

When it comes to predicting the future, Hollywood has got a lively **(0)** *IMAGINATION*.   **IMAGINE**

In *The Day After Tomorrow*, **(1)** .... warming causes huge devastation. Too much   **GLOBE**
(2) .... from factories and exhaust fumes creates a new Ice Age. We see the scientist,   **POLLUTE**
Dr Jack Hall, walk across **(3)** .... lakes and snow drifts to save his son. He arrives just   **FREEZE**
in time – but **(4)** .... there's no happy ending for planet Earth.   **FORTUNATE**

It seems that directors take a **(5)** .... view of the future – perhaps because it's   **GLOOM**
more **(6)** .... that way. If they aren't warning us about climate change, they're   **DRAMA**
concerned about our health. Films like *Blindness* and *28 Weeks Later* imagine how a terrible
(7) .... might affect us. Aliens are another worry, as *The War of the Worlds* and   **ILL**
Independence Day predict – yes, they both foresee lots of fighting and **(8)** .... !   **VIOLENT**

But don't despair. Hollywood is fascinated by the apocalypse, but it loves superheroes too. In
Batman and *Spiderman*, heroes find **(9)** .... to all kinds of problems, including saving   **SOLVE**
the world. Maybe we don't have to feel quite so **(10)** .... about the future, after all!   **DEPRESS**

Prepare

1 Look at the photos. How are these people raising money for charity? Can you think of any other ideas?

2 Quickly read the advertisement in Activity 3. Which of the ideas in the photos does it mention?

Analyse the task

3 Read the advertisement and the notes again carefully. Imagine you are going to write a Part 1 email and answer the questions.

1 How many notes do you have to address in your reply?
2 Do you need to use formal or informal language?

4 Read Saira's email. Which information does she miss out? Correct her mistake.

To:	enquiries@green.rock.festival
From:	Saira Ahmed
Subject:	Volunteering

Dear Sir or Madam,

I am writing in response to your advertisement for the Green Rock festival.

I was extremely interested to read about this event, because I believe that saving the environment is very important. I think that global warming will be a serious problem in the future, so we must do all we can to prevent it from getting worse.

For this reason, I would welcome the opportunity to help at your festival. I could work for two hours. I would prefer to serve food, as I already have some experience as a waitress.

I would be very grateful if you could tell me more about the music at the festival. Would it be possible to let me know which bands are going to play?

I look forward to hearing from you.

Yours faithfully,

Saira Ahmed

5 Read the email again. Why does Saira:

1 begin the email with the expression *Dear Sir or Madam*?
2 use indirect questions rather than direct questions in the final paragraph?
3 end the email with the expression *Yours faithfully* rather than *Yours sincerely*?

Improve your writing:

linkers (3): purpose, reason and result

6 Read sentences A–H. Then answer the questions in pairs.
1 Do you agree or disagree with the statements? Why?
2 Can you add any more linkers to each of the categories in red?

Purpose
A I donate money **in order to** help charities.
B I believe my government must do more **to** help the environment.
C My whole family recycles **so as not to** create waste.
D Everyone should get rid of their cars **so that** we can have a greener planet.

Reason
E We must save all endangered species **because** every animal's life is important.
F My country is already experiencing problems **because of** climate change.

Result
G I care about my world, **so** I read the news every day.
H We shouldn't waste electricity. **Therefore** we should only use computers for work, not for fun.

7 Which of the linkers above do we use before:
1 an infinitive form?
2 a subject and a verb?
3 a noun?

8 Complete the advertisement with suitable linkers from Activity 6.

Volunteers needed (1) _____ save turtles!

Illegal hunting kills thousands of turtles annually, **(2)** _____ many species have become endangered. At our Mexican centre, we breed turtles **(3)** _____ populations can increase. We are looking for summer volunteers to look after the young turtles before setting them free. — *When? For how long?*

(4) _____ waste time travelling, you will both live and work near the beach. There will be opportunities to go surfing or diving at the weekends! — *What accommodation?* — *Great, because ...*

(5) _____ summer is our busiest time of year, all volunteers will work hard.

(6) _____ this, the summer programme is only suitable for people who are absolutely passionate about animals or conservation. — *Yes, give details.*

Enquiries: admin@turtle-centre-mexico.com

Ready to write!

You have seen an advertisement on a website for a conservation holiday. Read the advertisement and the notes you have made. Then write an email, using **all** of your notes. Write your answer in 120–150 words in an appropriate style.

9 Read the task above and the advertisement in Activity 8. Why is the centre looking for volunteers? What kind of volunteers are they looking for?

Writing Part 1: *informing the reader* — *Exam tip*

Try to keep the reader fully informed in your writing.
➤ You *must* address all four notes. You will lose marks if you miss one out!
➤ Address each note appropriately. For example, the note *Give details* asks you to give factual information, whereas *Say why* or *... because ...* asks you to explain something.
➤ Where appropriate, add relevant extra information to support your ideas. For example, it is a good idea to give reasons for arguments, opinions or preferences.
➤ Use a range of linkers to add and organise ideas.

Writing reference ▶ p. 168

10 Read the *Exam tip*. Then read each note in Activity 8 carefully. First decide what the function of each note is, then write down some ideas on how you're going to answer it in your email.

Note	Function, e.g. giving information	Ideas
Red	Asking for information	
Blue		
Green		
Orange		

11 Write a plan and decide which information you are going to include in each paragraph.

12 Now write your email. Remember to use formal language and include a range of linkers. When you have finished, look at the checklist on p 169. Check your email and make any corrections.

Unit 4

1 Complete the sentences with the correct form of the verbs.

0 By the end of the year, what (**you / do**) to help the environment?
By the end of the year, what will you have done to help the environment?

1 It's very dark outside. There (**be**) a storm soon.
2 There's a lot of litter here. Perhaps I (**clean**) it up later.
3 He's not very fond of (**work**) with animals.
4 The bus to the nature reserve always (**leave**) at 11.15.
5 At this time tomorrow, I (**interview**) a famous conservationist.
6 It's everyone's responsibility (**recycle**).
7 Many scientists think that global warming (**destroy**) the Earth.
8 I (**meet**) some friends at the zoo at 2.00 tomorrow.
9 Hurry up! The nature documentary is about (**start**).

2 Complete the crossword with the correct words.

Across
2 We throw … rubbish. (4)
4 solve = … out (4)
5 noun formed from *stupid* (9)
8 … dioxide; … emissions (6)
9 Cars pollute the air with … *fumes*. (7)
10 rare kind of animal = *endangered* … (7)

Down
1 large amount of water covering an area which should be dry (5)
3 take care of = *look* … (5)
6 noun formed from *please* (8)
7 We're going to … a month on the island. (5)

Units 1–4

3 Complete the text using the words in the list. There is one word you will not need to use.

a   any   ~~enough~~   some   that   the   too   very   which   who   whose

For some people, it isn't good **(0)** *enough* to walk instead of drive, or to remember to recycle. **(1)** _____ environmentalists, **(2)** _____ are sometimes called 'eco warriors', go to extremes to help save the planet!

Alain Robert, also known as 'Spiderman', believes that modern society is **(3)** _____ materialistic. To draw attention to environmental issues, he climbs enormous buildings – without using **(4)** _____ ropes! When Robert climbed up the New York Times building in the USA, **(5)** _____ is a **(6)** _____ tall skyscraper, he held up a banner protesting about global warming.

Another famous protester, **(7)** _____ name is Julia 'Butterfly' Hill, spent two years living up a tree! She didn't want developers to cut down **(8)** _____ beautiful old forest in California. Luckily, her protest was successful, and most of **(9)** _____ forest was saved.

4 You are going to talk for one minute on one of the topics in the list. Choose a topic, then write notes. Think about:

1 *why* this is an important issue.
2 *what* the main problems are.
3 *how* we can improve the situation in the future.

climate change   conservation   pollution   recycling

5 Take turns to give your presentation in pairs. The partner who is listening should give the presentation a mark out of 10, explaining why!

UNIT TARGETS

Topic vocabulary: places ● advertising ● city life
Grammar: conditionals 0-3 ● conditional linkers
Word building: compound nouns ● collocations (1) ●
easily confused verbs
Writing: an essay ● linkers (4)
Exam preparation: Reading Part 1 ● Use of English
Parts 1 and 4 ● Listening Part 1 ● Speaking Parts 3
and 4 ● Writing Part 2

Places

1 In pairs, compare photos A–C, and say why you think people might choose to live in each place.

Useful language

In photo A you can see ... , while in photo B ...
One thing these photos have in common is ...
Unlike photo A, photo B ...
One small / major difference is that ...

2 🔊 5.1 Listen to three people talking about the places where they live. For each of the speakers 1–3, answer the questions.

1 Which place is the speaker describing: photo A, B or C?
2 What are the advantages and disadvantages of living in each place?

3 🔊 5.1 How did the speakers describe each place? Listen again and write the adjectives.

Speaker 1: remote, ...

4 What do the expressions in **bold** mean?

1 We live **in the middle of nowhere**.
2 Some districts are a bit **run down**.
3 There's **a strong sense of community** here.

5 Write short descriptions (20–50 words each) of two places in your area. Then compare with a partner. Can they guess which places you're describing?

Word boost ▶ Places ▶ Workbook p. 28

Over to you!

6 In groups, decide whether photo A, B or C shows the best place to live for a) teenagers, b) young families, c) retired people. Give reasons for your opinions.

A

B

1 Look at the photos and discuss the questions in pairs.

1　What are the differences between place A and place B?
2　Why do you think place B looks like this?
3　Which place do you think looks more attractive? Why?

2 You are going to read an article about advertising in different cities. Quickly read the article on page 55 and find out where the places in photos A and B are.

Exam practice

3 Read the article again carefully. For questions 1–8, choose the answer (A, B, C or D) which you think fits best according to the text. Use the ideas in the *Exam tip* to help you.

1　What is the main point of the first paragraph?
  A　We see more adverts than we realise.
  B　Many people are annoyed by television advertising.
  C　We do not pay enough attention to adverts.
  D　Advertising has increased in towns and cities.

2　What do we learn about the writer's opinion of advertising in Tokyo in the second paragraph?
  A　It lacks a personal appeal for him.
  B　He thinks that it is very creative.
  C　It seems excessive to him.
  D　He thinks it is Tokyo's main attraction.

3　Why do advertisers see Tokyo as important?
  A　It sets trends which are often copied.
  B　Its distinctive style is popular with everyone.
  C　It reflects trends that are popular elsewhere.
  D　Its style is imitated in every city.

4　What does the writer mean by 'sets it apart' in line 30?
  A　makes it seem individual and different
  B　is something which visitors find very inviting
  C　gives it something in common with other cities
  D　lends it a highly unattractive appearance

5　In the fourth paragraph, Roberta Calvino suggests that
  A　the largest adverts can usually be found in rural areas.
  B　advertising is a particularly bad problem in Austria.
  C　outdoor advertising extends beyond urban areas.
  D　modern adverts are continuing to grow in size.

6　What does Roberta tell us about urban advertising in the fifth paragraph?
  A　It can be rather unconvincing.
  B　It helps us to fulfil our dreams.
  C　It particularly affects women.
  D　It can lower our self-confidence.

7　What comparison does Roberta make between urban advertising and TV advertising?
  A　TV advertising is more effective in the long term.
  B　It is easier to ignore urban advertising.
  C　Urban advertising can have more impact.
  D　There is greater variety in urban advertising.

8　What response did the mayor get when he removed advertising from São Paulo?
  A　The majority of private individuals and commercial people supported him.
  B　Advertisers were willing to display fewer advertisements in the city.
  C　Local artists were unsure how attractive the office blocks would look.
  D　Most of the people who lived in the city welcomed his decision.

How many adverts do you think you'll see today? 10? 30? Astonishingly, according to the market research firm *Yankelovich*, some of us see as many as 2,000–5,000 adverts a day! As well as commercial breaks, those irritating interruptions to our TV viewing, there are adverts all around us. Most of the time we're not even consciously aware of them. But think about your town or city. How many billboards does it have? What about shop signs and posters?

Tokyo, in Japan, takes urban advertising to the extreme. Flashing neon lights and gigantic outdoor TVs blaring out advertising slogans make the city seem like something from science fiction. Although the city temples may still lay claim to being more impressive, the explosion of sound and colour in the commercial centre can take your breath away. Whether you find the overall effect stunning or nightmarish is a question of personal taste. However, it would be hard not to admire the advertisers' ingenuity. Recent innovations include interactive games projected onto walls for people to play with (all featuring a company logo, of course!). 'Smellvertising' is also catching on – that's the idea of using pleasant smells like chocolate to attract consumers' attention!

Innovations in Tokyo are of huge significance in the world of advertising because where Tokyo leads, other cities soon follow. Big cities from New York to London already have outdoor television screens, although 'smellverts' are still relatively unusual. Although Tokyo is far from being universally admired, many urban authorities find its approach to advertising exciting and dynamic. So what's the problem?

'If every city copied Tokyo, it would be absolutely terrible!' exclaims Roberta Calvino of the advertising watchdog group, *Ad Alert*. 'At the moment, Tokyo's futuristic style sets it apart. It invites our attention even if not necessarily our appreciation because there's simply nothing like it. But we don't need 100 poor imitations. Do you want

tourists visiting your city to notice the wonderful architecture, the upmarket shopping boutiques, or the millions of signs and flyers? In many cities, advertising is as bad as litter or vandalism – it spoils our environment. Go beyond the city outskirts and you'll find that advertising is taking over the countryside, too. The world's biggest advert was actually in a field in Austria, below the flight path to Vienna airport. It was the size of 50 football pitches!'

According to Roberta, advertising can also influence the way we think and feel. 'Advertisers want to convince us that their products will make us happy or successful, just like the celebrities in the promotions. Unfortunately, that's all an illusion – you can't simply "buy" a celebrity lifestyle at the shops! Nevertheless, advertisers work hard to get us to swallow this message. For instance, fashion brands prefer to advertise using images of glamorously made-up supermodels because they want "ordinary" girls to feel inadequate in comparison. The logic goes that the more dissatisfied we feel with our lives, the more we'll spend to cheer ourselves up! Although outdoor advertising may seem to make less of an immediate impression than TV commercials, its message can have greater force. If we don't want to watch a TV ad, we can turn over, or switch off. We can't be so choosy about our surroundings.'

Or perhaps we *do* have a choice? In 2007, one Brazilian city made a radical protest. Gilberto Kassab, the mayor of São Paulo, ordered the removal of more than 15,000 adverts! In justification, he condemned urban advertising in very strong terms as 'visual pollution'. Unsurprisingly, this made many local businesses unhappy. One marketing executive argued that adverts 'are more like works of art, hiding grey office blocks and industrial estates,' a view which had some backing from a number of the city's residents. However, a more typical response can be summed up in this statement from Isuara dos Santos, 19. 'If we'd known what a difference it would make, we'd have got rid of the adverts years ago. Now we can see the *real* São Paulo, and it's wonderful!'

Vocabulary in context: *advertising*

4 Find words and phrases in the article which mean:

1 adverts shown between TV programmes (*paragraph 1*)
2 large panels or signs displaying advertising (*paragraph 1*)
3 advertising messages (*paragraph 2*)
4 symbol or trademark used by a company (*paragraph 2*)
5 shoppers (*paragraph 2*)
6 small advertising leaflets (*paragraph 4*)
7 advertising campaigns (*paragraph 5*)
8 product or company names (*paragraph 5*)
9 person who decides how a product or service should be advertised or sold (*paragraph 6*)

Word boost ▶ Advertising ▶ Workbook p. 28

Over to you!

5 Tell your partner about adverts you've seen which you really liked / hated. Do they share your opinion? Why? / Why not?

6 Do you think there is too much advertising? Should any kinds of adverts be banned or restricted? Discuss the questions in groups, thinking about the following:

1 product promotion in films
2 educational advertising
3 the advertising of cigarettes and alcohol
4 advertising in schools.

A If cats **could speak**, we **wouldn't need** to advertise.

– *Kitty Chow (pet food)*

B You **won't get** it completely clean unless you **get** it *Splenda* clean.

– *Splenda (washing powder)*

C If nature **had intended** man to fly, it **would have given** him wings.

– *Coach Express (cross-country coach travel)*

D If something **sounds** too good to be true, it probably **is**.

– *Campaign for Advertising Standards*

1 Read the advertising slogans. Which did you find the most convincing? Why?

2 Complete the rules by matching slogans A–D to the conditional forms and their uses.

Conditionals 0–3

Conditional	Used for ...
zero	general truths
first	possible future actions or events
second	unlikely, imaginary or impossible present or future actions
third	hypothetical past actions or events (things which did not happen)

Language summary ▶ p. 160

3 In pairs, write rules for forming conditionals 0–3. When do we use a comma to separate the two clauses?

Zero: If + present tense, present tense

4 Decide what type of conditional (0–3) the sentences below are. Complete them using the correct form of the verbs in the list.

be   bring   buy   not see   spend   want

1 If the company _____ more money on advertising they might have been more successful.
2 Shoppers can get a discount on their purchases if they _____ along one of these flyers.
3 If you _____ a celebrity, would you be happy to appear in advertising promotions?
4 You _____ many adverts if you visit São Paulo!
5 If you _____ to work in an advertising agency, you need to be very creative.
6 _____ you _____ that particular brand if you hadn't seen the advert?

5 Complete the conditional questions with your own ideas. Then ask and answer your questions with a partner. What was the most interesting thing you found out?

0 What *will* you (**buy**) *buy if you go shopping this week* ?
1 If you (**go**) into town this weekend, ...?
2 If you (**live**) alone on a tropical island ...?
3 How ... your town or city (**be**) different if ...?
4 If you (**see**) a really good advert ...?
5 If you (**be**) in charge of your district ...?
6 Where ... you (**buy**) your dream house if ...?

6 How would things be different if situations 1–5 had happened? Write sentences using third conditional.

1 the government banned all adverts last year
2 you were born in New York
3 no one invented cars
4 you grew up in a remote village
5 you spent all your money at the shops yesterday

Over to you!

7 If you were in charge of your town or city, what would you change? Discuss your ideas in groups, using photos A–D to help you. Agree which **three** things you would change first and why.

Get ready: *conditional linkers*

1 A girl is trying to persuade her friends to come shopping. Read what her friends say by matching 1–6 to A–G. **Which friend sounds the most enthusiastic?**

0 I'm working today, so I can't come,
1 OK, but I need to find an umbrella first
2 Shopping is boring! We can go into town
3 Definitely! I'll make it into town
4 Mum says I can't go out
5 Sorry, I'm busy. I'll let you know
6 I'm skint. I'll come with you

A **as long as** we can do something else afterwards.
B **unless** my room's spotless. Right now, it's a tip!
C **when** I'm free.
D **in case** it rains. And a coat …
E **even though** I'd much rather go shopping!
F **providing that** you buy me a coffee.
G **even if** I have to walk the whole way there!

2 Look at the linkers in **bold** above. Which linker or linkers mean:

1 if not
2 but only if
3 because something might happen
4 as soon as; at a particular time
5 whether or not ('strong' *if*)
6 despite the fact that

3 Write your own advertising slogans! Complete the sentences with your ideas. Look at a partner's slogans: which of theirs do you think would be more effective than yours? Why?

1 When you use *MagicWash* shampoo, …
2 As long as you brush with *Minty* toothpaste, …
3 Unless you read *What's On* magazine, …
4 Always carry an *X-Talk* mobile, in case …

Grammar boost ▶ Conditional linkers ▶ Workbook p. 31

Exam Practice

4 Complete the exam task.

Use of English Part 4: *key words*

Exam tip

➤ Look at the key word and identify what kind of word it is (e.g. *a verb, a noun, a linker*).
➤ Consider how we use this kind of word – think about grammar and collocations.

For questions **1–8**, complete the second sentence so that it has a similar meaning to the first sentence, using the word given. **Do not change the word given.** You must use between **two** and **five** words, including the word given.

0 I'll get there by six if the train is on time. **AS**

I'll get there by six *AS LONG AS THE TRAIN* is on time.

---

1 Both of the villages are equally picturesque. **JUST**

This village .... that village.

2 You might want to buy something, so take your wallet with you. **CASE**

Take your wallet with you .... to buy something.

3 Please take care of your little brother while I'm out. **LOOK**

I want .... your little brother while I'm out.

4 If we catch the bus, we should reach the shop before it shuts. **MISS**

We should reach the shop before it shuts as long .... the bus.

5 Going shopping at the mall always makes me feel happier. **IF**

I always feel .... at the mall.

6 My preference is for leaving early rather than late. **SET**

I would rather .... early than late.

7 We visited the outdoor market despite the rainy weather. **EVEN**

We visited the outdoor market .... raining.

8 He got lost in the city because he forgot to take his map with him. **LEFT**

If he .... behind, he wouldn't have got lost in the city.

Get ready: *city life*

1 Read these extracts from travel guides. What is unusual about each city? Which would you most like to visit?

Motorbikes are the most popular way to get around in Ho Chi Minh City! Motorcycle taxis are speedier than public transport so fasten your helmet before you set off! If you want to escape the congestion, take a detour down the backstreets. You'll find thousands of bargains on sale on market stalls, so go on, treat yourself ...

Head to Bloomington, Minnesota, for the biggest shopping mall in the US! With over 400 stores, from high street names to designer outlets, in addition to movie screens, fast-food diners, and even an indoor theme park, there's always a lot going on. Getting there is easy – visitors can land at a local airport, or catch a train directly to the mall!

Venice is famous for culture and canals – much of the city is accessible only by waterways! Boasting Europe's largest car-free zone, much of the commercial centre is completely pedestrianised. Visitors can admire the historic architecture, explore the chic boutiques, or take in a gallery.

2 Complete the table with expressions from Activity 1. How many more ideas can you add in **one** minute?

traffic	shopping	things to do
get around	on sale	a lot going on

3 Write a mini (50-80 word) travel guide for a town or city near you. Compare your descriptions with a partner. Whose sounds more exciting? Why?

Word boost ▶ City life ▶ Workbook p. 28

Exam Practice

Listening Part 1: *opinions*

Exam tip

➤ People often use set phrases to give opinions, e.g. *I think.*
➤ Some opinions may be negative, *I don't think*, etc.
➤ Watch out! Speakers do not *always* use set phrases, so listen carefully!

4 🔊 **5.2** You will hear people talking in eight different situations. For questions 1-8, choose the correct answer, A, B or C.

1 On the radio, you hear a review of *The UK City Guide for Teenagers*. Which aspect of the book disappointed the reviewer?
  A the size of one of the sections
  B the writing style of the authors
  C the lack of any cultural information

2 You hear a man talking about his journey to work. What does he think about in the car?
  A his interest in nature
  B having a country home
  C plans for the rest of his day

3 You hear a boy and a girl talking about life in their village. Which problem are they discussing?
  A boredom   B crime   C tourism

4 You hear some information about a holiday. The speaker's main recommendation for summer visitors is to visit ...
  A the city centre attractions
  B the coast
  C the countryside

5 You hear part of a programme about a new village. What are the speakers doing?
  A discussing reasons for creating the village
  B giving advice on starting up a new village
  C describing everyday life in the village

6 You overhear a conversation between a boy and a girl. Where does the girl prefer to shop?
  A in small boutiques
  B at shopping malls
  C on the high street

7 You overhear a woman talking on her mobile phone. What change would she like to make to the city centre?
  A create more parking
  B stop people from driving
  C open better cafés

8 You hear a part of a radio programme. What is the man talking about?
  A a treatment for stress
  B the beauty of the countryside
  C his research into urban lifestyles

Over to you!

5 Which speaker said these things? What do you think? Discuss your ideas with your partner.

1 It's greener to take the bus.
2 Just because you're a teenager it doesn't mean you're a shopaholic!

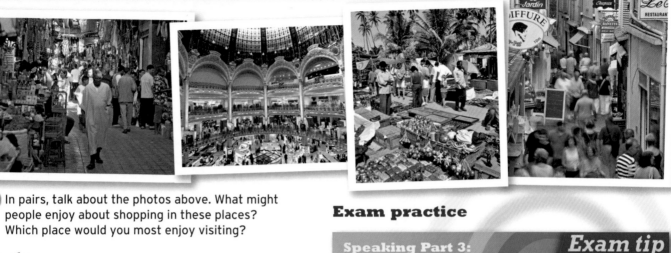

1 In pairs, talk about the photos above. What might people enjoy about shopping in these places? Which place would you most enjoy visiting?

2 🔊 **5.3** Listen to two students answering part of a Part 3 task. Which of the places in the photos do they like the most / least? Why? Is there anything they disagree about?

3 Work in pairs. How many different expressions can you think of to complete the table?

Asking for an opinion	Giving your opinion	Responding to your partner
Would you agree with that?	*I strongly believe ...*	*That's an interesting idea.*

4 🔊 **5.3** Listen to the recording again. How many of your ideas do the speakers use?

Exam practice

Speaking Part 3: *discussing opinions*

Exam tip

In Speaking Part 3, you must interact with your partner.
➤ Ask your partner's opinion.
➤ Respond to what your partner says, e.g. *That's an interesting idea, but ...*
➤ Use a range of interaction language. Just saying *I think* or *What do you think* can sound repetitive.

5 Look at photos A–H and discuss these Part 3 questions in pairs. Use as many expressions from Activity 3 as you can.

• How do these things improve the quality of life for families in a city?
• Which two things are the most important?

6 In pairs, discuss these Part 4 questions.

1 Do you think that teenagers and older people enjoy the same things in a city? Why? / Why not?
2 Is it better to live in lots of different places, or just one place for your whole life? Why?

Compound nouns

1 Complete the compound nouns 1–8. Use the words in the list. Then find examples of each compound noun in the illustration.

> exhaust fast- one-way pedestrian
> push steering traffic under

1 _____ fumes   5 _____ food restaurant
2 _____ lights   6 _____ ground station
3 _____ wheel   7 _____ street
4 _____ crossing   8 _____ chair

2 Read the rules and find **one** example of each of A–D in Activity 1. More than one correct answer may be possible.

Compound nouns

A compound noun is a noun formed from two or more words, for example:
A noun + noun
B verb + noun
C adjective + noun
D preposition + noun

Compound nouns can be written as one word, two or more words, or with a hyphen.

3 Make compound nouns from the words in list A and list B. Then complete the sentences.

A: cycle   housing   ~~night~~   out
     rush   sky   taxi   traffic

B: estate   jam   lane   ~~life~~   hour
     rank   scraper   skirts

0 The city boasts a fantastic _nightlife_ , with many wonderful restaurants and bars.
1 People with bikes can use the special _____ to get to work more quickly.
2 She worked in an office at the top of a really high _____ .
3 There was a huge _____ so he was late for class.
4 We're living in a large _____ . There are 1,000 houses here but only one shop!
5 It's really stressful driving at _____ - everyone's trying to get to work at the same time!
6 They lived on the _____ of the city, only five minutes away from the countryside.
7 Luckily, there was a _____ right outside the station, so they got home quickly.

Collocations (1): *prepositions + nouns*

4 This student is having a bad day! Choose the correct options in **bold** to complete what he says. Have you ever been late for something important? What happened?

"Normally, I go to class **(0)** by / in / on bus, but today I decided to go **(1)** by / on / with foot **(2)** for / from / with a change. **(3)** In / On / During the way, I met a few friends, and we chatted **(4)** for / on / about a while. Then I looked at my watch – it was ten minutes to the start of class! I didn't want to be **(5)** around / in / of trouble for being late, so I decided to run. **(6)** At / For / On the beginning it was OK, but after a few minutes, I was exhausted. I didn't realise how **(7)** out of / without / into shape I was! Amazingly, I arrived **(8)** at / with / on time – but I couldn't talk **(9)** at / for / in all for the first five minutes because I was completely **(10)** of / out of / without breath! I'm definitely going to catch the bus home ..."

Over to you!

5 Complete the questions. Then ask and answer the questions in pairs.

1 Do you prefer to travel _____ **bus**, car or bike, or _____ **foot**? Why?
2 Would you enjoy living at the top of a **sky**_____ or other high rise building? Why? / Why not?
3 Do you find it easy or difficult to be _____ **time** for things? Why?
4 Would you prefer to live in the city centre or on the **out** _____? Why?

Word boost ▶ Workbook p. 80

Get ready: *easily confused verbs*

1 Complete the sentences. Use the words in the lists.

been
gone

lost
missed

beat
won

get
go

bring
take

1 We've just _____ to the shopping centre, but we didn't see her there.
2 He's _____ to the shops. He'll be back later.
3 He _____ the train this morning.
4 She _____ her way and had to ask for directions.
5 Congratulations! You've _____ a holiday competition!
6 She _____ him at a game of squash at the leisure centre.
7 I usually _____ to work by bus.
8 It took me half an hour to _____ to class today.
9 _____ your friends to visit me!
10 You should _____ your cousin to the museum in town.

2 Write gapped sentences like those in Activity 1 for three of the verb pairs below. Can your partner complete them?

borrow / lend   expect / hope   deny / refuse
hear / listen   look / see   remember / remind

Word boost ▶ Easily confused verbs ▶ Workbook p. 29

Exam practice

3 Complete the exam task.

> **Use of English Part 1:** *easily confused words*
>
> **Exam tip**
>
> ➤ Look at the words just before and after the gap. Is the missing word part of a collocation?
> ➤ Complete the sentence with one of the options. Then read the whole sentence. Does it make sense?

For questions **1–12**, read the text below and decide which answer (**A**, **B**, **C** or **D**) best fits each gap.

The Game of Life!

Since *SimCity* first went **(0)** ...*ON*........ sale in 1989, it has become one of the most successful computer games of all **(1)** ....

The popularity of the game **(2)** .... most people by surprise. At **(3)** .... , retailers didn't **(4)** .... to sell many copies. After all, the game didn't have any heroes or villains, and there were few exciting **(5)** .... scenes. Instead, *SimCity* offered something completely different – an element of realism!

Players of *SimCity* have to think **(6)** .... a variety of real-life issues. For example, they have to consider transport issues. Can the people in their city get to work on time? Will there be lots of **(7)** .... jams at rush hour? Players must also consider residents' **(8)** .... of life. Is there too much crime in the city centre? Are there slums on the **(9)** .... ? The game is so **(10)** .... that some schools and universities have used it to teach students about urban planning!

So, why did *SimCity* become such a success? It seems that lots of people enjoyed the creativity of the game. Many also liked the fact that it wasn't competitive – players don't **(11)** .... or lose in *SimCity*. They just **(12)** .... on playing!

0	(A)	on	B	at	C	with	D	for
1	A	age	B	moment	C	time	D	period
2	A	brought	B	got	C	affected	D	took
3	A	beginning	B	once	C	first	D	start
4	A	hope	B	imagine	C	suppose	D	expect
5	A	action	B	movement	C	activity	D	performance
6	A	to	B	from	C	about	D	in
7	A	car	B	vehicle	C	traffic	D	road
8	A	value	B	quality	C	merit	D	worth
9	A	outside	B	outskirts	C	outdoors	D	outlet
10	A	realistic	B	actual	C	true	D	reliable
11	A	beat	B	defeat	C	win	D	overcome
12	A	remain	B	keep	C	continue	D	stay

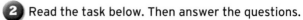

Prepare

1 Discuss the photo in groups.

1 What kind of problems can traffic cause in city centres?
2 Do you think city life would be better or worse if your government banned all cars from cities? Why?

Analyse the task

2 Read the task below. Then answer the questions.

> You have had a class discussion about travel and transport. Your teacher has asked you to write an essay giving your opinion on the following statement.
>
> *People should not use cars in city centres.*
>
> Write your essay in **120-180** words in an appropriate style.

1 Who will read your essay?
2 Do you have to agree with the statement?

3 Read one student's answer to the task in Activity 2. Does he / she include any of the ideas you discussed in Activity 1?

4 Read the essay again. Which paragraph includes:

1 arguments *for* the essay statement?
2 general statements about the topic?
3 a personal opinion?
4 arguments *against* the essay statement?

5 Is the language mainly formal or informal? Find examples to support your answer.

People should not use cars in city centres.

A There is usually a lot of traffic in city centres, especially at rush hour. Many people enjoy using cars to travel around cities, while others think that they have too many disadvantages.

B On the one hand, cars create a lot of pollution. This makes cities less pleasant to live in or visit, and it can also cause health problems. What is more, a lot of traffic can make city centres dangerous places for cyclists and pedestrians.

C On the other hand, going by car can be a very convenient way to travel. Public transport is not always very reliable, and it often takes more time to reach your destination. In addition, travelling in a crowded bus or train is not very enjoyable for passengers.

D Overall, I agree with the statement. In my opinion, city centres would be much cleaner and quieter places if we banned cars. However, I think that cities also need to have good public transport systems as an alternative.

Improve your writing:

linkers (4): addition, contrast and summarising

6 Complete the table using the linkers in the list. Then add more ideas from the essay on page 62.

~~although~~   as well   despite   furthermore
in conclusion   in spite of   moreover   nevertheless
on the whole   to sum up   whereas

Addition	
Contrast	*although*
Summarising	

7 Choose the correct alternatives.

1 **In spite of / Although** the traffic, I love living in a city!
2 My favourite city is Paris. I like New York **moreover / as well**.
3 Big cities are usually busy, **whereas / what is more** market towns are more peaceful.
4 **To sum up, / Despite** I disagree that living in a village is boring.
5 Many people enjoy going shopping, **while / also** others hate it!
6 Cars emit pollution. **In addition, / Nevertheless,** they can put cyclists at risk.

8 Look at the people in the photos and imagine what they think about life in the city / countryside! Write at least three sentences for each person using linkers from above.

I love city life. However, I hate commuting!

9 Compare your sentences with a partner's. Which one was the funniest / most original?

Ready to write!

You have had a class discussion about cities. Your teacher has asked you to write an essay giving your opinion on the following statement.

Living in a city is better than living in the countryside.

Write your essay in **120-180** words.

10 Read the task above. In groups, discuss the following.

1 What arguments can you think of *for* the statement?
2 What arguments can you think of *against* the statement?
3 What is your opinion?

11 Read the *Exam tip*. Then copy the Paragraph Plan into your notebook and complete it with your own ideas.

Writing Part 2: *an essay*   *Exam tip*

When you have to write an essay:
➤ Think about *who* you're writing for. In most essays you will need to use a more formal style of writing.
➤ Give an introduction to the topic in the first paragraph.
➤ Use a different paragraph for each main argument. Include points *for* or *against* a statement in different paragraphs.
➤ Give a conclusion in the final paragraph and state your opinion clearly.
➤ Use linkers like *in addition* to add ideas, and linkers like *however* to contrast ideas.

Writing reference ▶ p. 172

PARAGRAPH PLAN

	Main topic	Points to include
Para. 1:	Introduction	....
Para 2:	....	*(tip: choose two ideas from exercise 8.1)* ....
Para 3:	....	*(tip: choose two ideas from exercise 8.2)* ....
Para 4:	Conclusion	....

12 Write your essay. When you have finished, look at the checklist on page 172. Check your work and make any corrections.

Unit 5

1 Complete the sentences. Use the correct form of the words in the list.

> be   buy   ~~even if~~   in case   not miss   not run
> provided that   rain   unless

0 I hate shopping, _*even if*_ it's online. I find all kinds of shopping boring!

1 We might go for a walk in the park unless it _____ .

2 I'll come to the cinema _____ you pay for my ticket!

3 If we got rid of all the adverts, the city centre _____ much prettier.

4 Take your wallet _____ you see something you want to buy.

5 If I'd left earlier, I _____ the bus.

6 _____ more people visit the museum, it will have to close.

7 They would have stayed longer in the city if they _____ out of money.

8 If I were rich, I _____ a big house in Hollywood!

2 Complete this article about an unusual kind of advertising with the words in the list.

> beat   ~~billboards~~   consumers   change   outskirts
> slogans   successful   underground   won

Selling on skin

Advertisers have a hard time attracting our attention. They have images plastered on **(0)** _*billboards*_ sited on the **(1)** _____ of every city, posters on buildings, walls, even at **(2)** _____ stations, and advertising **(3)** _____ splashed across nearly every page of the internet. And yet **(4)** _____ still continue to look the other way! Tattoo advertising is an attempt to make us sit up and take notice for a **(5)** _____ . One of the most effective tattoos was that worn by the boxer Bernard Hopkins during a 2002 match, for a fee of $100,000. Hopkins **(6)** _____ his opponent and **(7)**_____ the title of world middleweight champion, and the website he was advertising became 200% more **(8)** _____! Since then, tattoo advertising has soared in popularity.

Units 1–5

3 Complete the fact file with the correct form of the verbs. Which **two** facts did you find the most surprising?

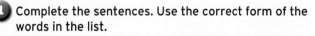

CAPITAL CITY FACT FILE

1 The Republic of South Africa (**have got**) _has got_ three capital cities – but the largest city in the country, Johannesburg, (**not be**) one of them!

2 In 1822, the original founders of Monrovia, Liberia, (**name**) their capital after a US President! Few people (**remember**) President Monroe now, but the city's inhabitants (**keep**) the name ever since.

3 The world's most heavily populated city is Tokyo, Japan, with over 12 million residents! The population (**continue**) (**grow**) even now – by the end of next year it (**expand**) by another 0.7%!

4 If you (**not like**) the cold, you (**should not**) (**go**) to Reykjavik in Iceland! It (**be**) famous for (**be**) the most northerly capital in the world.

5 Quito, Ecuador, (**lie**) close to an active volcano! At the moment, scientists (**monitor**) the volcano closely in an attempt (**prevent**) any disaster.

6 Washington D.C. (**not be**) the capital city of the US throughout the history of the States. While Americans (**fight**) in the Civil war, Philadelphia (**serve**) as the temporary capital. After the war (**finish**), the government then (**move**) to Washington.

UNIT TARGETS

Topic vocabulary: health and fitness ● food ● movement
Grammar: modal verbs (1) ● permission
Word building: adverbs ● phrasal verbs (3) ● adverb collocations
Writing: a report ● formal language
Exam preparation: Reading Part 3 ● Use of English Parts 1 and 2 ● Listening Part 2 ● Speaking Part 1 ● Writing Part 2

Health and fitness

1 Discuss the photos in pairs. How important do you think health and fitness is to these celebrities? Why?

2 🔊 6.1 You are going to hear a health and fitness expert discussing celebrity lifestyles. Whose lifestyle does she think is the healthiest? Why?

3 🔊 6.1 In pairs, try to complete these expressions from the recording. Which expressions did Dr Williams use to describe each celebrity? Listen again and check.

This person ...

0 *keeps* **fit** by dancing. *Beyonce*

1 **is** _____ **great shape**.

2 **goes** _____ **lots of diets**.

3 **has got quite a few** _____ **habits**, including smoking.

4 **allows themselves the** _____ **treat**.

5 **pushes themselves too** _____ with their training and rather _____**does** it.

6 frequently **puts** _____ **weight** then rapidly _____ **it** again.

7 **eats a lot of junk** _____ especially snacks, and **rarely** _____ **any exercise**.

Jack Black   Beyonce

Watch out! *over-* and *under-*

The prefixes *over-* and *under-* usually mean 'too much' / 'too little', e.g. *overdo* (=do too much) or *underweight* (=weigh too little).

4 Do you agree with Dr Williams that 'beauty comes in all kinds of shapes and sizes'?

Word boost ▶ Health and fitness ▶Workbook p. 34

Over to you!

5 Tell your partner about your own approach to health and fitness, using at least **three** expressions from Activity 3. How similar / different are you?

'I don't do a lot to keep fit, apart from walking the dog after school.'

Useful language

I would(n't) describe myself as (+ noun / gerund) ...
I almost always / hardly ever ...
I try to ... but I don't always succeed.
I'm (not) very worried about ... so I ...

Brad Pitt   Madonna

1 What do you think the typical diet is for the people in the photos? Which diet would you most / least like to eat for a week? Why?

Watch out! *diet*

The word *diet* can mean either:
1 the food usually eaten by a person or group:
 She used to have an unhealthy diet.
2 the food eaten by someone who wants to lose weight:
 Now she's gone on a diet. She only eats salads!

2 Quickly read the article on page 67 and match the people to illustrations E-H. Which person is the most positive about their diet?

Exam practice

Reading Part 3: **Exam tip**
synonyms and paraphrasing
Words used in the questions may not exactly match those in the text. Think about:
➤ **synonyms** (different words which have a similar meaning), e.g. *ill* has a similar meaning to *unwell*.
➤ **paraphrasing** (different ways of expressing similar ideas), e.g. *this can make you put on weight* has a similar meaning to *it may cause people to get fatter*.

3 You are going to read an article about four people who tried an unusual diet for a week. For questions 1-15, choose from the people (A-D). The people may be chosen more than once.

Which person:

1 ate with other people?
2 was ordered to end their diet early?
3 has changed their eating habits as a result of the experiment?
4 is usually very active?
5 did not enjoy a food they had previously liked?
6 spent a lot of time eating?
7 ate in an unusual position?
8 enjoyed doing other activities while eating?
9 was looking forward to trying the diet?
10 respects the philosophy behind the diet?
11 had to stop doing an activity they enjoyed?
12 felt guilty about something?
13 mentions learning something that they found upsetting?
14 thought that the diet had a positive effect on their health?
15 was reassured by the example set by someone else?

Vocabulary in context: *food*

4 Work in pairs. Find words in the article on page 67 to complete the table.

the way food tastes	the way food is prepared / cooked
spicy	baked

5 Look at the *taste* adjectives. For each adjective, write a food that matches this flavour.

6 Compare your list with a partner's. Do you agree with your partner's choices? Which of the foods on his / her list do you like or dislike the most? Why?

7 Explain the difference between the adjectives *tasteful*, *tasty* and *tasteless* as they are used in paragraphs C and D.

A Elisa Riedo *tried a medieval European diet (fifteenth century)*

Life expectancy in the middle ages was much lower than today, and now I understand why. At one dinner I ate a baked goose stuffed with a chicken, a partridge and a blackbird! I ate so much meat that I started dreaming about vegetables. Actually, since the experiment I've turned vegetarian, so that tells you how bad it was! Cooks used to heavily season meat to preserve it, so it was very spicy. This made me thirsty, so I drank a lot. That was a mistake! I was horrified to discover that medieval people always drank beer or wine, even for breakfast – apparently because the water was very polluted. Eventually I felt so unwell that I had to see a doctor, who wouldn't let me continue. Although it's never nice to let people down, I admit that this was something of a relief!

B Wang Fei *tried the 'fruitarian' diet (popularised in the nineteenth century)*

Nineteenth-century fruitarians believed you should never cause harm to any living thing, which is a principle I admire in theory. But it's an extreme diet. In order to show respect to plants and trees, fruitarians can only eat fruit or nuts which have fallen to the ground, they aren't allowed to pick them! You also aren't allowed to cook – you have to eat everything raw. I spent several hours a day just looking for food, because of course you can't just pop into a supermarket. I thought I'd feel really healthy, but instead the diet made me tired and weak. I'm normally quite sporty, and I go running daily, but I just couldn't manage to keep it up. I got so desperate for something warm, sweet and sugary that I eventually gave in and bought a fried doughnut. Of course, I felt awful about breaking the rules. Afterwards I read that the famous spiritual leader Gandhi had once experimented with fruitarianism, but he also struggled to stick to it. That made me feel slightly better!

C Alicja Kolub *tried an ancient Roman diet (c. 200 AD)*

In search of an authentic experience, some friends and I hired an old Mediterranean villa, which had a huge dining room. We replaced the chairs there with couches from the lounge. Apparently, Romans preferred to dine lying down, in the belief this aided digestion! I don't know if that's true, but it definitely wasn't good for my table manners. I think I spilled as much as I ate! Romans believed mealtimes should delight all the senses, so during dinner we listened to music and admired the **tasteful** artwork on the villa walls. In films, Roman dining seems pretty unhealthy – too many rich foods, too much drinking. But this turned out to be something of a myth. The diet included lots of fresh salads and fruit, and I was allowed to dilute my wine with water, so I never felt drunk. Several dishes were very **tasty**, although I didn't take to those flavoured with garum, a sauce with a salty taste and overpowering smell. I wasn't surprised to discover it was made from old, rotting fish!

D Jake Brown *tried an early American weight-loss diet invented by Horace Fletcher (1903)*

I was keen to volunteer for this, as I'd put on rather a lot of weight over Christmas! Horace Fletcher was one of the first people to recommend a low-fat diet, and I must admit, I did seem to be in better shape afterwards, which was great. Unfortunately, he also advised people to chew each mouthful thirty two times before swallowing. As you can imagine, this makes meals stretch on forever, and by the end of the process most food seems completely bland, even **tasteless**. I used to think roast chicken was delicious, but when you've reduced it to mush, you might as well be eating cardboard. Even worse, no one would dine with me. My girlfriend said watching me turn food into liquid was too disgusting!

---

8 Tell your partner about the most a) delicious, b) disgusting things you've ever eaten, using words you found in the article.

Word boost ▶ Food
▶ Workbook p. 34

Over to you!

9 Your school is going to open a new, 'healthy living' café. There is a prize of a term's free food to the students with the best ideas. Work in groups and agree on the following:

- what the café should look like
- what kind of food and drinks it should serve
- anything else you think would make the café appealing to students

10 Present your ideas to the class. When everyone has finished, decide as a class which students should win the prize!

1 Look at the picture of an unusual competition and read the extracts from the competition handbook. Would you be good at this type of competition? Why? / Why not?

Competitors:

1 **have to** be over 18. The competition is for adults only.
2 **need to** be in good health, or they won't be allowed to take part.
3 **must** eat every single sandwich in order to win.
4 **mustn't** spit out any food, or they'll be disqualified.
5 **don't have to** use sauces – they're optional.
6 **needn't** eat sitting down if they prefer not to. Standing up is fine.
7 **ought to** stop eating if they feel unwell.
8 **should** remember that this competition is just for fun!

2 Complete the rules with the verbs in **bold** above.

Obligation, necessity and advice

Function	Verb form
1 advice *(it's a good / bad idea)*	_____ OR _____
2 obligation or necessity *(it's necessary)*	*have to,* _____ OR _____
3 NO obligation or necessity *(it isn't compulsory)*	_____ OR _____
4 prohibition *(it's forbidden)*	_____

Language summary ▶ p. 161

3 Read one competitor's comments after the race and answer the questions in pairs.

1 *'In order to win, I **had to eat** 50 hotdogs in one go, but I only managed 45!'*

Can we use **must** in this sentence? Why? / Why not?

2 *'It was awful. I **shouldn't have entered** the competition – I **should have stayed** at home.'*

Did the speaker enter the competition? Did he stay at home? How does he feel about this?

3 *'I felt very full afterwards. My friends weren't very sympathetic because I **needn't have entered** the competition – it wasn't compulsory. But on the plus side, I **didn't need to buy** any dinner that evening!'*

Did the speaker enter the competition? Did he buy dinner that evening?

4 In pairs, choose a competitive sport or hobby you both know well. Write a 'competition handbook' like the one in Activity 1, including at least five of the forms in **bold**.

5 Read another pair's 'handbook'. Imagine you have just taken part in this competition – and lost! Describe what happened and how it made you feel. Include at least three of the verb forms in **bold** from Activity 3.

6 Read the text. How well does this person run now? How well did they use to run? How do you compare with them?

Last year I **couldn't** even run for the bus – now I **can** run for thirty kilometres without stopping! Getting fit wasn't easy. The first time I went jogging, my ten-year-old sister **was able to** overtake me! She even **managed to** beat me home! But I've improved a lot since then. By the end of next year, I'll **be able to** complete a whole marathon.

7 Look at verb forms in **bold** in the text above, and complete the rules.

Ability

Use	Verb form
1 general ability in the past	_____
2 general ability in the present	_____
3 general ability in any tense	_____
4 ability on a specific occasion	_____ OR _____

Language summary ▶ p. 161

Over to you!

8 Have you ever learnt a new skill? How difficult / easy was it? Tell your partner, using verb forms from the rules box above. Who had the most challenging experience?

Get ready: *permission*

1 Read the text. Why does the writer want a new teacher? Do / Did you enjoy sports at school? Why? / Why not?

> Help! My new sports instructor is really strict. Last year we **could** relax if we were feeling tired, but this year we **can't** take any breaks! On my last birthday I **was allowed to** leave early, but this year the teacher made me stay extra late! What next? Soon we **won't be allowed to** do anything, apart from following orders! I thought sport was supposed to be fun?

2 Complete the table with the verb forms in **bold** in Activity 1.

Permission	any tense	present only	past only
Permission in general		can	
Permission on a specific occasion			

3 Read the complaint below and find two verbs which mean 'give permission'. Which do we use before:

1 object + infinitive with *to*,
2 object + infinitive without *to*?

> Our last teacher allowed us to talk during lessons, but our new teacher won't let us chat!

Grammar boost ▶ Permission ▶ Workbook p. 37

Exam practice

4 Quickly read the exam task, ignoring the gaps. What unusual way to get fit does it recommend? Can you think of any other interesting or unusual ways to get fit?

5 Complete the exam task.

Use of English Part 2: *verb forms* — *Exam tip*

In a Part 2 task, you may need to complete some gaps with verbs. Always think about *form* as well as *meaning*.
➤ What kind of verb form do you need to use? Look at the context carefully for clues. Think about modal verbs, auxiliary verbs (*do, have* etc.), infinitives and gerunds.
➤ Does the verb form match the subject? E.g. *he does* (not *do*).
➤ Have you used the correct tense? E.g. *He had* (not *has*) *left by the time we arrived.*

For questions **1–12**, read the text below and think of the word which best fits each gap. Use only **one** word in each gap.

Home gym?

(0) ......*DO*...... you want to get fitter, but it seems difficult to know where to start? Perhaps you'd **(1)** .... not join a sports class, or you're **(2)** .... allowed to take up any expensive new hobbies? Then maybe you should consider the 'home gym'. At the 'home gym', you don't **(3)** .... to learn any new skills, or even buy any equipment. Even better, you can impress your family **(4)** .... the same time!

It's a surprising fact that doing housework can actually burn as **(5)** .... fat as doing some sports! When someone cleans energetically, their face gets red, they start to sweat, they may even get out **(6)** .... breath! That's because they're using a **(7)** .... of energy. Half an hour of cooking can burn 40–50 calories, and gardening an impressive 100–200 calories!

(8) .... not ask your parents or partner to allow you **(9)** .... help around the home? They're bound to agree! If you spend at least thirty minutes every day doing housework, you'll soon be **(10)** .... to feel a real difference in your health. But you **(11)** .... work really hard to get the full benefit – that's essential. Try dancing around while you tidy **(12)** .... your room. You may feel silly, but you'll improve your overall fitness, and have more fun too!

Get ready: *movement*

1 Look at the sports in the pictures. In pairs, discuss which sports you think would best improve your:

1 strength
2 agility *(the ability to move quickly and easily)*
3 posture *(the way that a person sits, stands or walks)*
4 coordination *(the ability to control the movements of your body so that they work together)*

2 In pairs, describe pictures A–L using the expressions in the list. How easy / difficult do you think each activity is?

balance on one leg	**bend** towards the ground
catch a ball in mid air	**hit** with a racquet
jog in the park	**jump** into the air
kick as hard as you can	**lift** a heavy weight
punch an opponent	**sprint** towards the finishing line
stretch as far as you can	**throw** a ball

3 Choose two sports you know well and complete the sentences. Include at least four of the verbs in bold from Activity 2.

Sport A
1 You need to _____
2 You mustn't _____
3 You can _____

Sport B
4 You are allowed to _____
5 You shouldn't _____
6 You must _____

4 Work in groups of four. Take turns reading out your rules. Can your group guess the sport?

Word boost ▶ Movement ▶ Workbook p. 34

Exam practice

5 What is the person doing in the photo? Have you ever tried this activity? If so, what did you think? If you haven't tried it, would you like to? Why? / Why not?

Exam tip

Listening Part 2:
giving relevant answers

➤ Don't make any changes to the words you hear. Thinking of synonyms or paraphrases will waste time.
➤ Use the correct spelling and make sure that the words you write are grammatically correct (e.g. do you need a singular or plural form?).
➤ Write between one and three words. Don't write more than this!

6 6.2 You will hear a radio review by a man called Graham Woodson, who recently tested the *Wii Fit* software. For questions 1–10, complete the sentences.

1 The people that Graham works with enjoy food like energy bars and _____ .
2 Graham tried out *Wii Fit* in his _____ .
3 Some people think that the _____ game on *Wii Fit* makes players look silly.
4 Both Graham and his _____ have played tennis on *Wii Fit*.
5 When he was young, Graham liked reading _____ .
6 In real life, Graham is _____ years old.
7 Graham's _____ laughed when he said he was taking up yoga.
8 *Wii Fit* has improved Graham's agility and _____ .
9 Graham would not recommend *Wii Fit* to _____ .
10 Graham once hurt his pet's _____ while using *Wii Fit*.

Over to you!

7 How could the government encourage more young people to exercise? Discuss the question in pairs then agree on your **three** best ideas.

1 Look at the photos below. In pairs, discuss the following.

1 What do you think the food and the atmosphere is like in these restaurants?
2 Which restaurant would you like to visit the most / least? Why?
3 What restaurants in your area would you recommend to a visitor, or advise them to avoid? Why? Think about *food*, *location*, *atmosphere* and *service*.

2 6.3 You are going to hear two people answer questions on the topic of *food and restaurants*. Listen and guess what questions they are answering.

Exam practice

Speaking Part 1: staying calm!

Exam tip

➤ If you need time to think, begin with one of these expressions: *Let me think / see ....That's difficult to say, really ...*
➤ Don't rush! Speak slowly and clearly and make sure that you answer the question.
➤ Try not to leave long silences. An easy way to expand your answers is to give reasons or examples. Use expressions like:
reasons: *as, because, so, so that, that's why*
examples: *for example, for instance, like, such as*

3 6.3 Read the *Exam tip*. Listen again and answer the questions.

1 Which expressions do Speakers 1 and 2 use to give themselves times to think?
2 What example does Speaker 1 give of the food at Doña Olga?
3 What two reasons does Speaker 2 give for preferring to eat at home?

4 Read the questions below. Add one more question to each category.

Likes and dislikes

1 What is your favourite food? (Why do you like it?)
2 Do you like cooking? (What kinds of things do you cook?)

Free time

3 What do you do to keep fit? (How often do you exercise?)
4 Have you got any plans for this weekend? (What are you going to do?)

Travel

5 Where did you spend your most interesting holiday? (What kind of things did you do?)
6 What's your favourite way of travelling? (Why do you like it?)

5 Work in pairs and follow the instructions.

Student A: Ask Student B the questions in red and your own questions from Activity 4. Answer Student B's questions.

Student B: Answer Student A's questions. Ask Student A the questions in blue and your own questions from Activity 4.

Unit 6   71

Super sized

In his documentary *Super Size Me*, Morgan Spurlock **(1) bravely** went on a fast-food diet for thirty days. He **(2) only** ate junk food, and he **(3) always** bought a 'super' size portion if it was offered to him. Morgan wanted to prove that too much fast food can be **(4) incredibly** bad for you. He started to gain weight **(5) very (6) rapidly**, and he suffered from headaches and other problems. **(7) Shockingly**, doctors became **(8) seriously** concerned about his health **(9) after just a few weeks**. **(10) Unsurprisingly**, Morgan has **(11) never** tried the experiment **(12) again**! He eats a much healthier diet **(13) now**.

Adverbs

1 Read the article above. How did Morgan Spurlock's diet affect his health?

2 Complete the table with the adverbs in **bold**. How do we form regular adverbs?

Adverbs	
We use adverbs to modify verbs, adjectives and other adverbs. Common examples include adverbs of:	
manner	*slowly, well*
comment or opinion	*amazingly, luckily*
degree	*quite, rather*
frequency	*often, sometimes*
time	*tomorrow, on Monday*

3 Where does each type of adverb usually go in a sentence? Check your answers on page 161.

4 Rewrite the sentences so that they include the adverb form of the word in **bold**.

1 Morgan prefers to eat a healthy diet.   **USUAL**
2 He was surprised by the results.   **TRUE**
3 His health deteriorated.   **FAST**
4 He gained 11.1 kilograms in one month!   **ALARMING**
5 Eating too much fast food is bad for you!   **REAL**

5 In pairs, choose the correct alternatives. Explain *why* you have chosen each answer.

1 That basketball player can jump really **high / highly**. I can **high / highly** recommend playing basketball.
2 He's **hard / hardly** training at all. He needs to do more. He's training really **hard / hardly**. He needs to rest.
3 They haven't gone out for dinner **late / lately**. They arrived **late / lately** for dinner.

Phrasal verbs (3): *health*

6 Read one person's list of resolutions (= *personal goals*). Do you make resolutions like these? Are you good at keeping them?

> My resolutions
> This year, I'm going to ..
> • **(1)** give up smoking.
> • **(2)** take up a new sport.
> • stop **(3)** eating out every night and cook my own meals instead.
> • **(4)** cut out all junk food from my diet.
> • **(5)** work out more at the gym.
> • **(6)** cut down on the amount of chocolate I eat!
> • **(7)** stick to my health plan – I'm not going to **(8)** give up this time!

7 In pairs, match the phrasal verbs in bold in Activity 6 to their meanings. One phrasal verb has *two* different meanings.

> continue with   going to restaurants   lift weights
> reduce   remove   start doing
> stop doing something you did before   stop trying

1 give up – stop doing something you did before

Over to you!

8 How satisfied are you with these areas of your life? Give each one a score from 1 (dissatisfied) to 5 (highly satisfied). Write **six** resolutions for yourself.

health   hobbies   studies   family and friends

Word boost ▶ Workbook p. 81

Get ready: *adverb collocations*

1 Music stars often make some strange food requests at concerts! Which of these is the most surprising?

Britney Spears - was **quite insistent** that she had her favourite breakfast cereal, Fruit Loops, backstage.

Metallica - said it was **extremely important** that bacon was available at every meal.

Van Halen - used to demand M&Ms. It was **absolutely essential** that none of the sweets were brown!

2 Answer the questions in pairs.

1 Which adjectives in **blue** are *normal / extreme*?
2 Which adverbs in **red** go with extreme adjectives?

3 Not every adverb can go with every adjective. Complete these celebrity complaints.

1 I'm a **highly / deeply** successful singer and I demand to be treated like a star!
2 I was horrified to see the chef was **fast / hard** asleep backstage. Fire him!
3 Why is this coffee **totally / terribly** different from the one you served me yesterday?
4 I'm always **wide / broad** awake at three in the morning so I need breakfast early.
5 I was **bitterly / completely** disappointed by the food. Please make more effort!

Word boost ▶ Adverb collocations ▶ Workbook p. 35

Exam practice

4 Read the exam task quickly. What are *cassava*, *fugu* and *ackee*?

5 Complete the exam task.

> **Use of English Part 1:** *meaning and usage*   **Exam tip**
> When you complete a gap, think about:
> ➤ the difference between similar meanings, e.g. *sprint* is faster than *jog*.
> ➤ how we use a word in context, e.g. the collocations.

For questions **1–12**, read the text below and decide which answer (**A**, **B**, **C** or **D**) best fits each gap.

Food to die for?

A **(0)** ...GREAT... number of plants and animals are edible, but not all of them! Every year, thousands of unlucky people fall ill as a result of **(1)** .... eating something poisonous. But some of us deliberately choose to eat dangerous food.

Cassava is an **(2)** .... popular vegetable which is enjoyed by more than 50 million people. However, it must be washed and cooked properly in **(3)** .... to remove all traces of a toxin called cyanide. Even a tiny **(4)** .... of this can be fatal, so it's absolutely **(5)** .... you seek help immediately if you feel unwell!

Parts of the *fugu* fish are **(6)** .... poisonous. Remarkably, this fish is considered to be a delicacy in Japan, in spite of the fact that it kills dozens of diners every year. Japanese chefs must cut the fish **(7)** .... accurately to prevent disaster!

Aficionados of the *ackee* in Jamiaca say that the ripe fruit has a very **(8)** .... but delicious flavour, like scrambled eggs! **(9)** .... you have to pick ackee at exactly the right time. If you pick it too soon or too late, it can **(10)** .... you very sick indeed.

Some people eat these foods simply because they are **(11)** .... whereas others enjoy the thrill of taking a risk. However, I think I'll stick **(12)** .... my usual diet for now!

0	A	terrible	(B)	great	C	giant	D	strong
1	A	casually	B	wrongly	C	accidentally	D	harmfully
2	A	extremely	B	entirely	C	intensely	D	utterly
3	A	purpose	B	hope	C	order	D	intention
4	A	number	B	amount	C	volume	D	supply
5	A	required	B	desirable	C	essential	D	important
6	A	widely	B	deeply	C	highly	D	greatly
7	A	incredibly	B	wholly	C	simply	D	greatly
8	A	strange	B	astonishing	C	irregular	D	rare
9	A	Moreover	B	However	C	Therefore	D	Despite
10	A	cause	B	get	C	create	D	make
11	A	tasteful	B	tasteless	C	tasty	D	distasteful
12	A	on	B	for	C	in	D	to

Prepare

1 Which of these activities are more popular with people under 25, and which with older people? Why do you think this is?

A

B

D

E

Analyse the task

> A local business wants to open a new sports centre in your area, and is keen to encourage younger people to join. The centre manager has asked you to write a report including the following information:
> - the most popular sports in your area
> - ideas for after-school activities
> - suggestions on what kind of food to serve in the sports centre café.

2 Read the task above. Who is the report for? How many topics *must* you include?

3 Read the report on the right and complete it with suitable headings from the list.

A delicious café

Beginning

Ideas for the café

Introduction

Popular local sports

Some activities

Sports I like

Suggestions for after-school activities

A new sports centre

1 _____

The aim of this report is to provide information for a sports centre which wants to appeal to young people. The report discusses popular local sports and makes recommendations for suitable activities and refreshments.

2 _____

The three most popular sports in my region are:
- football
- basketball
- swimming.

In addition, many younger people enjoy martial arts and dance. Skateboarding is also quite popular. However, there are currently no suitable facilities for this in the area.

3 _____

Many people already play football and basketball at school. Therefore I would suggest that the centre offers afternoon and evening classes teaching other popular sports, such as modern dance or judo. Moreover, I believe that there would be considerable interest in a supervised skate area, especially if the centre also ran a skateboarding club.

4 _____

As many students have little money, I would strongly recommend that the café sells a range of cheap but healthy food, such as sandwiches and fruit. This will encourage younger customers to visit.

Improve your writing:
formal language

4 In a report, you should use more formal language. Which of 1-9 are more formal and which are more informal? Explain your answers.

1 I think it would be a brilliant idea if ...
2 This report is intended to ...
3 I would strongly recommend that ...
4 It seems pretty clear to me that ...
5 I would suggest that ...
6 Let's start with ...
7 Another possibility might be to ...
8 The purpose of this report is ...
9 It's a bit difficult to say whether ...

5 Which expressions from Activity 4 could you use to *start* your report? Find an expression with a similar meaning in the report on page 74.

6 Decide which of these linkers would **not** be suitable in formal writing.

although	anyway	by the way	furthermore
however	in addition	mind you	moreover
therefore	well	you see	

7 In groups, complete the table with the formal linkers from Activity 6. Can you add any more?

addition	contrast	result
what's more	*despite*	*as a result*

8 Expand on the ideas in the sentences using suitable linkers.

0 Yoga can help to improve your posture. *(addition)*

   What's more, it can help you to relax.

1 A certain amount of regular daily exercise can be good for you. *(contrast)*
2 Some parents do not allow children to watch any television. *(result)*
3 Drinking alcohol can make you feel unwell. *(addition)*

Ready to write!

Your school wants to encourage students to improve their health and fitness. Your teacher has asked you to write a report for students about things they can do in your local area. Include advice on local sports facilities, cafés and restaurants which serve healthy food, and the best places to relax in.

Write your report in **120-180** words in an appropriate style.

9 Read the task above. Which **three** topics must you include in your report?

10 In pairs, brainstorm ideas for each topic. Then choose the **three** best ideas from each category to include in your report.

11 Read the *Exam tip*. Look at the report on page 74 and:

1 decide how many paragraphs you are going to include.
2 think of a suitable heading for each paragraph.
3 choose at least four formal expressions and linkers to include in your report.

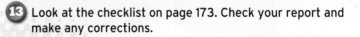

Writing Part 2: *a report* — *Exam tip*

➤ Think about who you are writing for (e.g. a teacher) and why (e.g. to encourage someone to do something).
➤ Organise your ideas into paragraphs before you write (there is time in the exam to plan!).
➤ Try to use suitable headings for each paragraph. If you would like, you can also include bulleted (•) or numbered (1) points.
➤ Begin with an introduction and end with a conclusion.
➤ Use more formal language.
➤ Include a range of grammar and vocabulary, but do NOT include a lot of descriptive language.

Writing reference ➤ p. 173

12 Write your report. Remember to organise your ideas clearly and to use a range of formal expressions.

13 Look at the checklist on page 173. Check your report and make any corrections.

Unit 6

1 Complete the second sentence so that it has a similar meaning to the first, using between two and five words, including the word given.

0 I was not allowed to cook in my parents' kitchen. **LET**
My parents _didn't let me cook_ in their kitchen.

1 The use of cutlery is not compulsory for contestants. **NOT**
Contestants _____ cutlery.

2 It wasn't necessary for him to eat the hot dogs, but he did it anyway. **NEED**
Even _____ to eat the hot dogs, he did it anyway.

3 It's a bad idea to push yourself too hard when you're exercising. **OVERDO**
You ought _____ when you're exercising.

4 Cheating in the contest is strictly forbidden. **ABSOLUTELY**
You _____ in the contest.

5 Participating in the competition was a mistake. **SHOULD**
He _____ part in the competition.

2 Choose the correct alternatives to complete the text.

The World's STRONGEST Men?

The World's Strongest Man competition tests entrants' **(O)** strong / (strength) and endurance. Competitors **(1)** get / take part in a number of **(2)** absolutely / very challenging events. They have to **(3)** lift / pick heavy stones above their heads, **(4)** hit / throw huge weights over the top of a wall using only their hands, and even **(5)** lift / pull along cars and trucks! You need to train **(6)** hard / hardly if you want to win. Entrants regularly work **(7)** out / up at a gym, and they **(8)** often exercise / exercise often for more than twenty hours a week. What's more, to develop their muscles they need to **(9)** put / get on a lot of weight! Some competitors eat more than 7,000 calories a day, including **(10)** frying / fried food and junk food!

Units 1–6

3 Only two of these sentences are complete. Add **one** extra word to the incomplete sentences.

0 This chilli dish is much hotter~~·~~the curry. _than_

1 I'm cutting down on sweets because I want lose weight.

2 By the end of this course, you will able to cook.

3 I'll join the gym as long you come with me.

4 Would you mind looking after the children while I'm cooking?

5 I always liked sweet foods, ever since I was a child.

6 She always buys milk and eggs from the farm.

7 Pablo, mother is a sports instructor, is very fit.

4 Join the sentences using the word or expression in brackets.

0 Mole is a type of sauce. It is made with chocolate. *(which)*
Mole is a type of sauce which is made with chocolate.

1 That is the chef. We were talking about her. *(who)*

2 I went jogging every day. I wanted to get fit *(in order to)*

3 You should go to the doctor's. It's possible your cough is serious. *(in case)*

4 He isn't very strong. He can't win the Strongest Man contest! *(enough)*

5 The restaurant stopped serving food. Then I arrived. *(by the time)*

6 I ate too much chocolate. Then I felt sick. *(if)*

5 Complete these health tips with suitable words.

0 Everyone needs to exercise, whether you're skinny, slim, or w_e_ l l-b _u_ _i_ l_t.

1 Keeping your back straight will improve your p _ _ _ _ _ e .

2 It is best to meditate in a quiet, p_ _ _ _ _ _ _ l place.

3 Always t_ _ _ w away out-of-date meat and fish.

4 Try not to be g _ _ _ _ y and only eat what you need.

5 If you're r_ _ _ _ _ _ g a temperature, you'd better see a doctor.

6 Yoga is a good way to improve your a_ _ _ _ _ _ y.

7 Hi-tech

UNIT TARGETS

Topic vocabulary: science and technology
● computers ● communication
Grammar: the passive ● *have / get something done*
Word building: negative prefixes ● collocations (2)
● word stem transformations
Writing: a formal letter ● pronouns
Exam preparation: Reading Part 1 ● Use of English
Parts 3 and 4 ● Listening Part 3 ● Speaking Part 2
● Writing Part 1

1 Which **chemist** and **physicist** carried out important experiments into radioactivity?

   A Thomas Edison   **B** Nikola Tesla   **C** Marie Curie

2 Which **astronomer** first worked out that the Earth orbits the sun?

   A Nicolaus Copernicus   **B** Aristotle   **C** Galileo Galilei

3 When did **scientists** first come up with the theory of 'global warming'?

   A 1976   **B** 1938   **C** 1896

4 Which **biologist** set out the first classification system for plant and animal species?

   A Charles Darwin   **B** Carl Linnaeus   **C** Richard Dawkins

5 Which **psychiatrist** looked into our subconscious mind in the book *The Interpretation of Dreams*?

   A Alfred Adler   **B** Sigmund Freud   **C** Carl Jung

6 Which invention did the artist, **mathematician** and **engineer** Leonardo da Vinci dream up?

   A a helicopter   **B** a freezer   **C** a camera

1. Geospiza magnirostris. 2. Geospiza fortis.
3. Geospiza parvula. 4. Certhidea olivacea.

Science and technology

1 7.1 How much do you know about science? Work in pairs and try to guess the answers to the quiz! Then listen and check your answers.

2 Look at the expressions in **red** in Activity 1. Which phrasal verb means:

1 organise systematically?   2 explore; investigate?
3 do; perform?

3 Look at the nouns in yellow, and complete the table for each noun. Some of the words may not have an adjective form.

person (noun)	science (noun)	adjective
chemist	chemistry	chemical

Word boost ▶ Science and technology ▶ Workbook p. 40

Over to you!

4 In pairs, discuss how you think these inventions or discoveries have changed the world. How would life be different without them?

   cars   electricity   the internet   music   printing
   space travel   television

Useful language

It's hard to imagine a world without ...
The world would be completely different if we +
past simple ... (**second conditional**)
If we hadn't invented / discovered ..., then we
wouldn't have + *past participle* (**third conditional**)

5 Together, decide what you think the world's **three** most important inventions or discoveries are, and why.

1 Look at the cartoons opposite. Discuss the questions in pairs.

1 Why are the cartoons funny?

2 Why do you think that the cartoonists have shown both computer users as male? Do you think this is fair?

3 Do you think people can become addicted to computers?

Exam practice

Reading Part 1:
thinking about the options

Exam tip

➤ Always read the question and each option carefully, and underline the key words.

➤ Read the text again carefully and eliminate (cross out) any wrong answers.

➤ Find and underline evidence for your answers in the text. Try not to guess unless you really have to!

A DEREK--I'M UNINSTALLING YOU

B "Dataholic."

2 Read the article quickly. How did Helen use to feel about computer games? How does she feel now?

3 For questions 1–8, choose the answer (A, B, C or D) which you think fits best according to the text.

1 What is the writer's main point in the first paragraph?
   A Addiction to gaming is a common problem.
   B The press exaggerates the negative side of gaming.
   C Gaming is as harmful as smoking.
   D Gaming seriously affects students' performance at school.

2 What does Helen mean by 'geek' in line 21?
   A someone who is obsessed by technology to an embarrassing degree
   B someone who is not very experienced at using technology
   C someone who is praised and admired for their technological expertise
   D someone who is not interested in technology

3 When her boyfriend first subscribed to *EverQuest*, Helen
   A did not say anything about the game.
   B found playing the game boring.
   C told him that the game was childish.
   D became enthusiastic about the game.

4 What does 'this' refer to in line 34?
   A damaging the computer
   B allowing Tom to play games
   C feeling upset and annoyed
   D arguing with Tom

5 What does Helen say she likes about *EverQuest* now?
   A It allows her to do whatever she likes.
   B It is full of realistic characters.
   C It is almost as good as real life.
   D It allows everyone to play as equals.

6 Why does Helen think that people are more critical of gaming than other hobbies?
   A It doesn't require much intelligence.
   B It is too time-consuming.
   C It is not a traditional hobby.
   D It does not offer many benefits.

7 The writer thinks some institutions are using computer games at work in order to
   A employ greater numbers of young people.
   B make employees more intelligent.
   C help employees to solve problems.
   D help employees to feel calmer and more relaxed.

8 What do we learn about the writer's opinion of computer games from reading this article?
   A They do not have any negative consequences.
   B They have been unfairly criticised.
   C They can be enjoyed by everyone.
   D They are superior to most other hobbies.

Vocabulary in context: *computers*

4 Find words or expressions in the text that match 1–8.

1 stop the flow of power to something (*paragraph 1*)
2 copying a file from the internet (*paragraph 2*)
3 leave a game or website (*paragraph 2*)
4 something you use to represent yourself in a computer game or online (*paragraph 4*)
5 not real; created by a computer (*paragraph 4*)
6 browsing different webpages (*paragraph 5*)
7 programs used to operate a computer (*paragraph 6*)

Word boost ▶ Computers ▶ Workbook p. 40

Over to you!

5 Design an avatar! Turn to page 153 and follow the instructions.

Only

Are computer gamers victims of addiction - or prejudice?

Sarah Dylan investigates.

Computer games are the latest media scare. If you believe the hype, they're highly addictive and almost as dangerous as cigarettes or alcohol. Features on gaming dwell on the horror stories – the players who stare at a monitor for days, weeks or months at a time, barely pausing to sleep or eat, never mind study or socialise. Mistakenly convinced that gaming ruins grades and lives, parents and teachers then demand that teenagers immediately put down their joysticks and switch off their computers. Some even call for all games to be banned! But is this concern really justified? Gaming is a hugely popular hobby, with millions of players worldwide. Surely not all of these people are hopeless addicts and loners?

Helen Mackay is one player who contradicts the stereotype. She is both a high-flying student at a prestigious US university, and a site administrator on *EverTalk* – a chatroom where fans of the online game *EverQuest* swap ideas and game cheats. But she wasn't always an enthusiast. "Until last year, my experience of computers was limited to checking emails and downloading music, and I prided myself on not being very technologically minded, in other words, not being a geek! I'd never even heard of *EverQuest* until my boyfriend Tom bought a subscription. Back then I didn't get the appeal and frankly, I thought Tom was too old for that kind of stuff. But I held my tongue, convinced he'd soon get fed up and log out for the last time."

"When months went by and he still showed no signs of losing interest, I got increasingly bothered. I even considered 'accidentally' spilling coffee over his keyboard so he'd be forced to stop – but I knew that would start a row and he'd only carry on playing anyway. And then I thought, this isn't me, why am I behaving like this? So I had a go in secret, in a bid to be more sympathetic. I didn't really expect to enjoy it. But after a few clicks of the mouse I was hooked!"

"The game was fun and surprisingly challenging. Every action has a consequence, so you have to think very carefully! Yes, the characters – or avatars as I've learned to call them – are rather silly (I'm an elf!). However, they're liberating too. When you're acting out a role in cyberspace, you can't be judged by your looks, age or background. Through the game I've made friends with a skater-punk in Alaska and a 91-year-old Korean physicist. So-called 'reality' could learn a lot from this virtual world."

Does Helen consider herself a computer addict? "Of course not. Tom and I play games for about ten hours a week. That's much less time than the average American spends surfing the internet – or watching TV! I think gamers are often treated very unfairly. We don't sneer at people in the same way for being sports fanatics, and compulsive readers are praised for being clever! But what's the difference? Just because some hobbies have been around for longer doesn't mean they're necessarily better for you. Different things suit different people, that's all."

However, anti-gaming prejudice may at last be starting to wane. Many professional organisations, including NASA, the Armed Forces and medical schools, are now designing computer game software especially for staff. Cynics have claimed that this is merely a gimmick to attract younger applicants. However, it seems more likely that employers have been influenced by the latest scientific research. Extensive studies have suggested that although playing computer games can't significantly alter IQ*, it does help people to become better at analysing details and working out solutions – all essential workplace skills. The fact that it also reduces stress is an added bonus!

Of course, as with any pleasure in life, you can have too much of a good thing. Devoting yourself entirely to one activity is never healthy, whether your passion is gaming – or studying! But maybe it's time for the technophobes to relax a bit? A few hours a week playing computer games might not be the end of the world, after all ...

* a measure of intellect

1 Read this article. What is special about ASIMO? In pairs, decide which of the verb forms in **bold** are *active* and which are *passive*. How do we form the passive?

(1) ASIMO **was designed** by Honda. (2) It is one of the most advanced robots that **has** ever **been created**! (3) It **has** the ability to walk. (4) The most advanced models **are equipped** to perform complex tasks, like negotiating obstacles, or answering questions. (5) Perhaps one day ASIMO robots **will be** able to help us in our everyday lives. (6) They **could be asked** to cook dinner, walk the dog, or even help with homework!

The Passive

We use the passive:
- to emphasise the **action** or the **object of the action** (= who or what an action is done to)
- when we do not know the **agent** (= who or what did an action), or the **agent** is not important.

When it is essential to say who or what does the action, we use *by* + agent.

Language summary ▶ p. 162

2 Read the rules and answer the questions.
1 Why does the writer choose the active or the passive form for sentences 1–6 in Activity 1?
2 Why does the first sentence include *by* + agent? Why doesn't the second sentence include *by* + agent?

3 Read sentences A–D, then answer questions 1–3 in pairs.
A Robots are expected to change the world for the better.
B Robots cannot be taught how to love, so they will never think like humans.
C It has been said that by 2100 every home will own a robot.
D If too many skills are given to robots, they'll take over the world!

1 Do you agree or disagree with the statements? Give reasons for your opinions.
2 How do we form the passive with reporting verbs (*think*, *believe*, etc.)? Find two ways.
3 How do we form the passive with verbs with two objects (*send*, *offer*, etc.)? Find two ways.

4 Read the article. Would you like to be a space tourist? Why? / Why not? Complete the text using the active or passive forms.

Space adventure!

Ever since Neil Armstrong and Buzz Aldrin (**1 land**) on the moon in 1969, we (**2 fascinate**) by space travel. In the seventies it (**3 predict**) that by 2000 flights to the moon would be a part of everyday life! Although that prediction (**4 not expect**) to come true for a few more years, things (**5 begin**) to change. Today, tourists as well as astronauts (**6 allow / travel**) into space! In 2001, the businessman Dennis Tito (**7 pay**) approximately $20 million to the Russian Space Agency. In return, Tito (**8 give**) the chance to go into space. He (**9 spend**) seven days orbiting the earth. Now, several companies hope to develop space tourism as an industry. It is possible that space 'buses' and even space 'hotels' (**10 might / build**) in the future!

5 These sentences from a science magazine would all be better written in the passive. Rewrite them in pairs.
0 People have found evidence of life on Mars.
   Evidence of life on Mars has been found.
1 Someone has invented a time travel machine.
2 The government may ban all scientific experiments on animals.
3 Scientists predict that average life expectancy will increase to 200 years.
4 Judges have awarded the Nobel Prize for Physics to a teenager.

Over to you!

6 In groups, write three *true* and three *false* sentences about famous achievements, using passive forms of verbs from the list.

compose build design direct discover elect invent open make paint show write

The film 2001: A Space Odyssey was directed by Ridley Scott. (Answer: FALSE. It was directed by Stanley Kubrick.)

7 Read your sentences to another group, and guess which of their sentences are true.

Get ready: *have / get something done*

1 In pairs, explain the difference between the two illustrations.

> **have / get something done**
>
> We use *have / get something done* to talk about things which someone else does for us (we do not do them ourselves).

2 Read the rules. Do sentences 1–3 describe picture A or B?

1 He's getting his car fixed. 2 He's fixing his car. 3 He's having his car fixed.

3 Write four sentences about your life using *get / have done*. Discuss your sentences with your partner, giving details.

One of my least favourite things is getting my teeth checked at the dentists. I'm glad I only have to go twice a year!

Grammar boost ▶ *have / get something done* ▶ Workbook p. 43

Exam practice

Use of English Part 4: *making changes*

Exam tip

➤ You will *always* need to make changes to grammar or vocabulary – and you will often need to change both.
➤ You usually need to change at least **two** things in your answer, e.g. *He prefers Science to Maths.* (**LIKE**)
He does not like Science as much as Maths.
➤ *Watch out!* You must never change the key word!

4 Complete the exam task.

For questions **1–8**, complete the second sentence so that it has a similar meaning to the first sentence, using the word given. **Do not change the word given.** You must use between **two** and **five** words, including the word given. Write **only** the missing words **IN CAPITAL LETTERS**.

0 Luckily, the car had enough petrol.   **RUN**
Luckily, we *DIDN'T RUN OUT OF* petrol.

---

1 A professional will be making repairs to my computer tomorrow.   **GETTING**
I will .... tomorrow.

2 According to the witness, the person flying the space ship was an alien!   **BEING**
According to the report, the space ship .... an alien!

3 I prefer writing emails to letters.   **RATHER**
I .... than a letter.

4 The scientists couldn't solve the answer to the problem.   **WORK**
The scientists weren't .... the solution to the problem.

5 The astronaut always hated having his photo taken.   **SOMEONE**
The astronaut didn't like it .... his photo.

6 We were prevented from using the computer room by a power cut.   **COULD**
A power cut meant .... the computer room.

7 People say that the first bicycle was invented by Leonardo da Vinci.   **SAID**
The first bicycle .... invented by Leonardo da Vinci.

8 Someone installed the programme for me a few minutes ago.   **JUST**
I .... installed.

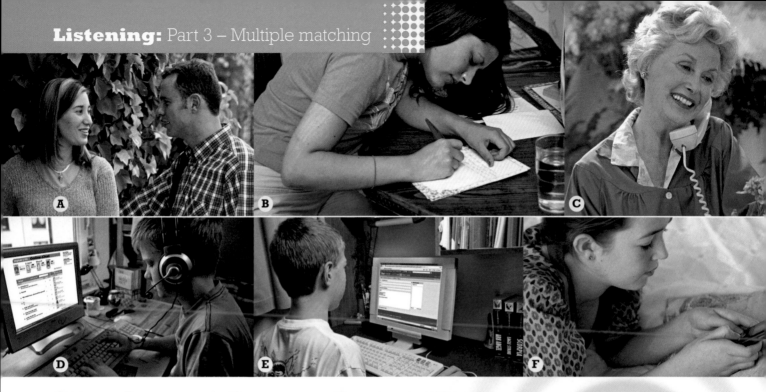

Get ready: *communication*

1 In pairs, describe what's happening in the photos. Then discuss questions 1–3.
1   What are the advantages and disadvantages of these different kinds of communication?
2   Which type or types of communication do you think would be best for:
   a   applying for a job?
   b   telling a friend you're going to be late?
   c   splitting up with a boyfriend or girlfriend?
3   Which of these forms of communication do you use most / least often? Why?

2 In pairs, complete the list of complaints about phones with the correct form of the words in the list. Which of these annoys you the most?

   call   cut   hang   lose   pick   tone   wrong

Phone moans!

1   leaving a message for someone who never _____ you back
2   someone _____ up while you're still talking
3   _____ the signal or getting _____ off during an important call
4   being too slow to _____ up the phone
5   accidentally calling the _____ number
6   hearing other people's awful mobile ring _____s!

Word boost ► Communication
► Workbook p. 40

Exam practice

Listening Part 3: *listening for clues*

Exam tip

➤ Listen for **synonyms** and **paraphrases**.
➤ Think about **topic vocabulary**.
➤ Make **inferences** about the information you hear, e.g. if you hear that someone can't stand animals, you could infer that they don't have a pet.

3 🔊 7.2 You will hear five people talking about mobile phones. For questions 1–5, choose from the list (A–F) what each speaker says. Use the letters only once. There is one extra letter which you do not need to use.

Speaker 1 ☐   Speaker 2 ☐   Speaker 3 ☐
Speaker 4 ☐   Speaker 5 ☐

A   Mobile phones are unnecessarily complicated.
B   Mobiles are more suitable for younger users.
C   Having a mobile can stop you feeling lonely.
D   People's mobiles can tell you about their personality.
E   Mobile phone users ought to be polite.
F   Some people use their mobiles too much.

Over to you!

4 🔊 7.2 Complete these statements about mobiles from the recording. Then listen again and match them to the speakers. Which statements do you agree with? Why?

1   It's no substitute for talking f_____-to-f_____.
2   Mobiles m_____ life so much less complicated.
3   A mobile is simply a tool, a handy way to s_____ in t_____ with people.
4   You've got to k_____ u_____ with the latest technology.
5   My ringtone says I don't t_____ myself too seriously.

What can be difficult about doing these jobs?

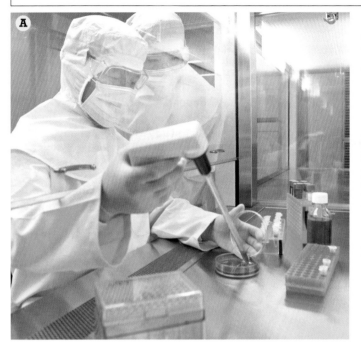

1 Look at photos A and B and read the question. In pairs, write down as many similarities and differences between the photos as you can think of. Then decide on your **four** best ideas.

2 7.3 Listen to a student comparing the two photos and answer the questions.

1 How many of your ideas from Activity 1 does she include?
2 Do you think she misses out anything important?
3 Does she add any new ideas?

3 Don't worry if you don't understand every detail in the photos – suggest your own ideas. Complete these expressions from the recording. Then listen again and check. Can you think of any other useful expressions you could use?

1 I don't t_____ many people c_____ do either of these jobs.
2 I i_____ that's difficult sometimes.
3 It looks as t_____ the scientists are working with chemicals.
4 I think he's p_____ making something but I'm not sure e_____ what.
5 M_____ it's some k_____ of machine?
6 I'd s_____ that both jobs are really dangerous.
7 If you a_____ me, there's a big difference between the attitude of the scientists.
8 It m_____ be a great feeling to build something l_____ that.
9 Well, that's my opinion, a_____ .

Exam practice

Speaking Part 2:
talking for one minute

Exam tip

Don't panic! Talking for one minute is easier than it sounds.

➤ Talk about **similarities and differences** between the photos.
➤ **Speculate** about *why* something is happening, or *what* people are feeling.
➤ Give **reasons** for your ideas.
➤ Don't waste time trying to think of the 'perfect' word – **paraphrase** instead.

4 7.4 Work in pairs. Student A, look at the photos on page 150. Student B, look at the photos on page 152.

• Listen to the instructions, then complete the task, using ideas from the *Exam tip*.

• Listen carefully while your partner is speaking. What expressions does he / she use for a) speculating, b) comparing and contrasting?

Negative prefixes

1 In 2080, Mr and Mrs Steel become dissatisfied with their son Max and replace him with the robot SuperMax 1.0! Complete the table with their criticisms, using prefixes from the list.

dis- il- im- in- ir- un-

	SuperMax 1.0	Max
0	is obedient.	*is disobedient.*
1	is considerate.	
2	is reliable.	
3	is responsible.	
4	is mature.	
5	acts logically.	

2 Complete the table below with the opposite forms of the words in the list. Then try to add one more word to each category.

accurate ~agree~ approve dependence employment important
legally literate moral probable regular reversible

1 dis-	*disagree*
2 il-	
3 im-	
4 in-	
5 ir-	
6 un-	

3 Complete the questions with words from Activity 2. Then ask and answer the questions with a partner. Find **two** things you agree about.

1 Do you think that having all the latest gadgets is essential or _____ ?

2 Do you agree or _____ that the subject of Computer Science is more difficult than English?

3 Have you ever read any _____ or misleading information on the internet? What was it?

4 Do you agree that people who _____ download music from the internet should go to prison?

Collocations (2):
verbs + prepositions

4 Match 1–6 with A–F to complete Mrs Steel's complaints about Max.

1	I **suspect** him	A	**on** him.
2	He never **thinks**	B	**of** lying.
3	I can't **depend**	C	**at** me!
4	He **laughs**	D	**with** the chores.
5	He doesn't **study**	E	**about** anyone else!
6	He never **helps**	F	**for** his exams.

5 Complete the sentences with the prepositions. In pairs, decide whether you agree with statements 1–7, explaining why.

about   in   in   from   on   to   with

1 Scientists shouldn't **interfere** _____ nature.

2 Most people **know** more _____ literature than science.

3 More time should be **dedicated** _____ scientific programmes on TV.

4 Science is a boy's subject. Girls should be **discouraged** _____ studying Science.

5 It's completely unethical for scientists to **experiment** _____ animals.

6 Hollywood has **succeeded** _____ making science look 'cool'.

7 It's illogical to **believe** _____ the supernatural. Everything can be explained scientifically.

Over to you!

6 In pairs, discuss how important each of these pieces of technology is to you personally and why. Then put the items in order of importance.

camera   microwave   computer   kettle
TV set   mobile   MP3 player   watch

> **Useful expressions**
> *I completely depend on …*
> *This really helps me to …*
> *I would find it impossible to live without …*
> *… is unimportant / inessential, because …*

Word boost ▶ Workbook p. 82

Get ready: *word stem transformations*

1 Read about the world's first real computer, ENIAC (1946). Label the photograph with the noun form of the words in **bold**.

ENIAC was 30.5 metres **long**, 2.4 metres **high**, 0.9 metres **deep**, and it **weighed** around 30 tons!

2 Creating word-building tables can be a good way to revise. Complete the table in pairs. Add five more rows with words you have learnt in this course.

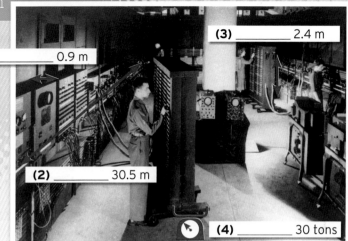

(1) _____ 0.9 m
(3) _____ 2.4 m
(2) _____ 30.5 m
(4) _____ 30 tons

	Adjective	Noun	Verb	Adverb
0	*competitive, competing*	*competition, competitor competitiveness*	compete	*competitively*
1		death		X
2			memorize	
3			believe	
4	destructive			
5		success		
6		life		X

Word boost ▶ Word stem transformations ▶ Workbook p. 41

Exam practice

3 Read the article below, ignoring the gaps. Why is Thomas Midgley 'the unluckiest inventor'?

4 Complete the exam task.

> **Use of English Part 3:** ***Exam tip***
> *the whole word*
> ➤ Add the correct **suffix**. Think about meaning as well as part of speech. Some words can form three nouns!
> ➤ Add a **prefix** if you need the *negative* form.

For questions **1–10**, use the word given in capitals at the end of some of the lines to form a word that fits in the gap **in the same line**. There is an example at the beginning **(0)**. Write your answers **IN CAPITAL LETTERS.**

The unluckiest inventor?

Thomas Midgley (1889–1944) is **(0)** ...*POSSIBLY*... the world's unluckiest inventor. He was incredibly   **POSSIBLE**
(1) .... in his day, patenting over a hundred different ideas and receiving   **SUCCEED**
(2) .... awards and medals. However, several of his inventions proved to be highly   **NUMBER**
dangerous. It has been suggested that Thomas Midgely is responsible for more **(3)** ....   **ENVIRONMENT**
damage than any other person!

One of Thomas Midgley's most significant inventions was leaded petrol, which turned out to produce
poisonous fumes which cause permanent, **(4)** .... damage to people's health. He also patented   **REVERSE**
a chlorinated fluorocarbon (CFC), which contributed significantly to the **(5)** .... of the ozone   **DESTROY**
layer. Midgley's inventiveness also ultimately cost him his **(6)** .... After a bad attack of polio left   **LIVE**
him with an **(7)** .... to walk without help, he invented a system of harnesses to support himself.   **ABLE**
Tragically, one day he became entangled in the harnesses, which resulted in his **(8)** ....   **DIE**

Thomas Midgley was an extremely unlucky inventor, whose best ideas **(9)** .... proved to   **FORTUNATE**
have terrible consequences. Perhaps not all **(10)** .... progress is good progress?   **SCIENCE**

Prepare

1 **In pairs, discuss the photos.**
1 What do you think the people will learn from these experiences?
2 How do you think we can encourage more people to study Science?

Analyse the task

2 Read the letter on the right. Which **three** things does Flavia write to complain about? What **one** positive thing does she say?

3 It is a good idea to use a range of language in a formal letter. Match the expressions and linkers in **bold** in Flavia's letter to the following categories.

1 Adding or ordering ideas	
2 Expressing contrast	
3 Giving a reason	
4 Making a suggestion	
5 Asking for something	
6 Expressing dissatisfaction	

4 Find examples of the passive in Flavia's letter. Why is it often a good idea to use the passive in this type of letter?

Dear Mr Watson,

I am writing to complain about the Science course which I recently attended at your college. **Although** it was certainly challenging, with interesting and demanding assignments, in other respects **it was unsatisfactory**.

First of all, the instructor was frequently late. **I felt this was unacceptable** as everyone had paid to attend. **Furthermore**, we were not provided with any books, which made it difficult to revise.

Last but not least, I must add **I was disappointed by the fact** that students were not allowed to do experiments themselves. These were all performed by the instructor and, **since** the class was very large, it was not always possible to see what was happening. **I would recommend** that students are given more practical experience on future courses.

I would like to request a partial refund of my fees in compensation. I look forward to hearing from you.

Yours sincerely,
Flavia D'Angelo

Improve your writing: *pronouns*

5 Complete the rules about pronouns with the words in the list. What other kinds of pronouns are there?

> It   This   They

> ### Pronouns
>
> To avoid repetition and to link ideas more effectively, we can use pronouns. For example, we can use pronouns to refer back to:
> - a singular noun *(I attended the course. ~~The course~~ _____ was terrible.)*
> - a plural noun *(We ordered some books. ~~The books~~ _____ never arrived.)*
> - a piece of information *(I complained to the manager. ~~Complaining to the manager~~ _____ was a mistake.)*

6 Read Flavia's letter again. What do the following pronouns refer to?

0 which *(line 3)* *the Science course*
1 it *(line 4)*
2 this *(line 8)*
3 which *(line 10)*
4 these *(line 14)*

7 Choose the correct alternatives to complete this extract from a publicity leaflet.

Thank you for visiting the *Science Today* museum. We welcome your feedback to help make **(1) it / them** even better!

First, we would like to know more about **(2) you / yourself**. Do you usually enjoy going to museums? Why?— *Tell him*

With over two hundred exhibits, we like to think that our museum offers **(3) anything / something** for **(4) all / everyone**. Our 'sky at night' and 'inside the mind' centres have proved particularly popular. **(5) Which / What** one did you prefer?— *Answer, giving reasons*

Last year we opened three new cafés. Did you visit **(6) any / some** of **(7) this / these**? What did you think?— *Yes - expensive and dirty. Complain*

Please write to Mark Clinton with comments and suggestions for improvements.— *Make a suggestion*

Ready to write!

> After you have visited a museum, you read a leaflet which asks for feedback. Read the leaflet and the notes you have made. Then write a letter, using **all** your notes. Write your answer in **120-150** words in an appropriate style.

8 Read the exam task. Then read the leaflet and all the notes in Activity 7 again.

1 What **didn't** you enjoy on your visit?
2 What opening and closing expressions will you need to include in your letter? Why?

9 Write down ideas about all four of the notes.

> *Note I*
> - *yes, really keen on museums*
> - *often go to museums on holiday*
> - *an interesting way to learn*
> - *more exciting than books!*

10 Look at the *Exam tip* and the notes you made in Activity 9. Decide:

1 how many paragraphs you will need to use.
2 how you can connect your ideas.

> **Writing Part 1:** *organisation and cohesion*   **Exam tip**
>
> ➤ Plan your ideas about all of the notes *before* you write.
> ➤ Use a new paragraph for each main topic.
> ➤ Begin and end a letter or email with suitable expressions.
> ➤ Make sure that your ideas 'flow'. Don't just address each point in turn – try to connect your ideas together.
>
> **Writing reference**   ▶ p. 168

11 Write your letter. Make sure you organise your ideas clearly and use a range of formal expressions and linkers.

12 When you have finished, look at the checklist on page 169. Check your letter and make any corrections.

Unit 7

1 Complete the sentences with the correct form of the verbs in the list. Include the words in **bold** where provided.

correct   estimate   guarantee   install
occur   ~~purchase~~   repair

Homework Whizz 3000

0 Congratulations! You _have just purchased_ (**just**) *Homework Whizz 3000* from the Online Superstore.

1 Once opened, the software _____ (**must**) on your computer immediately.

2 Installation _____ to take ten minutes.

3 All homework assignments _____ by our '100% accuracy' programme.

4 In the unlikely event that any faults _____, please contact our helpline.

5 It is important to get faulty software _____ by a professional.

6 Customer satisfaction _____ (**always**)!

2 Write words for the definitions. Write the correct form of the words in **bold**.

0 not **accurate** _inaccurate_
1 something which has been **invented**
2 a doctor who is trained in **psychiatry**
3 find a **solution** to a problem
4 the opposite of **upload**

3 Complete the text about some unusual museums. Would you like to visit any of these? Why? / Why not?

In Oregon, USA, there's a museum which is completely dedicated (**0**) with / (to) telephones! The museum includes some of the earliest mobile phones. Expensive and (**1**) **un-** / **ir-** reliable (users were regularly cut (**2**) **off** / **out**), they nevertheless had one big advantage – they didn't have any annoying (**3**) **call** / **ring** tones!

Have you ever thought (**4**) **about** / **of** how pencils were made? The Cumberland Pencil Museum in the UK sets (**5**) **for** / **out** the complete history of this tool. People first came (**6**) **on** / **up** with the idea of writing with graphite in the 1500s, but it wasn't until much later that people worked (**7**) **out** / **for** that soft graphite was easier to hold in wooden cases!

Units 1–7

4 Choose the correct option to complete each sentence.

0 We're looking _into_ why the experiment failed.
  A up   Ⓑ into
  C out   D at

1 The Science Museum is not to be _____ !
  A left   B missed
  C escaped D lost

2 It _____ years for him to perfect his invention.
  A last   B spent
  C passed D took

3 This new weight-loss machine will help you stay in great _____ !
  A shape   B width
  C size   D build

4 The scientists _____ out over the disaster and never spoke again.
  A went   B fell
  C got   D split

5 Complete the text with the words in the list.

although   as well as   ~~despite~~   if
like   many   much   since   too

UNIT TARGETS

Topic vocabulary: emotions ● abstract nouns
● laughter
Grammar: modal verbs (2) ● coordinating linkers
Word building: responses ● phrasal verbs (4)
● *make* and *do*
Writing: an informal letter ● word order
Exam preparation: Reading Part 2 ● Use of English
Parts 1 and 2 ● Listening Part 4 ● Speaking Parts
3 and 4 ● Writing Part 1

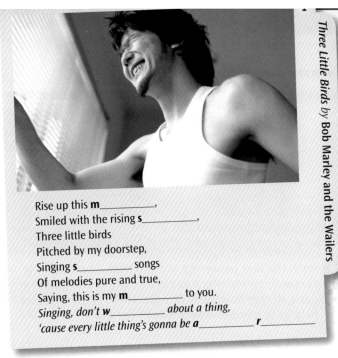

Three Little Birds by Bob Marley and the Wailers

Rise up this **m**_____,
Smiled with the rising **s**_____,
Three little birds
Pitched by my doorstep,
Singing **s**_____ songs
Of melodies pure and true,
Saying, this is my **m**_____ to you.
Singing, don't **w**_____ about a thing,
'cause every little thing's gonna be **a**_____ **r**_____

2

Lay All Your Love on Me, by ABBA

I wasn't **j**_____ before we met,
Now every woman I see is a potential threat.
And I'm **p**_____, it isn't nice.
You've heard me saying that **s**_____ was my only vice.
But now it isn't **t**_____, now everything is new,
And all I've learned has overturned, I **b**_____ of you:
Don't go wasting your e_____,
Lay all your love on me.

3

Heartbreak Hotel by Elvis Presley

Well, since my **b**_____ left me,
I found a new place to dwell.
It's **d**_____ at the end of Lonely Street
At Heartbreak Hotel.
You make me so lonely baby,
I get so lonely, I get so lonely I could d_____
And although it's always **c**_____,
You still can find some room.
Where **b**_____-hearted lovers
Do **c**_____ away their gloom.

Emotions

1 Quickly read the song lyrics, ignoring the gaps. Are these songs happy or sad?

2 🔊 8.1 In pairs, try to guess which words complete the lyrics. Then listen and check your answers.

3 Work in groups. Match the emotion adjectives to songs 1–3. Which other emotion words appear in the songs? How many more emotion words can you think of in one minute?

> anxious   chilled-out   despairing   insecure   gloomy
> light-hearted   miserable   suspicious   upbeat

4 Discuss which emotions the words in **bold** are expressing in the song lyrics 1–5. What do you think the songs are about?

1 He just walked away ... I cried like a baby, it hurt me so much and I'm **down**. - *Dolly Parton, Down*

2 Look what I found: the way to heaven. I'm **over the moon** ... since I found you. - *Liv Kristine, Over the Moon*

3 Stop just what you're doing to me. You **drive** me **mad**! Oh baby, why can't you see that I'm sad? - *Duffy, Stop*

4 I just can't help myself, don't want nobody else, I'm so **crazy about** you. - *Master P, Crazy About Ya*

5 You're **fed up with** all my bad habits, you're **sick of** me.
- *Green Day, Sick of Me*

Over to you!

5 What kind of music do you listen to when you're feeling a) upbeat, b) gloomy, c) chilled-out? Why? Do you listen to the same kind of music as your partner?

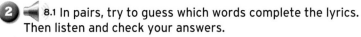

Word boost ▶ Emotions ▶ Workbook p. 46

A

B

C

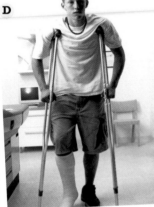

E

D

G

F

Reading Part 2:
reference words

Look for reference words (pronouns, linkers and time expressions), to understand how a text is organised.
➤ Underline any reference words in the sentences.
➤ Underline any reference words in the text before and after each gap.
➤ Working out what these words refer to will help you to complete each gap correctly.

4 Read the first paragraph in the article. Then read the sentence below, which completes gap Ø in the text. In pairs, decide how the reference words in **red** and **blue** help us to place this sentence in the gap.

At first this seems a slightly strange thing to do.

5 Seven sentences have been removed from the article. Choose from the sentences A–H the one which fits each gap (1–7). There is one extra sentence which you do not need to use.

A Nevertheless, it takes time and effort for people to improve their basic level of happiness.

B What's more, there is evidence that it can even extend your life by up to nine years.

C It can seem profound, whereas happiness is often unfairly linked to superficiality.

D However, it seems that we are surprisingly bad at predicting what will bring us long-term happiness.

E Well, it seems that the exact recipe for this varies from person to person.

F Unfortunately, it isn't a very profound emotion, and it doesn't usually last for long.

G But despite this general interest, happiness is still a little-discussed topic in academic circles.

H Prof. Mead thinks that the rest of us should be inspired by this example.

1 In pairs, match photos A–G to the topics in the list. How can these factors affect our happiness?

> family and friends   health   money   school or work
> the weather   where you live   your personality

2 Rank the factors in order of importance, from 1–7. Decide as a class which is the most important factor for happiness!

3 You are going to read a magazine article about a professor who studies and writes about happiness. Read the article opposite quickly, ignoring the gaps. What are the three main levels of happiness?

6 In pairs, discuss the following questions.

1 What does Professor Mead mean when she says that 'there's a certain glamour attached to misery'? *(paragraph 3)* Do you agree? Why? / Why not?

2 Why is Costa Rica 'the happiest place in the world'? *(paragraph 8)* Which places make you happy? Why?

The secret of *happiness*

Professor **Clarissa Mead** teaches and writes on the subject of happiness.

When I arrive at her office, Professor Mead <u>is watching a Japanese comedy while making lots of notes.</u> **0** *At first this seems a slightly strange thing to do.* But Prof. Mead <u>soon</u> reassures me with an explanation. "I'm not just watching for entertainment – this is part of my work! By investigating the things which bring us enjoyment, I can learn more about what cheers us up, or brings us down. I'm on a mission to uncover the secrets of happiness!"

Happiness is a topic that has fired the popular imagination, as demonstrated by the growing market for personal development books, each promising to bring bliss and fulfilment to our lives. **1** According to Prof. Mead, depression is still a more fashionable topic in university departments.

"Strangely, I think there's a certain glamour attached to misery, which is associated with poets and musicians. **2** This drives me mad, especially when people expect me to have a passion for kittens and rainbows!"

I observe that her office is very plain and businesslike. "That's quite deliberate! I want to encourage people to take my subject more seriously, because in my eyes it is hugely important. Happiness offers us an impressive array of benefits. For instance, it boosts your confidence, which in turn can help you achieve greater success. **3** This means it's almost as essential for your health as exercise and a balanced diet!"

Prof. Mead believes there are three levels of happiness. At the bottom, there's pleasure, which is the feeling we get from having fun. However, this type of enjoyment has its downside. **4** So when it passes, we can feel flat. That's why some people become thrill-seekers, addicted to pleasure. Not all happiness is good for us!

The next level is the feeling of intense joy, such as that experienced by lottery winners or newly dating couples. We often wrongly assume that if only we were wealthy, famous or in love then we could be joyful forever. **5** In fact, studies have shown that only one year after realising these dreams, our sense of well-being will have returned to previous levels.

For Prof. Mead, the best and most sustainable form of happiness is contentment, a basic satisfaction with our lives as a whole. So how do we become content? **6** However, it seems to consist of certain key ingredients, including living in a pleasant environment and having the freedom to pursue our interests and ambitions. Our relationships with other people are even more significant – it seems it's harder to be happy alone!

Close-knit families and communities are both highly valued in Costa Rica, which recently came top in the Happy Planet Index. The Happy Planet Index rates countries in terms of sustainable well-being. The project found that Costa Ricans have the highest life satisfaction in the world and high life expectancy, yet are among the lowest resource consumers on the planet. Despite being a so-called 'developing' country, most of the members of this beautiful and friendly nation enjoyed a very high quality of life. **7** "Living in a place we love surrounded by people we care about may not seem as exciting as becoming a millionaire, but it's more likely to make us happy. Luckily, it's much more achievable too!"

Vocabulary in context:
abstract nouns

7 Abstract nouns describe emotions or ideas. Form nouns from the following adjectives and verbs. Then find and check your answers in the article.

1 entertain	4 passionate	7 content
2 enjoy	5 succeed	8 satisfy
3 depress	6 please	9 free

Word boost ▶ Abstract nouns ▶ Workbook p. 46

Over to you!

8 Write around 50–80 words on the subject of what *happiness* means to you. Include at least **four** abstract nouns.

*To me, **happiness** means having the **freedom** to live by my own rules. It drives me mad when people try to tell me what to do!*

9 Compare your ideas with a partner. Which of your partner's ideas do you agree or disagree with?

1 This man is always happy! What's his secret? Read one student's ideas, then work in pairs and add **two** more ideas of your own.

A He **might be pretending** to be cheerful. That's one explanation, anyway!

B He **must be** a very chilled-out person. That much is obvious!

C I'm not sure, but he **may have come** from a wealthy background.

D He **can't have had** many problems in his life, that's for sure.

E He **couldn't be living** in poverty, or he wouldn't look so cheerful.

F He **must have grown** up in a very close family. That's essential for happiness.

2 Look at the ideas in Activity 1 again. Complete the table with the modal verbs in **red**.

Deduction

Modal verb	Used when we are ...
1 could, _____ OR _____	not sure about something
2 _____	sure that something is true
3 _____ OR _____	sure that something is NOT true

`Language summary` ▶ p. 163

3 In which sentences above do the modal verbs refer to:

1 the present simple?
2 the present continuous?
3 the past?

Watch out! couldn't

We use *might not (have)* or *may not (have)* to talk about something that **possibly** isn't true.

*Jack's late. He **might not** / **may not** / ~~couldn't~~ have got my message about the party.*

We use *could not (have)* to talk about something that **definitely** isn't true.

Oh no! Jack ~~might~~ / ~~may~~ / couldn't have got your message because I forgot to send it!

4 Read the *Watch out!* box, then complete the sentences. Use your imagination!

1 That athlete looks disappointed. He can't ...
2 Why is that girl crying? Her boyfriend may ...
3 I'm worried about yesterday's test. I might not ...
4 That couple look over the moon. They must ...

5 Read the dialogue quickly, then discuss these questions:

1 What did Jack dream about?
2 What does Kasia think it might mean?
3 Do you agree that dreams can have meanings? Why? / Why not?

Jack: I had a weird dream last night. I was being chased by a wild animal – **(0) it's possible that it was a lion or a tiger**. Or **(1) perhaps it wasn't a cat** – **(2) perhaps it was some kind of monster!** What do you think it means?

Kasia: Well, it doesn't sound very pleasant, so **(3) I'm sure it doesn't mean anything good! (4) I'm certain that you're feeling anxious** – that's why you're having bad dreams. **(5) It's possible that the animal represents a problem**, like your exams, or your job at the shop.

Jack: Hmm, **(6) it's definitely my exams** – I'm very worried about them. What do you think, Ela?

Ela: I think you're both talking rubbish! **(7) It's possible that the animal doesn't represent anything at all**. You watched a horror film last night, didn't you? **(8) I'm quite sure it gave you nightmares** – that's the most rational explanation!

6 Rewrite 1–8 in Activity 5 using modal verbs.

0 it could have been a lion or a tiger.

Over to you!

7 Work in pairs. Turn to page 153 and discuss the questions.

Get ready: *coordinating linkers*

1 Read the extract from a dream dictionary. Have you ever dreamt of these things? Do you agree with the explanations?

2 Look at the coordinating linkers (= *linkers with two parts*) in **bold**. Which can we use:
1 to say that two things are true?
2 to say that two things are not true?
3 to express a choice between two possibilities?

3 Complete the sentences with your own ideas, then compare your sentences with a partner.

1 If I want to cheer myself up, I **either** …
2 **Neither** … are good to do when you're stressed.
3 I don't get annoyed easily, but **both** …. drive me mad!
4 When I'm feeling over the moon about something I **not only** …

Grammar boost ▶ Coordinating linkers
▶ Workbook p. 49

flying
Dreaming of flying is very positive! It **not only** means you're happy with life **but also** that you're well on the way to achieving your ambitions.

being chased
Dreaming that you're being chased means you're struggling with a problem. Right now, you're **neither** facing up to your worries **nor** trying to change the situation, so the problem's getting worse!

falling
Dreaming of falling has **both** positive **and** negative interpretations, depending on whether you felt happy or sad in the dream. It can **either** mean that you feel confident enough to take risks, **or** that you feel down and anxious.

Exam Practice

4 Quickly read the exam task, ignoring the gaps.
Do people all over the world a) feel the same emotions, b) use the same body language?

5 Complete the exam task.

Use of English Part 2:
the whole context
Don't just look at the words around a gap.
➤ Key information may appear at the start, middle or end of a sentence, or elsewhere in the text.
➤ Remember, some expressions consist of two or more separate parts, e.g. *neither … nor*.

Exam tip

For questions **1–12**, read the text below and think of the word which best fits each gap. Use only **one** word in each gap. There is an example at the beginning **(0)**.
Write your answers **IN CAPITAL LETTERS**.

Express yourself!

What does a Kazakhstani tribesman have **(0)** ......*IN*........ common with a Brazilian student? Scientists **(1)** .... discovered that, while languages and cultures can vary widely around the world, in **(2)** .... respect we're all very much alike. Both the Kazakhstani **(3)** .... the Brazilian are capable of feeling and expressing **(4)** .... same six basic emotions: sadness, happiness, fear, anger, surprise and disgust.

Remarkably, we use similar facial expressions for each **(5)** .... these emotions, regardless of our background. For instance, most people either smile **(6)** .... laugh to express happiness.

But **(7)** .... these similarities, interpreting other people's emotions isn't always easy. In the US and Latin America, people usually prefer a big, wide smile. In contrast, people in Asia not **(8)** .... use smaller movements, but they also smile **(9)** .... frequently. People who smile a lot may be seen as insincere, rather **(10)** .... friendly!

Scientists believe that as much **(11)** .... 70% of all communication is non-verbal, so understanding different expressions and gestures is very important. **(12)** .... avoid embarrassment, travellers should remember that looking directly into someone's eyes is considered aggressive in the West Indies, and nodding the head up and down means 'no', not 'yes', in Bulgaria!

Get ready: *laughter*

C: Sitcom

B: Stand-up comedy

A: Cartoon

1 Match the reviews 1–3 to topics A–C above. Which is the most positive / negative review? Why?

1 Some of the dialogue is extremely **witty**. Unfortunately, the script is let down by the acting - some of the actors **take themselves too seriously**. They need to relax and **have some fun**!

2 It's impossible to read this without **laughing out loud**! Both the drawings and the captions are absolutely **hilarious**. I'd recommend it to anyone with **a sense of humour**!

3 I think the act needs more work. He **told a lot of jokes**, but I didn't **laugh at** very many. I'm not really keen on comedians who **make fun of** other people – it was cruel rather than **amusing**.

2 Work in pairs and write definitions for five of the words and expressions in **bold** in the reviews.

witty – funny and clever

3 What's the difference in meaning between the words in **bold** in these sentences?

A The comedian was **funny**. We couldn't stop laughing.

B What's making that **funny** noise? I don't know what's causing it.

C We should invite Rob to the party. He's great **fun**!

4 Write a short review of a funny show, film or cartoon you've seen recently. Include expressions from Activities 1 and 3.

Word boost ▶ Laughter ▶ Workbook p. 46

Exam practice

5 8.2 You will hear an interview with Zadie Mack, a comedian who has just toured America. For questions 1–7, choose the best answer (A, B or C).

1 What does Zadie say about performing live on stage?

A It's sometimes boring.
B It isn't well-paid.
C It can be very tiring.

2 Why did Zadie decide to follow a career in comedy?

A Her parents encouraged her.
B Her grandfather inspired her.
C Her teachers suggested the idea.

3 Zadie got on well with her teachers because they thought she was

A a good-natured girl.
B an intelligent student.
C a talented performer.

4 For Zadie, what was the most difficult part of getting started in comedy?

A learning how to cope with criticism
B working for extremely long hours
C having to develop her act by herself

5 What is Zadie's best source of ideas for jokes?

A reading stories in the news
B watching other comedians' acts
C listening to people's conversations

6 As a result of Zadie's success,

A her shows are completely full.
B some people recognise her.
C she has changed her image.

7 Zadie thinks that comedians should try to be

A honest.
B original.
C likeable.

Over to you!

6 Discuss these questions in pairs.

1 Would you like to be a comedian? Why? / Why not? What aspects of the job do you think you'd find the most difficult?

2 What's your favourite joke? Tell your partner. Did you make them laugh?

1 In pairs, compare the photos and answer the questions.

1 Why are the people celebrating?
2 Which party looks like the most fun and why?
3 What do you think makes a successful party?

2 🔊 **8.3** Listen to two students talking about parties. Are they answering a Part 3 or a Part 4 question? Which of the topics below do they discuss, and in what order?

decorations   food   gifts   guests   music   fireworks

Exam practice

3 Read the *Exam tip* and these extracts from the dialogue. How does the next speaker respond to each of 1–4? Listen and check your answers.

1 People need to be able to chat, too.
2 Do you think food's important?
3 I don't think you need a big meal, do you?
4 I really hate those parties where no one talks!

4 Work in pairs. Match these expressions from the dialogue (1–7) with their function (A–G). Add at least **two** more expressions for each of A–G.

1 Well,	A sequencing your ideas
2 First of all,	B giving yourself time to think
3 Personally,	
4 So, we've agreed that ...	C responding to the other speaker
5 What else?	
6 And another thing,	D asking for input
7 Yeah, good point.	E adding ideas
	F expressing an opinion
	G concluding / summarising

5 In pairs, look at the pictures on page 155 and discuss these Part 3 questions.

• How can these things make people feel happier if they are feeling sad?
• Which **two** of these things would be the most effective?

6 Read these Part 4 questions, then write one more of your own. Discuss each question with a partner and try to find one thing you have in common.

1 When you're feeling sad, do you think it's better to be alone or with friends? Why?
2 What's more important, being successful or being happy? Why?

Responses

1 It's important to respond appropriately to what another person says. In pairs, match 1-4 to the responses A-L. Can you think of any other possible responses to 1-4?

1 *You've just won the lottery!*

2 *Our first date didn't go well.*

3 *Can I stay with you?*

4 *I'm so happy. I've passed FCE!*

A I don't believe it!
B What a shame!
C Congratulations!

D You must be joking!
E That's fine by me.
F You can't be serious!

G Good for you!
H Of course.
I Never mind.

J No problem.
K Well done!
L Oh dear!

2 Work in pairs. Take turns to give news and respond appropriately on the following topics, using expressions from Activity 1.

1 You want to borrow a book.
2 You think you've just seen an alien!
3 You've just been offered a job in Hollywood!
4 You're upset because your favourite football team lost a match.

Phrasal verbs (4): *behaviour*

3 Do you read your horoscope regularly? Why? / Why not? Quickly read the text below. Do you agree with what it says about your star sign?

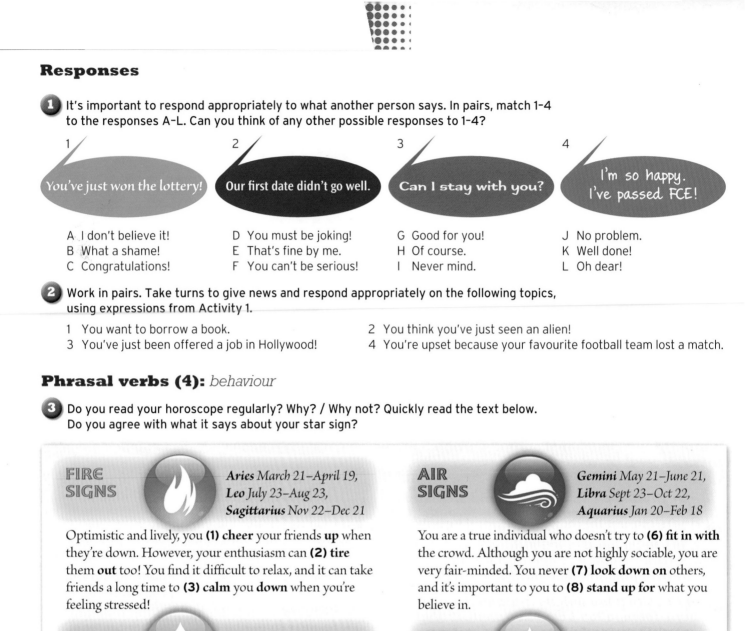

FIRE SIGNS — *Aries* March 21–April 19, *Leo* July 23–Aug 23, *Sagittarius* Nov 22–Dec 21

Optimistic and lively, you **(1) cheer** your friends **up** when they're down. However, your enthusiasm can **(2) tire** them **out** too! You find it difficult to relax, and it can take friends a long time to **(3) calm** you **down** when you're feeling stressed!

EARTH SIGNS — *Taurus* April 20–May 20, *Virgo* Aug 23–Sept 22, *Capricorn* Dec 22–Jan 19

`Earth` people are reliable and honest. They rarely tell lies or **(4) make** things **up**. They tend not to **(5) rush into** things, but they're very determined and hardworking when it comes to achieving their goals.

AIR SIGNS — *Gemini* May 21–June 21, *Libra* Sept 23–Oct 22, *Aquarius* Jan 20–Feb 18

You are a true individual who doesn't try to **(6) fit in with** the crowd. Although you are not highly sociable, you are very fair-minded. You never **(7) look down on** others, and it's important to you to **(8) stand up for** what you believe in.

WATER SIGNS — *Cancer* June 22 –July 22, *Scorpio* Oct 23–Nov 21, *Pisces* Feb 19–March 20

Relationships are very important to 'water' types. They are generous and kind-hearted, and friends can always **(9) rely on** them for help. A 'water' person hates to **(10) let** anyone **down**.

4 Work in pairs. Match five of the phrasal verbs in **bold** in Activity 3 to the meanings A-E. Write definitions for the five remaining phrasal verbs.

A to hurry to do (something)
B think that you are better than (someone)
C invent (something)
D disappoint (someone)
E make (someone) feel happier

5 Which phrasal verbs in Activity 3 are *separable* (we can separate two parts of the phrasal verb by an object)?

Over to you!

6 Choose **one** of the topics below and make notes about a time when:

• you successfully stood up for someone or something
• you did something which completely tired you out
• you managed to cheer someone up
• someone really let you down.

7 Take turns to talk about your situation with a partner. Your partner should listen and respond appropriately.

Word boost ▶ Workbook p. 83

Get ready: *make* and *do*

1 Read part of a personality questionnaire and look at the answers that a student called Luke has circled. What do you learn about Luke?

How good a friend are you?

1 A relative asks you to do them a favour and babysit tonight but you've made **plans** to go out! Do you:

(A) make an excuse and go out anyway?
B do your relative a good turn and agree?

2 You notice that your friend, who usually does well in class, has made a **mistake** in her homework. Do you:

A make a suggestion to your friend that she checks her work again?
(B) do nothing? After all, it's her fault!

2 Complete the table with the expressions in **blue** from Activity 1. Add the expressions in the list below. Can you add any more?

a course   a living   an appointment   an effort
an offer   badly   business   harm   homework
housework   money   the best of something   your best

make ...	*plans*	do ...	*someone a favour*

3 Write **four** more questions using expressions with *do* and *make*. Ask your partner the completed questionnaire. Did you learn anything interesting?

Word boost ▶ *make* and *do* ▶ Workbook p. 47

Exam practice

4 Complete the exam task.

5 Do you agree with the final question in the text?

Use of English Part 1: *collocations*

Exam tip

You may need to think about **how** we use a word, as well as what it means.
➤ Does an option fit in the sentence? Read the whole sentence carefully.
➤ Think about collocations, e.g. *pay attention to, make a decision about.*

For questions **1–12**, read the text below and decide which answer (**A**, **B**, **C** or **D**) best fits each gap.

All in the mind?

Many great magicians are **(0)** EXPERTS in analysing human emotions and behaviour. Performers such as David Blaine and Derren Brown **(1)** .... to have the ability to read people's minds, for example by asking them to **(2)** .... a choice between several cards and then correctly 'guessing' their selection. But is this **(3)** .... a feat of mind-reading, or is it just a very clever **(4)** ....?

Derren Brown says that it's all a **(5)** .... of psychology. By paying **(6)** .... attention to people's body language, he has become skilled at **(7)** .... out what they're thinking and feeling. **(8)** .... addition, he has learnt how to use his own body language to make subtle **(9)** .... to his audience. If he does this **(10)** ...., he can influence the way people act.

But some people are critical of Brown's act, expressing **(11)** .... that he may be doing **(12)** .... to people by manipulating their responses. Is magic simply a bit of fun – or does it have a darker side?

	A		B		C		D	
0	scientists		authorities		artists		(D) experts	
1	appear		look		show		demonstrate	
2	do		take		get		make	
3	certainly		really		utterly		surely	
4	magic		disguise		trick		fake	
5	substance		matter		measure		state	
6	near		deep		close		hard	
7	working		solving		getting		turning	
8	On		For		In		With	
9	opinions		offers		ideas		suggestions	
10	right		truly		good		really	
11	concern		sympathy		care		consideration	
12	hurt		destruction		harm		danger	

Prepare

1 Compare the photos in pairs. How do you think the people are feeling and why? How are you going to celebrate finishing your FCE course?

2 Quickly read the letter. How might Lucy celebrate the end of her exams?

Analyse the task

3 The expressions below can be used to reply to the notes in Lucy's letter. Work in pairs and complete the table. Then add **one** more expression to each category.

> I'd love to come   If I were you, ...
> I haven't decided how ...
> Good luck   I think you should ...
> ... is the best time for me
> I'm planning to ...
> ~~You must be feeling ...~~

red note	*You must be feeling ...*
blue note	
green note	
purple note	

4 Complete Claudio's reply below with **six** of the expressions from Activity 3.

5 To get high marks for writing, you need to vary your language. Read Claudio's letter again and find at least **two** examples of each of the following:

1 modal verbs
2 adverbs
3 different tenses
4 adjectives
5 phrasal verbs
6 linkers

Sorry I haven't written sooner. As you know, I've got my final exams next month, so I've been revising really hard! ————— *Poor you!*

Anyway, when it's all over I want to celebrate! My parents say I could either have a party or they'll give me some money to go to a football match (our local team are really good). What do you think? ————— *Make a suggestion*

It would be great if you could come too. You could stay for the week if you like. Are you free any time in July? ————— *Say yes and suggest a time*

Let me know, anyway. Write soon!

Lucy

PS How are you going to celebrate finishing your English exam? ————— *Tell Lucy*

Hi Lucy,

Poor you, **(0)** <u>*you must be feeling*</u> stressed! **(1)** _____ with your exams, though I'm sure you won't need it. You always seem to do brilliantly!

I think it's a great idea to celebrate. **(2)** _____, I'd throw the biggest party I could. That would cheer me up the most, anyway!

(3) _____ to stay with you, thanks for asking. The first week in July **(4)** _____, as I think we're going on a family holiday later that month.

My English exam's in June, so I'm also revising quite hard. But **(5)** _____ have some fun soon! **(6)** _____ I'm going to celebrate yet. I might have some friends round, or maybe we'll go out for a nice meal.

Looking forward to seeing you soon!

Claudio

Improve your writing: *word order*

6 Add the words in **bold** to the sentences, making any other changes if necessary.

1 She laughed at his jokes. (**never**)
2 He told the joke. (**badly**)
3 They're both Italian actors. (**funny**)
4 That performer isn't confident. (**enough**)
5 She told a joke. (**me**)
6 The comedian explained it. (**us**)

7 Choose the correct word to complete the rules.

Common word order errors!

1 Frequency adverbs (e.g. *often, always*) go **before / after** a main verb and **before / after** the verb *be*.

2 Evaluating adverbs (e.g. *well, badly*) usually go at the **beginning / middle / end** of a sentence or clause.

3 Adjectives expressing an opinion or evaluation (e.g. *kind, ugly*) go **before / after** adjectives with a more specific or objective meaning (e.g. *red, Argentinean*).

4 *Enough* goes before a noun and **before / after** an adjective.

5 With verbs with two objects, the **direct / indirect** object usually goes before the **direct / indirect** object.

6 BUT with some verbs (*announce, describe, explain, introduce, suggest, say*), the **direct / indirect** object is used before *to* + **direct / indirect** object.

8 Write the phrases in **bold** in the correct order.

Do you remember that short story competition I entered? Well, **(1) will / you / believe / never / it** – **(2) well / really / did / I** and **(3) me / awarded / the second prize / the judges**! ⎯⎯ *Well done!*

The prize includes two tickets to go to the International Film Festival in July. This year it's being held in my town! Would you like to come? You could stay for the week, and we could go swimming or play some football too, ⎯⎯ *Yes, because ...* **(4) have / we / enough / time / if**!

I love films, **(5) especially / really / comedies / Hollywood / funny**. What's the funniest film you've seen? ⎯⎯ *Answer, and say why*

I've also won a small amount of money. **(6) to / me / explained / the judges** that I can either keep it or give it to a charity. What do you think I should do? ⎯⎯ *Give advice*

Write soon!

Jon

Ready to write!

Your friend, Jon, has written you a letter. Read Jon's letter and the notes you have made. Then write a letter to Jon, using **all** your notes. Write **120-150** words in an appropriate style.

9 Read the exam task above, and the letter in Activity 8. Write down ideas for replying to each of the notes.

Writing Part 1: *range* *Exam tip*

➤ **Vocabulary**
Don't copy word-for-word from the notes. Use a variety of language, including more complex structures like phrasal verbs and collocations.

➤ **Grammar**
Use different tenses and structures. Try to avoid using too many short, basic sentences in the present simple.

➤ **Linkers**
Use a variety of linking words and expressions, not just *and, but* and *because*!

Writing reference ▶ p. 168

10 Read the *Exam tip*, and look at the ideas you wrote in Activity 9. For each note, think of useful vocabulary, grammar and linkers you could include.

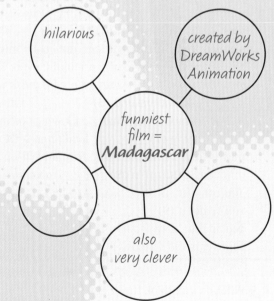

11 Write your letter. Use a range of language with the correct spelling, punctuation and word order. When you have finished, check your letter and make any corrections. Use the checklist on page 169 to help you.

Unit 8

1 Complete the second sentence so that it has a similar meaning to the first sentence. Use between two and five words, including the word given.

1 Maybe she broke his heart. **HAVE**
  She _____ his heart.

2 There's no chance of me ever forgiving him. **CAN**
  I _____ him.

3 It's possible that this song will help him relax. **MIGHT**
  This song _____ down.

4 It's impossible that the magician knew what we were thinking. **COULD**
  The magician _____ what we were thinking.

5 As well as acting, he also performed comedy routines. **ONLY**
  He was not _____ also a comedian.

6 I don't feel any fear or anxiety. **NEITHER**
  I feel _____ anxious.

2 Complete the text using the words in the list.

cheer	crazy	down	feelings	joy	out
sense	take	tell	up		

Do you know what **:-)** means? Turn it sideways, and you can see a smiling face. It means 'happiness' or **(1)** _____ . You can use this symbol in a text or email to **(2)** _____ someone up or to show them that you're trying to **(3)** _____ a joke. In contrast, **:-(** means that you're feeling depressed or **(4)** _____ . These symbols, also called *emoticons*, are commonly used in texts and emails. People originally made them **(5)** _____ because they wanted a quick way to express emotions and **(6)** _____ . Other common emoticons include **:-D** which means 'I'm laughing **(7)** _____ loud', and **:-X** which means 'love'. You could send it to a boyfriend or girlfriend to say 'I'm **(8)** _____ about you!' You can also use a winking sign **;-)** to show that you've got a **(9)** _____ of humour, and warn people that they shouldn't **(10)** _____ your comments too seriously!

3 What do you think these emoticons mean? Suggest definitions for 1–4.

:-| *I think this emoticon means that you're neither happy nor sad. Or it could mean that you aren't sure about something.*

1 **=O**   2 **:-?**   3 **:'-(**   4 **|-O**

Units 1–8

4 Complete the quotations with the correct form of the words in **bold**.

1 Happiness _____ (**not give**) but exchanged. *Anon.*
2 The secret of happiness is to make others _____ (**believe**) they are the cause of it. *Al Batt.*
3 Happiness is often the result of _____ (**be**) too busy _____ (**be**) miserable. *Anon.*
4 Happiness seems made _____ (**be**) shared. *Pierre Corneille.*
5 Happiness is the art of never _____ (**hold**) in your mind the memory of any unpleasant thing that _____ (**happen**). *Anon.*

5 Complete the article by writing the correct form of the words in brackets. Think about prefixes, suffixes, and internal changes.

therapy

9 Go for it!

Topic vocabulary: success and failure ● sport ● body idioms
Grammar: wishes and regrets ● mixed conditionals ● be / get used to
Word building: words with similar meanings ● collocations (3) ● word families
Writing: set text (an article) ● appropriate language
Exam preparation: Reading Part 3 ● Use of English Parts 3 and 4 ● Listening Part 1 ● Speaking Parts 3 and 4 ● Writing Part 2

Ⓐ   Ⓑ   Ⓒ   Ⓓ

Success and failure

① How do you think these people are feeling? Why?

② What makes people successful? Why? In groups, agree on the three most important ingredients for success in: a) business, b) entertainment, c) sport.

> ambition   confidence   famous relatives
> hard work   good looks   good planning
> luck   money   qualifications   talent

③ Read the notes opposite from a course called *Reach for the Stars*, ignoring the gaps. Which tip do you agree with the most and why?

④ 🔊 9.1 In pairs, guess which words might complete the gaps. Then listen to someone presenting the course and complete the notes.

⑤ Did you find the speaker convincing? Why? / Why not?

Word boost ▶ Success and failure ▶ Workbook p. 52

Reach for the Stars
The Six Secrets of Success!

1 Be positive. **The sky's the** _limit_ if you **believe** _____ **yourself**!

2 **Set** yourself _____. You need to have a plan if you're going to _____ your **ambitions**.

3 _____ **action**. Don't wait – your future starts now!

4 Work hard. Only time and effort can _____ your dreams **into** reality.

5 Be different. **Stand out from the** _____ – don't follow it!

6 Don't let negative thoughts **get the** _____ **of** you, and never _____ **up**! Remember: failure is just a stage on the way to success!

Over to you!

⑥ Work in pairs. Read a set of challenges to your partner, and answer the challenges your partner gives you. Each successful answer scores one point.

Student A: turn to page 153.
Student B: turn to page 155.

A B

C `00:01`

1 You are going to read an article about five young sportspeople. Look at the illustrations. What pressures do you think young sportspeople face?

2 Quickly read the article on the right. Which sport does each person play?

Exam practice

3 Read the *Exam tip*. For questions 1–15, choose from the sportspeople (A–E). The sportspeople may be chosen more than once.

Which person mentions ...

... preferring individual to team sports?	1	☐
... needing expensive equipment?	2	☐
... a negative opinion of the way some sportspeople behave?	3 ☐	4 ☐
... the effect that their sport has had on their social life?	5	☐
... having made money from their sport?	6	☐
... having a very competitive attitude to winning?	7	☐
... having hurt themselves while doing their sport?	8	☐
... almost giving up their sport?	9	☐
... having some enthusiastic supporters?	10	☐
... not being taken seriously by others?	11	☐
... learning from observing other sportspeople?	12	☐
... feeling exhausted as a result of training?	13 ☐	14 ☐
... the way their sport reflects their attitude to life?	15	☐

Going for gold

Five young sports stars tell us what it's really like ...

A Django

Coming second in the free running world championships has landed me roles in music videos, but it doesn't bring in quite enough to get by, so I'm also a bike courier. That isn't ideal, but it won't make me quit, and I try to stop it getting me down. I'm always looking out for new opportunities. For instance, I'm currently working on a deal with a potential sponsor – a sportswear company called Free Spirit. That's me! I don't run on a track, I go wherever I want. I don't let any obstacles or worries about danger hold me back. Not when I'm running, nor any other time! There are too many distractions when you play sports in groups. Alone, you can concentrate on each movement, completely in tune with your body and your surroundings.

B Tomas

When I lost the junior championships, my coach refused to speak to me. Devastated, I practised alone with a racquet for hours, until I was practically falling asleep on my desk at school. It took me months to get my confidence back and it nearly put me off tennis for life. The funny thing is, since I got rid of my coach, I've been doing much better! I've won some awards and I'm hoping to earn some money as a professional one day. I think

it's important to keep things in perspective, and it's a shame that some people take it all too seriously. You see players trying to cheat by intimidating opponents or shouting at referees. I really can't relate to that. At the end of the day, it's just a game.

C Gabrielle

When I tell people what I do they often laugh, which drives me mad. If I hadn't trained really hard, I wouldn't be where I am today. Looks aren't enough; you've got to have talent, determination and strength. And I mean that in both ways. I work out a lot, often to the point of being completely worn out. As part of an acrobatic routine I sometimes have to carry other girls on my shoulders, and they're not as skinny as they look on TV! You also need inner strength. Cheerleading is largely an amateur sport, so you don't get paid, but that doesn't stop it from being very competitive. I have seen instances of bullying among team mates, which is just terrible. I wish it wasn't an issue; I want to feel proud of my sport.

D Monica

There's still this stereotype of the laid-back, supercool surf 'dude'. If only it were true! You can't be laid-back if you want to succeed, and for me, second place is

as bad as last place. If I see someone doing a new trick it obsesses me. I study all their moves and work out how to copy them. I don't care how many times I fall off the board or how many bruises I get as long as I can do it perfectly in the end! It can be a lonely sport. If you're getting up at dawn every day to catch the best waves, then you don't want to go out much in the evenings. But I figure, I'm young, and all that can wait – I just want a few more trophies first!

E Mario

My parents were initially against my taking up wheelchair rugby because it's often perceived to be dangerous. Some people even call it 'murderball'! So far I've managed to avoid any crashes on the court myself, although I've had a few near misses. I reckon if you're speedy enough you can avoid most collisions! Anyway, luckily, I managed to persuade my parents to change their minds and so I wasn't forced to give it up. Now I regularly hear them cheering in the stands – they nearly deafen me each time I score! Wheelchair rugby's so exciting it's becoming increasingly popular with spectators, which is great because that may mean more funding. Sadly, the modified chairs don't come cheap! It'd be a shame if that put anyone off the sport.

Vocabulary in context: *sport*

4 Find as many words relating to sport as you can in the text. Which describe these things?

sports   people   equipment   places
actions   competitions   other

5 Write five rules for your favourite sport. Can your partner add any more ideas?

In this sport you have to run on a track.

Word boost ▶ Sport ▶ Workbook p. 52

Over to you!

6 Work in teams to argue *for* or *against* statements 1-4.
Team A: You are *for* 1 and 2 and *against* 3 and 4.
Team B: You are *for* 3 and 4 and *against* 1 and 2.
First brainstorm ideas in your teams.

1 Winning is the most important thing in sport.
2 Top footballers are paid too much money.
3 Dangerous sports like boxing should be banned.
4 Sports lessons at school should be compulsory.

7 Debate statements 1-4. Try to convince the other team that you are right!

1 Read the extract on the right from a press announcement. What is the footballer apologising for? Do you think there's too much bad behaviour in professional sport? Why?

2 Look at the expressions in **bold** in the text in Activity 1, and complete the rules with A–F.

A *wish / if only* + past simple
B *wish / if only* + past perfect
C *wish / if only* + *would*
D *wish / if only* + *could* + infinitive
E *regret* + gerund
F *should(n't)* + *have* + past participle

Wishes and regrets

1 _____	to make a wish about a present state or situation
2 _____	to make a wish about a present action
3 _____ , _____ , _____	to express a regret about or criticism of the past
4 _____	to make a wish that probably won't come true

Language summary ▶ p. 164

3 Choose the correct alternatives to complete what an athlete said to a friend after being disqualified for cheating.

" I wish today **(1) were / had been** over – it's been the worst day of my life! If only everyone **(2) stopped / would stop** shouting at me – I can't take any more! I wish I **(3) could go / went** home. I really regret **(4) to cheat / cheating** in the race, it was a stupid thing to do. I **(5) couldn't / shouldn't** have tried to trip anyone up, especially not with all my friends and family watching. If only no one **(6) saw / had seen** me do it! "

4 Work in pairs and write **two** wishes or regrets for each speaker.

A If I**'d trained** harder, I **would** still **be** in the team.
I shouldn't have been so lazy!

B I **would be** rich today if I**'d won** the contest!

C If I **was fitter**, I **would have won** the race.

5 Read the rules below. <u>Underline</u> the clauses in sentences A, B and C in Activity 4 which refer to the past, and circle those which refer to the present.

Mixed conditionals

We can sometimes use a mixture of conditional forms, for example: <*if* + past perfect>, <*would* + infinitive> shows how an unreal past event would affect the present.
<*if* + past simple>, <*would* + present perfect> shows how an unreal present or general situation would have affected the past.

Language summary ▶ p. 164

" What I did was completely wrong. I shouldn't have shouted at the referee! **If only I'd kept** my temper on the pitch. Then I wouldn't have been sent off, and we might have won the match. I really regret letting my fans down and **I wish I could** make it up to them. I know that people are claiming I've set a bad example for younger players and I'm really sorry about that. **I wish I was** a better role model. But right now, **I wish** that the press **would leave** me in peace! "

6 Answer the questions using mixed conditional forms. How would things be different if:

1 your parents were both professional sportspeople?
2 no one had ever invented the sport of football?
3 you'd gone to a football match instead of coming to class?

Over to you!

7 Work in pairs. Student A is going to be an interviewer and Student B is going to be a celebrity in the news. Choose your celebrity, 1 or 2. Then Student A, prepare five questions and Student B, prepare your story.

1 A pop star who was late for a concert, then played badly. (He / She didn't refund the tickets!)
2 A famous sportsperson who insulted an opponent live on TV. (He / She was disqualified!)

8 Perform your interview. When you have finished, decide together whether the celebrity has made a good impression, and why.

Get ready: *be / get used to*

1 Read this extract from a biography. How has Vinnie's life changed? Which of Vinnie's two careers would you prefer to have? Why?

> The British actor Vinnie Jones **used to be** a professional footballer! He doesn't have any regrets about his career change. At first, it took a while to **get used to** all the new challenges. He'd never done any acting before in his life. But Vinnie had one big advantage – he **was** already **used to** working long hours in a very competitive field. It wasn't long before he landed roles in films, as well as the hit US show *24*.

2 Look at the expressions in **bold** in Activity 1, then complete the rules. Which two expressions can we use before a noun or a gerund (*-ing* form)?

be used to / get used to / used to	
1	to refer to a past habit or state
2	to mean 'be accustomed to'
3	to mean 'become accustomed to'

3 In pairs, write sentences comparing these people's lives before and after the event in red.

0 (*Marcella*) never did any exercise - decided to get fit - now a marathon runner

> *Marcella used to spend her free time watching TV. She found it really hard to get used to exercising. Now, she's used to running 10 km every day!*

1 (*Luis*) a poor student - won a sport competition - now a very wealthy tennis player

2 (*Serena*) a school sports teacher - joined an expedition - currently walking to the South Pole

3 (*Marcin*) a famous footballer - thrown out of the team for bad behaviour - now works in a supermarket

Grammar boost ▶ *be / get used to*

▶ Workbook p. 55

Exam practice

4 Complete the exam task.

Use of English Part 4: *keeping the meaning*

Exam tip

➤ Make sure that you make all necessary changes. Don't miss anything out!
➤ Don't over-transform. Only make necessary changes. Never add anything else!

For questions **1–8**, complete the second sentence so that it has a similar meaning to the first sentence, using the word given. **Do not change the word given.** You must use between **two** and **five** words, including the word given. Write **only** the missing words **IN CAPITAL LETTERS**.

0 I wish I'd worked harder at school. **REGRET**
I ...*REGRET NOT WORKING*... harder at school.

---

1 It was a mistake not to tell my fans the truth. **LIED**
I wish .... my fans.

2 I regret failing to take action sooner. **TAKEN**
If .... action sooner.

3 People applauding me isn't something I'm familiar with. **USED**
I .... applauded.

4 Letting my doubts get the better of me was a bad idea. **SHOULD**
.... my doubts get the better of me.

5 My current success is a result of believing in myself in the past. **SUCCESSFUL**
If I hadn't believed in myself in the past, I .... today.

6 These awards have not been given to many sportspeople. **FEW**
Only .... given these awards.

7 At first, I found it difficult to work for long hours, but eventually I became accustomed to it. **GOT**
I eventually .... for long hours, although I found it difficult at first.

8 It wasn't a habit of his to set himself daily goals. **USE**
He .... himself daily goals.

Get ready: *body idioms*

 1 Quickly read the text and choose a suitable title.

2 Find idioms in the text which match the definitions. Can you think of any more body idioms?

1 helped him
2 a lot of money
3 she didn't find something interesting
4 very busy with
5 agree about things
6 a natural ability for

3 You are going to interview your classmates for your school magazine. Write **four** questions using idioms from Activity 2.

*When was the last time you **gave a stranger a hand** with something?*

4 Interview at least four other students. Then summarise the most interesting things you found out in a short article for the magazine.

Word boost ▶ Body idioms ▶ Workbook p. 52

Exam practice

Listening Part 1: *the exam*

Exam tip

➤ Read the eight questions and options and <u>underline</u> any key words.
➤ Listen for synonyms and paraphrases.
➤ Think about *purpose* (why are the people speaking?) and the speakers' *opinions*.

5 🔊 9.2 You will hear people talking in eight different situations. For questions 1-8, choose the best answer (**A**, **B** or **C**).

1 You hear part of a radio programme where listeners phone in with their views. What does the man want to do?

A defend a politician
B criticise the media
C discuss a crime

2 You overhear two people talking about an exam. How does the girl feel about failing it?

A guilty   B disappointed   C relieved

3 You hear a woman talking about some dinners she's been invited to. Why does she think she was invited?

A She's a local teacher.
B She knows a lot about football.
C She's got a famous relative.

4 You hear part of a radio interview with a successful actor. What does he say about his first job?

A It taught him something useful.
B It was an enjoyable experience.
C It helped him to get acting work.

5 You hear a man giving a speech at a school careers day. What is his job?

A a journalist   B a politician   C a lawyer

6 You overhear two friends talking. Why is the girl worried about her application to join a music academy?

A She believes she isn't as talented as the other applicants.
B She doesn't think her application will stand out.
C She fears she may not do very well in the interview.

7 You hear part of a radio interview with a former ballerina. Why did she give up ballet?

A She was concerned about her health.
B She wasn't very successful.
C She wanted to start a different career.

8 You hear part of a radio play in which a couple are arguing. What is the woman most upset about?

A not being told the truth
B having spent too much money
C her husband being unemployed

1 Look at the photos and discuss the questions in pairs.

1 What is special about these achievements?
2 Which achievement do you think is the most impressive?

A

B

C

D

Exam practice

Speaking Parts 3 and 4:
a full response

Exam tip

Say as much as you can about each task.

➤ Always say something. Don't let your partner do all the talking!
➤ Always give an opinion - but don't worry: the examiner is assessing your speaking, not your ideas!
➤ Add details and explain your opinions. Don't just say *I agree!*

2 🔊 9.3 Read the *Exam tip*. You are going to hear three pairs of students (A, B, C) discussing the questions in Activity 1. Write *A*, *B*, or *C* where you think they belong on the line.

◄──────────────────────────────►

least successful   most successful

3 Explain your answers to a partner. Do you both agree?

4 🔊 9.4 Listen again to the most successful pair of students and complete the table with the expressions they used. Then add your own ideas.

Adding points	Giving examples	Responding to your partner
What's more ...	For example ...	Right, ...

5 In pairs, discuss these Part 3 questions. Use the ideas above to help you.

• What might be difficult about learning these skills?
• Which two skills are the most difficult to learn?

A   B

C   D

E   F

G

6 Discuss these Part 4 questions. Is there anything you and your partner disagree about?

1 Do you think it's better to learn new things from a book, from the internet or from a teacher? Why?
2 What are the advantages of learning a foreign language?
3 What kind of skills would you like to learn in the future? Why?

Words with similar meanings

1 Quickly read the text, ignoring the gaps. Whose behaviour do you think is the strangest? Why do you think very talented people are often a bit eccentric?

BRILLIANT but ECCENTRIC!

1 The famous boxer Muhammad Ali, who **(1)** _____ the title of World Heavyweight Champion three times, used to recite poems before fights predicting that he would win.

2 Björk has won awards for both her songs and her **(2)** _____ in films. But her unusual behaviour also attracts attention – she once wore a swan costume to an Oscar awards ceremony!

3 The World Chess Champion Bobby Fischer played endless **(3)** _____ of chess by himself every day. He was said to prefer the logic of chess games to the irrationality of people!

4 The surrealist artist Salvador Dalí once amazed **(4)** _____ watching the *Tonight Show* on TV by refusing to sit on anything other than a leather rhino!

5 Walt Disney, who **(5)** _____ millions of dollars from cartoons and films, took a childlike pleasure in toys and built a model railway that ran around his whole property!

2 Many words in English have similar (but not identical!) meanings. Work in pairs and complete gaps 1–5 above with A, B, C or D.

	A		B		C		D	
1	A	succeeded	B	achieved	C	realized	D	scored
2	A	exhibitions	B	performances	C	displays	D	acts
3	A	matches	B	contests	C	races	D	games
4	A	spectators	B	onlookers	C	audience	D	viewers
5	A	earned	B	profited	C	won	D	gained

3 Choose a different word from each group and write **five** more sentences about famous people. Leave a blank space instead of the target word.

1   When Pelé _____ his 1,000th goal, he dedicated it to the children of Brazil. (answer: scored)

4 Swap your sentences with a partner. Can they complete them correctly?

Collocations (3): *adjectives + prepositions*

5 In pairs, match the people in the list to the descriptions. Then choose the correct prepositions.

author   chef   environmentalist   football manager
nurse   police officer   prime minister   psychiatrist
songwriter   spy   website designer

A successful …

0 *author* is interested **by** / **for** / **in** creating stories and characters.
1 _____ is brilliant **at** / **to** / **with** finding out what other people are up to.
2 _____ is concerned **about** / **at** / **for** global warming.
3 _____ can get obsessed **on** / **for** / **with** trying to make the perfect dish!
4 _____ is experienced **in** / **about** / **to** politics.
5 _____ arrests people who are guilty **at** / **of** / **about** an offence.
6 _____ is kind and considerate **by** / **for** / **to** patients.
7 _____ is fascinated **on** / **by** / **in** the human mind.
8 _____ feels responsible **to** / **for** / **at** the success of their team.
9 _____ is keen **about** / **on** / **with** working with computers.
10 _____ is passionate **for** / **to** / **about** music.

6 In pairs, add ten more sentences like this describing the people above. Which job do you think is the most difficult? Why?

*O   An author also needs to **be good at** describing people and places.*

Over to you!

7 You are going to write a description of someone you consider exceptionally talented for a website called *The World's Greatest Geniuses*. Make notes about *who* this person is, *what* they achieved, and *why* they should be on the website.

8 Write your description in 120–150 words.

 **Word boost** ▶ Workbook p. 84

Get ready: *word families*

1 **Some words have large 'families'.**
1 Identify the part of speech for each word below.
2 **Three** words have the *same* part of speech. What is the difference in meaning?

2 **In pairs, can you create word families for these words?**

> reason   imaginative   possible   uncritical

Word boost ▶ Word families ▶ Workbook p. 53

> compete – competition – competitor – competitiveness – competitive – competitively – uncompetitive

Exam practice

3 **Read the exam task, ignoring the gaps.**
1 According to the author, what do Pelé, Shakespeare, Rembrandt and the Beatles have in common?
2 If you could spend an afternoon with **one** of these people or groups, who would you choose and why?

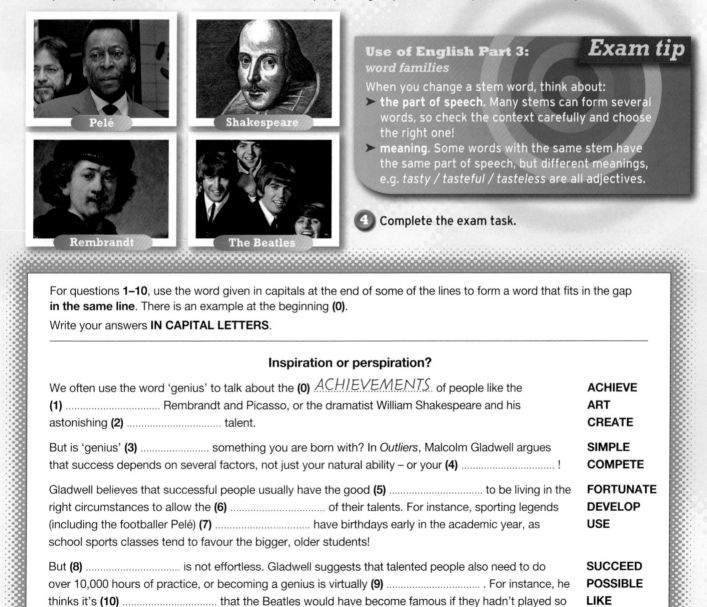

Pelé

Shakespeare

Rembrandt

The Beatles

Use of English Part 3: *word families*   **Exam tip**

When you change a stem word, think about:
➤ **the part of speech.** Many stems can form several words, so check the context carefully and choose the right one!
➤ **meaning.** Some words with the same stem have the same part of speech, but different meanings, e.g. *tasty / tasteful / tasteless* are all adjectives.

4 **Complete the exam task.**

For questions **1–10**, use the word given in capitals at the end of some of the lines to form a word that fits in the gap **in the same line**. There is an example at the beginning **(0)**.
Write your answers **IN CAPITAL LETTERS**.

Inspiration or perspiration?

We often use the word 'genius' to talk about the **(0)** *ACHIEVEMENTS* of people like the   **ACHIEVE**
(1) .... Rembrandt and Picasso, or the dramatist William Shakespeare and his   **ART**
astonishing **(2)** .... talent.   **CREATE**

But is 'genius' **(3)** .... something you are born with? In *Outliers*, Malcolm Gladwell argues   **SIMPLE**
that success depends on several factors, not just your natural ability – or your **(4)** .... !   **COMPETE**

Gladwell believes that successful people usually have the good **(5)** .... to be living in the   **FORTUNATE**
right circumstances to allow the **(6)** .... of their talents. For instance, sporting legends   **DEVELOP**
(including the footballer Pelé) **(7)** .... have birthdays early in the academic year, as   **USE**
school sports classes tend to favour the bigger, older students!

But **(8)** .... is not effortless. Gladwell suggests that talented people also need to do   **SUCCEED**
over 10,000 hours of practice, or becoming a genius is virtually **(9)** .... For instance, he   **POSSIBLE**
thinks it's **(10)** .... that the Beatles would have become famous if they hadn't played so   **LIKE**
many long gigs. It seems the old saying is true: "there's no inspiration without perspiration"!

Prepare

1 There are many interesting characters in fiction. Look at the pictures, then answer the questions in pairs.

 1 What is unusual about these people?
 2 How might their lives be different or interesting?
 3 Do you recognise which books or comics they appear in?

2 Who are your **three** favourite fictional characters? Why?

Analyse the task

3 Read the task below. Have you read this book? (If so, did you enjoy it?) Who are your favourite British or American authors?

Great Expectations by Charles Dickens

You see the following notice in a magazine:

We are looking for articles about unpleasant characters in fiction. The best articles will be published next month!

Write an article for the magazine about one of the characters in *Great Expectations*, describing why they are unpleasant and what factors have affected their personality.

Write your answer in **120–180** words in an appropriate style.

---

4 Read the article. What is the writer's opinion of Miss Havisham? What reasons does the writer give to support this opinion?

Miss Havisham: villain or victim?

Miss Havisham is one of the nastiest and least likeable characters in Dickens' *Great Expectations*, yet in some ways it is possible to feel sorry for her, too.

She is unkind to her adopted daughter, Estella, who she teaches to be completely heartless. And she is cruel to Pip, who she encourages to fall in love with Estella, knowing that she will break his heart.

However, Miss Havisham's behaviour is influenced by an awful personal tragedy. She used to dream of marriage, but the man she loved let her down, leaving her just before their wedding. This ended her hopes and left her with just one passion – revenge!

For this reason, I feel sympathetic towards Miss Havisham, even though she does some terrible things. At the end of the book, she changes her mind about revenge and tries to make things up to Pip. But it's too late. As Pip leaves, her dress catches fire and she burns to death. Surely no one deserves that, not even someone as unpleasant as Miss Havisham?

5 Look at the article again. Why has the writer used four different paragraphs? What is the main topic of each paragraph?

Improve your writing:
appropriate language

6 It is very important to use the right style of writing for a task. Look at the extracts below. Do you think they are more likely to belong to *articles* or *essays*? Why?

1   It is my opinion, therefore, that this is the most important event in the whole novel. Moreover, it is the most tragic.

2   If you're looking for a book that will have you crying with laughter, then read on.

3   **What's amazing about this character is that she's completely unpredictable. No one can guess what she'll do next!**

4   *In conclusion, I believe that the author is very successful in showing us how personal conscience can affect a person's character.*

7 In an article, use a lively style and a wide range of vocabulary. Read the article on page 110 again and find as many examples as you can of the following:

1   rhetorical questions
2   adjectives + prepositions
3   idioms
4   phrasal verbs
5   relative clauses
6   linkers.

8 Read an extract from an article. Why do you think it **didn't** get a high mark? Rewrite the extract in a more interesting style. Write between 50-100 words.

> Dracula is a very interesting character. He is not very nice. He kills people. That isn't a very nice thing to do. Many characters in the book are frightened of him. At the end, the heroes of the book kill Dracula, so then he is dead. It is an exciting end. You'll like it.

Ready to write!

> Your English teacher has asked you to write an article about an important event in which a character was either successful or unsuccessful. Choose one event in one of the set texts, describe what happens and explain why it is important.
>
> Write your article in **120-180** words in an appropriate style.

9 Read the task and decide which set text you are going to write about. If you haven't read either, choose another novel.

10 Choose an event to discuss and make notes about:

1   what happened
2   why the event was a success or failure
3   what the consequences were
4   why this event is important or interesting.

11 Decide how many paragraphs you will need and which information you are going to include in each paragraph.

12 Look at the *Exam tip* and the task. What *type* of writing task do you have to do? What kind of language will you need to use?

Writing Part 2:
a set text   **Exam tip**

➤ *Never* answer question 5a or 5b if you haven't read the set text. It's optional!
➤ In the exam, you *must* write about the text in the question. Don't write about other books.
➤ Make sure you answer the question – don't just write everything you know about the book!
➤ Think about what *type* of task you have to write. You need to use a different style and format depending on whether you write an essay, article or letter.

Writing reference ➤ p. 170–175

13 Write your answer. When you have finished, look at the checklist on page 170. Check your work and make any corrections.

Unit 9

1 Complete the sentences with the correct form of the verbs in **bold**.

0 I did terribly in the interview. I wish I _had made_ (**make**) a better impression.

1 If I'd spent more time practising, I (**be**) _____ a famous musician today.

2 Stop obsessing! I wish you (**stop**) _____ talking about him.

3 She (**should not / copy**) _____ her essay from the internet. Now she's in trouble!

4 I would have more friends now if I (**keep**) _____ in touch with people.

5 If only I (**be**) _____ wealthy. Then I could spend all my time surfing.

2 Rewrite the sentences. Use the word in **bold** followed by a suitable preposition.

0 My parents take great pride in my achievements.
My parents _are very proud of my achievements_ (**proud**).

1 Thank you for all your support!
I _____ (**grateful**).

2 We feel bad about disappointing our fans.
We _____ (**sorry**).

3 He doesn't like competitive sports.
He _____ (**keen**).

4 She finds Law really interesting.
She _____ (**fascinated**).

5 I did not predict the election results correctly.
I _____ (**wrong**).

3 Complete the slogans from internet adverts. Write the correct form of the words in **bold**.

0 Buy now and turn your dreams into _reality_ (**real**)!

1 How to start your own business _____ (**success**).

2 Read this book and achieve all your _____ (**ambitious**).

3 Life is a _____ (**compete**) – make sure you're a winner.

4 Let your dreams be as big as your _____ (**imagine**).

5 Our prices are so cheap they're almost _____ (**believe**).

Units 1–9

4 Complete the sentences. Write **one** word in each gap.

0 He definitely isn't at the stadium. He __must__ have left.

1 I _____ never won a competition in my whole life.

2 I won't get the gold medal _____ I finish first!

3 She didn't like being photographed at first, but after a while she _____ used to it.

4 They were not _____ rich but also very famous.

5 That's the writer _____ novel has just won a prize.

6 The boys weren't as successful _____ the girls.

5 Complete the text. Use the correct form of the verbs in the list.

beat	carry	do	look	~~realise~~
score	take	tire	turn	win

WINNERS and LOSERS

For every sporting champion, there are thousands more who never (**0**) _realise_ their ambitions by (**1**) _____ the competition or (**2**) _____ goals. But some of these people have (**3**) _____ losing into a success story! Eric Moussambani, nicknamed 'Eric the Eel', hit the headlines in the 2000 Olympics when he (**4**) _____ part in the 100 metres swimming freestyle race. He (**5**) _____ his first race with a finish time of more than twice the world record ... because he was the only competitor! Many people admired Eric for the fact that he (**6**) _____ on swimming even when it was obvious that the effort was (**7**) _____ him out! Another famous 'loser' is Michael Edwards, also known as 'Eddie the Eagle', who was the first person to represent Britain in Olympic ski-jumping. Eddie was hopeless at skiing, but instead of (**8**) _____ down on him, many viewers praised his determination. It seems we can admire people for simply (**9**) _____ their best – even when their 'best' is terrible!

10 ...ockbuster

UNIT TARGETS

Topic vocabulary: film, fiction and TV ● action and atmosphere ● thought
Grammar: reported speech ● reporting verbs
Word building: expressions with *mind* ● phrasal verbs (5) ● words with similar forms
Writing: a review ● opinions
  Exam preparation: Reading Part 1 ● Use of English Parts 2 and 3 ● Listening Part 2 ● Speaking Part 1 ● Writing Part 2

Film, fiction and TV

1. In pairs, discuss the photos. How often do you do these activities? Which one do you prefer? Why?

2. 🔊 **10.1** Listen to three people talking about films they have just seen. What types of film did they watch?

   animated film   historical drama   romance
   musical   science fiction film   thriller

3. 🔊 **10.1** Listen again and write down any nouns that relate to *films* (F), *TV programmes* (T) or *novels* (N), or more than one of these.

   heroine   F, T, N

4. What adjectives do the speakers use to describe a) the *actors / acting,* b) the *plot*? Can you think of any more adjectives for talking about films, TV programmes or novels?

    ▶ Film, fiction and TV ▶ Workbook p. 58

Over to you!

5. In pairs, imagine you are on a radio programme called *Arts Review*. Take turns to talk for **one** minute about a book, film or TV programme you've seen recently, saying what you liked and didn't like about it.

   Useful language
   The highlight of ... is the fantastic ...
   ... is let down by the terrible ...
   I have mixed feelings about ....
   On the one hand ... but on the other hand ...

6. Listen carefully while your partner is speaking. Would you like to see or read this book, film or TV programme? Why? / Why not?

1 The films in the photos are based on famous novels. Can you name any of the novels and authors?

2 🔊 10.2 Listen to a film studies class discussing the photos and check your answers.

3 Hollywood wants your ideas! What books or comics do you think would make a good film? Why?

Exam practice

Reading Part 1: *the exam*

Exam tip

➤ Read the whole text quickly first for gist.
➤ Read the questions, but not the options. Reread the text carefully, underlining the answers as you find them.
➤ For each question, go back and read the options. Choose the one which best matches the evidence in the text.

4 Read the extract from a novel. For questions **1–8**, choose the answer (**A, B, C** or **D**) which you think fits best according to the text.

1 We know thirteen-year-old Briony is enthusiastic about her play because she has:
   A missed all her meals since writing began.
   B spent two whole days writing the play script.
   C persuaded her cousins to prepare the theatre.
   D been revising her work since it was finished.

2 What is the main theme of Briony's play?
   A Love rarely leads to a happy ending.
   B People in love never act rationally.
   C Lovers must not be too sensitive.
   D Love should be based on reason.

3 Briony uses the phrase 'a prince in disguise' about the doctor to show that
   A he is not who he appears to be.
   B he is afraid to appear in public.
   C he is surprisingly aristocratic.
   D only her heroine appreciates his goodness.

4 Briony examines her mother's face because she
   A wants to see how the play affects her mother.
   B worries that the play might upset her mother.
   C doesn't understand her mother's feelings.
   D wants the play to make her mother happy.

5 What do we learn about Mrs Tallis?
   A She thinks Briony is highly talented.
   B She wants to make Briony happy.
   C She thinks Briony is too childish.
   D She wants to help improve Briony's play.

6 What does 'it' mean in line 40?
   A this time
   B this play
   C this poster
   D this word

7 Briony's main reason for writing the play is to
   A provide entertainment for her cousins.
   B convince her brother to move back home.
   C be a bridesmaid.
   D help her brother become an actor.

8 What do we learn about Briony from this extract?
   A She is good at understanding feelings.
   B She doesn't like being told what to do.
   C She likes things to be organised properly.
   D She does not mind what people think of her.

Vocabulary in context:
action and atmosphere

5 The writer uses a range of language to describe action and atmosphere. Find words or expressions which mean:

1 think about; look at (*paragraph 1*)
2 extremely (*paragraph 1*)
3 left alone (*paragraph 1*)
4 changing (*paragraph 2*)
5 saying quietly (*paragraph 2*)
6 dark (*paragraph 3*)
7 talking with a lot of pride (*paragraph 3*)
8 in a kind or pleasant way (*paragraph 3*)

Word boost ▶ Action and atmosphere ▶ Workbook p. 58

The play – for which Briony had designed the posters, programmes and tickets, constructed the sales booth out of a folding screen tipped on its side, and lined the collection box in red crêpe paper – was written by her in a two-day tempest of composition, causing her to miss a breakfast and a lunch. When the preparations were complete, she had nothing to do but contemplate her finished draft and wait for the appearance of her cousins from the distant north. There would be time for only one day of rehearsal before her brother arrived. At some moments chilling, at others desperately sad, the play told a tale of the heart whose message, conveyed in a rhyming prologue, was that love which did not build a foundation on good sense was doomed. The reckless passion of the heroine, Arabella, for a wicked foreign count is punished by ill fortune when she contracts cholera during an impetuous dash towards a seaside down with her intended. Deserted by him and nearly everybody else, bed-bound in a garret, she discovers in herself a sense of humour. Fortune presents her a second chance in the form of an impoverished doctor – in fact, a prince in disguise who has elected to work among the needy. Healed by him, Arabella chooses judiciously this time, and is rewarded by reconciliation with her family and a wedding with the medical prince on 'a windy sunlit day in spring'.

Mrs Tallis read the seven pages of *The Trials of Arabella* in her bedroom, at her dressing table, with the author's arm around her shoulder the whole while. Briony studied her mother's face for every trace of shifting emotion, and Emily Tallis obliged with looks of alarm, snickers of glee and, at the end, grateful smiles and wise, affirming nods. She took her daughter in her arms, onto her lap – ah, that hot smooth little body she remembered from its infancy, and still not gone from her, not quite yet – and said that the play was 'stupendous', and agreed instantly, murmuring into the tight whorl of the girl's ear, that this word could be quoted on the poster which was to be on an easel in the entrance hall by the ticket booth.

Briony was hardly to know it then, but this was the project's highest point of fulfilment. Nothing came near it *line 40* for satisfaction, all else was dreams and frustration. There were moments in the summer dusk after her light was out, burrowing in the delicious gloom of her canopy bed, when she made her heart thud with luminous, yearning fantasies, little playlets in themselves, every one of which featured Leon. In one, his big, good-natured face buckled in grief as Arabella sank in loneliness and despair. In another, there he was, cocktail in hand at some fashionable city watering hole, overheard boasting to a group of friends: Yes, my younger sister, Briony Tallis the writer, you must surely have heard of her. In a third he punched the air in exultation as the final curtain fell, although there was no curtain, there was no possibility of a curtain. Her play was not for her cousins, it was for her brother, to celebrate his return, provoke his admiration and guide him away from his careless succession of girlfriends, towards the right form of wife, the one who would persuade him to return to the countryside, the one who would sweetly request Briony's services as a bridesmaid.

She was one of those children possessed by a desire to have the world just so. Whereas her big sister's room was a stew of unclosed books, unfolded clothes, unmade bed, unemptied ashtrays, Briony's was a shrine to her controlling demon: the model farm spread across a deep window ledge consisted of the usual animals, but all facing one way – towards their owner. In fact, Briony's was the only tidy upstairs room in the house.

Over to you!

6 Work in pairs. Choose **one** of these first lines, and write a story of 120-180 words. Include a wide range of adjectives, adverbs, verbs and nouns.

- That was the summer that changed my life.
- At midnight, there was a knock at the door.
- He was the strangest man I had ever met.
- She wished she'd stayed at home.

7 Read the rest of the class's stories. Which story do you think would make the best novel / film? Why?

1 Read an interview with a film star, then a report of the interview on the TV show *Celebrity Gossip*. What does Josh think of what Adora said?

Josh Adora! Hi! Tell me, is it true that you're seeing the actor Brett Dean?

Adora Oh, you shouldn't listen to rumours! As I said the last time we met, we've been friends since we worked together on a film last year.

Josh So why did Brett fly over to be with you yesterday?

Adora He's just here on holiday! He'll be staying until next week – not that this is any of your business! Now, can you please ask me about something else?

Josh Newsflash: Adora says she's still single! I asked her if it was true she was seeing the actor Brett Dean. She said I shouldn't listen to rumours! She told me that, as she'd said the previous time we'd met, they'd been friends since they worked together on a film last year. So I asked her why Brett had flown over to be with her the day before. She looked annoyed and said that Brett was just there on holiday! She told me he would be staying until the following week, not that that was any of my business. Getting crosser, she asked if I could please ask her about something else! Was it something I said, I wonder – or something she was trying to hide ...?

2 Read the rules below. Then look back at the reported interview and find examples of 1–4.

Reported speech

1. We usually change the verb by moving it **back one tense**.
2. If what the person says is still true now, **change is optional**.
3. With the past perfect, *would*, *could*, *should* or *must*, there is **no tense change**.
4. BUT *can* → *could*, *will* → *would*.

3 Find three reported questions in Activity 1. Then choose the correct words to complete the rules.

Reported questions

1. We use **question / affirmative** word order.
2. We **use / don't use** auxiliary forms or question marks.
3. We use *if* or *whether* with **yes or no / open** questions.

Language summary ▶ p. 165

4 Look at the reported interview again and answer the questions in pairs.

1. What's the difference in use between *say* and *tell*?
2. How do these words and phrases change in reported speech? Can you think of any more?
   a) last time   b) yesterday   c) next week
   d) here   e) this
3. Why does *last year* not change in Activity 1?

5 Work in pairs and rewrite these film quotations in reported speech. Which film sounds the most interesting? Why?

1. 'I've got a feeling that we're not in Kansas any more.' (*The Wizard of Oz*) Dorothy told Toto ...
2. 'A boy's best friend is his mother.' (*Psycho*) Norman Bates says ...
3. 'What are you rebelling against?' (*The Wild One*) Mildred asked Johnny ...
4. 'Some of you may die, but that is a sacrifice I am willing to make.' (*Shrek*) Lord Farquaad said ...
5. 'What planet did you come from?' (*10 Things I Hate about You*) Bianca asked her sister ...

Over to you!

6 In groups of three, choose a celebrity and the reason why he / she is in the news. Make notes about questions 1–3.

actor / actress   comedian   director
TV presenter   screenwriter

fired from their job   received an award
photographed in an embarrassing situation

1. Who is the person and what are they like?
2. What happened and why?
3. How will this event affect their feelings / career?

7 Role-play an interview. Student A, turn to page 150. Student B, turn to page 152. Student C, turn to page 154.

Get ready: *reporting verbs*

1 Read the Oscar trivia file. Whose behaviour do you think is the strangest? Why?

Oscar Trivia

- Marlon Brando once **refused** to collect his Oscar in person. He **asked** an American Indian woman to collect it instead. He **explained** that his action was a protest against Hollywood's portrayal of American Indians.

- Oscar winner Jack Palance surprised viewers by doing exercises on stage! He **denied** that this was a publicity stunt, **insisting** that he didn't know what else to do.

- When the presenter **congratulated** Gwyneth Paltrow on winning an Oscar, the actress burst into tears and **insisted** on thanking absolutely everyone she knew!

- Sound technician Kevin O'Connell has lost out on winning an Oscar over 20 times! He **denies** feeling upset, and once **informed** journalists that his losing streak has made him famous!

2 Add the verbs in **bold** in Activity 1 to the table below. How many more verbs can you add?

	Reporting verb	Structure
1	agree, offer, *refuse*	+ infinitive
2	order, remind, warn	+ object + infinitive
3	announce, recommend, suggest	+ *that* + subject
4	remind, warn	+ object + *that*
5	recommend, suggest	+ *-ing*
6	apologise (for)	(+ object) + preposition + *-ing*

3 In pairs, take turns to talk about a time when you:
- denied doing something (which you really did!).
- wrongly blamed someone for something.
- had to apologise for something.
- were warned not to do something.

Grammar boost ▶ Reporting verbs ▶ Workbook p. 61

Exam practice

4 Read the article below, ignoring the gaps. Who is Nick Park? Why did his films take so long to make?

5 Complete the exam task.

Use of English Part 2: *usage* — **Exam tip**

Always think about *usage* as well as *meaning*, e.g.:
➤ common expressions, e.g. phrasal verbs, collocations.
➤ grammar and word order.

For questions **1–12**, read the text below and think of the word which best fits each gap. Use only **one** word in each gap. Write your answers **IN CAPITAL LETTERS**.

Getting animated!

Nick Park **(0)** .....*HAS*..... won several Oscars. But he's **(1)** .... an actor nor a director. Instead, the Academy wanted to congratulate him **(2)** .... creating some of the most endearing characters in film – all made out of clay!

(3) .... Nick Park's famous *Wallace and Gromit* films may look simple, anyone who thinks clay modelling is easy should be advised **(4)** .... think again! In interviews, Nick has explained **(5)** .... moving the models is very time-consuming work. **(6)** .... a result, creating just a second's worth of film can take a full day!

Some of the biggest blockbusters in recent years have been animated, **(7)** .... as *Ice Age* and *Madagascar*. However, most of these were very hi-tech compared to the *Wallace and Gromit* films, being designed on computers! Computer-generated imagery (CGI) **(8)** .... now used in a wide range of mainstream films, **(9)** .... science fiction to thrillers. But some campaigners have been encouraging studios to use less CGI. A number of actors and stunt artists have blamed it **(10)** .... reducing their chances of employment. They accuse producers **(11)** .... preferring 'virtual' stars because they're cheaper and **(12)** .... reliable!

Get ready: *thought*

1 Do the quiz, then check your answers on page 152. Do you agree? Discuss the results in pairs.

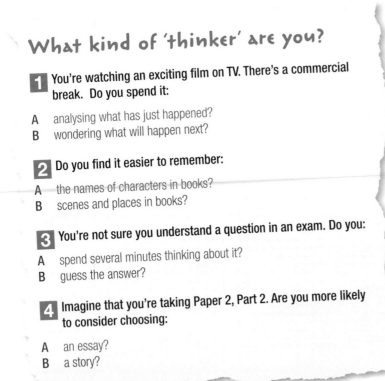

What kind of 'thinker' are you?

1 You're watching an exciting film on TV. There's a commercial break. Do you spend it:

A   analysing what has just happened?
B   wondering what will happen next?

2 Do you find it easier to remember:

A   the names of characters in books?
B   scenes and places in books?

3 You're not sure you understand a question in an exam. Do you:

A   spend several minutes thinking about it?
B   guess the answer?

4 Imagine that you're taking Paper 2, Part 2. Are you more likely to consider choosing:

A   an essay?
B   a story?

2 Look at the quiz again and <u>underline</u> all the verbs connected with thinking (mental processes). Can you think of any more thinking verbs?

3 In pairs, discuss which qualities you think are **essential** for a successful a) actor, b) novelist, c) newspaper editor. Why? Which job would you be best at? Why?

> a good memory   a logical mind
> an eye for detail   creativity   empathy
> imagination   intelligence

Word boost ▶ Thought ▶ Workbook p. 58

Exam practice

4 In pairs, look at these book covers.

1   What do you think these books are about? Do you enjoy books like these?
2   If you were a writer, what kind of book would you most like to write?

Listening Part 2: *the exam*

Exam tip

➤ Read the ten sentences before you listen and try to predict what's missing (e.g. a number, a job, etc.).
➤ Write the *exact* words you hear. Don't change them!
➤ Check that your answer makes sense in the sentence, e.g. does it fit the grammar?
➤ Always give an answer. You don't lose marks for wrong answers!

5 10.3 You will hear a woman called Kelly Good talking to students about a summer writing course that is held on the island of Majorca. For questions **1-10**, complete the sentences.

Get it 'write' summer course

1   Kelly is currently a _____, a teacher and an artist.
2   Kelly started working in Majorca at the *School of Culture* in _____.
3   The villa where the writing course is held is on a _____ in Majorca.
4   Students can enjoy every _____ as free time.
5   Workshop leader Scott McBride is an author whose first book was called _____ *in the Night*.
6   There is a visit to a local _____ for writers on the horror course.
7   One student in the screenwriting workshop will win an original _____.
8   Ghost-writers should write for _____ if they want to get rich.
9   The most important quality a good ghostwriter needs to have is _____.
10   Kelly will be in the _____ immediately after her talk.

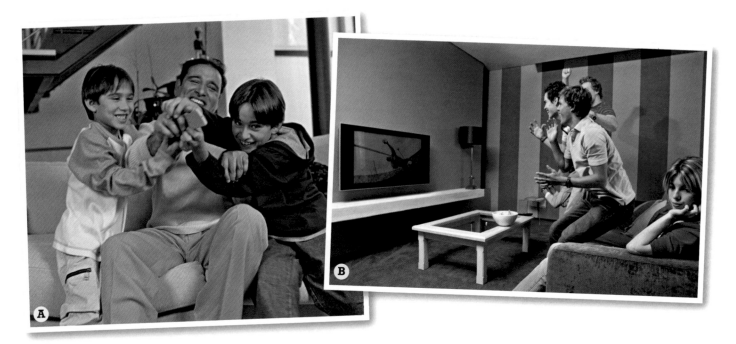

1 In pairs, compare the photos. What problems are people having? Have you ever had similar experiences?

2 Find out what your partner thinks about TV. Choose **four** of the prompts and write questions. Then ask and answer your questions in pairs.

1 How often ...
2 What kind ...
3 Do you and your family ...
4 Who decides what ...
5 Do you think ...
6 What's your ...

3 🔊 10.4 Listen to three students answer questions about TV in a Part 1 task. What questions did they answer? Did they use any of your ideas from Activity 2?

> ### Speaking Part 1: *Exam tip*
> **the exam**
>
> ➤ Listen carefully to each question, and don't be afraid to ask for it to be repeated.
> ➤ Make your answers interesting by using a range of language.
> ➤ Talk about your opinions and feelings, and give reasons and examples to support your ideas.
> ➤ Make sure you answer the question – DON'T give a speech that you prepared in advance!

Exam practice

4 Work in pairs and follow the instructions. Listen carefully while your partner is speaking.

Student A: Ask Student B the green questions (1 and 2), and the red questions (3, 5 and 7). Then answer Student B's questions.

Student B: Answer Student A's questions. Then ask Student A the green questions (1 and 2), and the blue questions (4, 6 and 8).

1 Where are you from?
2 What do you like about living here?

Free time
3 Have you got any plans for the weekend? (What are you going to do?)
4 When did you last go out with your friends? (What did you do?)

Media
5 What's the difference between watching films on TV and at the cinema? (Which do you prefer?)
6 Do you spend more time watching TV, using a computer, or reading? (Why?)

Work and education
7 Do you prefer working on your own or with other people? (Why?)
8 Is there something new you'd like to learn about in the future? (What is it?)

5 Tell your partner about **two** areas in which you are similar or dissimilar.

Expressions with *mind*

1 There are many expressions with *mind*! What might these people be saying? Fill in the speech bubbles.

> That's a weight off my mind.   Would you mind ... ?   You're out of your mind!   Never mind.
> Mind your own business.   Don't mind me.   I've changed my mind.   Mind out!   Make up your mind!
> I don't mind.   What's on your mind?   Do you mind!   My mind went blank.

A

B

C

D

E

F

2 Which expression with *mind* means:

1 I think you're mad!
2 Make a decision!
3 I couldn't remember anything.
4 That's a relief.
5 Hey! / That's annoying!

3 Work in pairs. Write three short dialogues of 40-80 words each. Each dialogue must **end** with a *mind* phrase from Activity 1.

4 Find another pair and take turns to act out your dialogues, but stop just before the final *mind* phrase! Can the other pair guess which expression completes your dialogue?

Phrasal verbs (5): *life's dramas*

5 In pairs, match each quotation to the films (A–C).

A *Love Hurts* (tragic romance)   B *Dreamcatcher*
C *You're Nicked!* (crime drama)   (basketball film)

1 You're **walking out**, after 40 years?   [A]
2 The training was tough, but I **got through** it.
3 The New York Giants **turned** me **down**.
4 She broke my heart. I'll never **get over** it.
5 She **turned out** to be the thief!
6 You need to **build** your strength **up**.
7 Behave, or you'll **end up** in prison.
8 That's it! I'm **calling** the wedding **off**.
9 OK, officer, I'll **own up**. I robbed him!
10 Go! I can't **put up with** your cheating!

6 Match the phrasal verbs in **bold** in Activity 5 to the meanings A-J.

A develop; increase
B complete a difficult experience
C be found to be
D admit to something
E eventually be
F recover from
G leave
H refuse or reject
I cancel
J tolerate

Over to you!

7 Work in groups and choose one of the films from Activity 5. What do you think the film is about? Write a short plot summary including at least **four** expressions or phrasal verbs from this page.

8 Find another group and compare your ideas. Do they think your film will be a Hollywood hit? Why?

Word boost ▶ Workbook p. 85

Get ready: *words with similar forms*

1 Some words look similar, but have different meanings. Choose the correct alternatives, and explain the difference.

1 A I was **bored** / **boring** of watching films.
  B The film was long and **bored** / **boring**.
2 A Going to the cinema is usually **fun** / **funny**.
  B It was so **fun** / **funny** she laughed out loud.

2 Complete the sentences. Use the words in the lists.

> historic   historical

1 The first ever film was a _____ event.
2 *Troy* and *Alexander* are _____ dramas.

> advice   advise

3 I _____ you not to buy this book.
4 Can you give me _____ on what to read?

> sensible   sensitive

5 She's very _____ . She cries during sad films.
6 He's very _____ . He plans what to watch in advance.

> breath   breathe

7 Take a deep _____ before you speak.
8 I can't _____ in this costume!

3 Choose **two** word pairs and write gapped sentences like those in Activity 2. Then swap with a partner and complete their sentences!

> childish / childlike   cook / cooker   horrible / horrific
> murder / murderer   practice / practise   terrible / terrific

Word boost ▶ Words with similar forms ▶ Workbook p. 59

Exam practice

4 Read the article below, ignoring the gaps. What is *Bollywood*? What is its connection to Arnold Schwarzenegger?

> **Use of English Part 3:**
> *words with a similar form*
> ➤ Think carefully about the meaning and the part of speech.
> ➤ Always check your spelling. Sometimes getting one letter wrong can change the whole meaning of a word, e.g. *whole / hole*.
>
> ***Exam tip***

5 Complete the exam task.

For questions **1–10**, use the word given in capitals at the end of some of the lines to form a word that fits in the gap in the same line. There is an example at the beginning **(0)**.

Write your answers **IN CAPITAL LETTERS**.

Hooray for Bollywood!

What's the world's largest film **(0)** ...*INDUSTRY*... ? If you answered Hollywood, you answered **(1)** ....! The Indian film industry, or 'Bollywood' as it is **(2)** .... known (after the old name for the capital, 'Bombay'), produces over 1,000 films a year – many more than Hollywood!   **INDUSTRIAL** **CORRECT** **HUMOUR**

Most Bollywood films are musicals, and themes from romances and **(3)** .... dramas are popular. The plots tend to be very melodramatic, featuring **(4)** .... characters such as unhappy lovers, deceitful villains and corrupt **(5)** .... If you fancy watching one, we'd **(6)** .... you to plan for a long evening: many films are over three hours long!   **HISTORY** **COLOUR** **POLITICS** **ADVICE**

Hollywood is becoming increasingly **(7)** .... to Bollywood's success and widespread **(8)** .... , and is not afraid to copy a few ideas. For example, the blockbusters *Moulin Rouge* and *The Guru* both include Hindi songs on their soundtracks. Many **(9)** .... are also keen to earn a Bollywood salary: the film *Kambakkht Ishq (Incredible Love)* features both Arnold Schwarzenegger and Sylvester Stallone. We are **(10)** .... to see many more Hollywood stars practising their singing and dancing skills in the future!   **SENSE** **POPULAR** **ACT** **LIKE**

Prepare

1. Work in pairs. Your school is organising a film club for students who want to watch films in English. Look at the posters and discuss the questions.
   - What might people enjoy about watching these types of film?
   - Which type of film would be the best choice for the opening night at the film club?

> **Useful language**
> *This film would appeal to ...*
> *This film might cheer people up / make people think.*
> *It would(n't) be popular with everyone, because ...*
> *I don't think this would be very suitable, because ...*

Analyse the task

2. What do you want to know when you read a film review? Tick (√) the most important information.

   1. a list of all the main characters
   2. the reviewer's opinion of the film
   3. a full description of the beginning, middle and end
   4. reasons why the film is good or bad
   5. a short summary of the plot
   6. biographical information about the actors / director

3. Read the review of *Watchmen* from the *MyFilm* website. Which points from Activity 2 are included?

4. What is the reviewer's opinion of the:
   1. plot?
   2. special effects?
   3. acting?
   4. characterisation?

Watchmen

Watchmen by Alan Moore is, in my view, the best graphic novel ever written. However, I walked away from the film version feeling disappointed.

Watchmen is a fantasy story set in New York, which centres on the lives of several unusual superheroes. Although they catch criminals, these 'heroes' have mixed moral values, which I think is a fascinating idea. Unfortunately, the characterisation in the film is weak, and we don't learn much about people's feelings and motives. In my opinion, this makes it difficult to sympathise with anyone. Consequently, the very complicated

Improve your writing: *opinions*

5 You need to include personal opinions in a review. Read the review again and find expressions for:

1 saying what you think.
2 making a recommendation / suggestion.

6 Match A-H to categories 1 and 2 in Activity 5. Decide whether each expression is *positive, negative* or *neutral*.

A I strongly feel that ...
B Personally, I believe ...
C Go and see / read / buy this ...
D I strongly recommend that ...
E I found it to be ...
F Don't bother watching / reading / getting ...
G It seems to me that ...
H Don't miss ...

7 Sometimes you may want to add emphasis. Which sentence in each pair expresses a stronger opinion? Underline the words which make the opinion strong.

0 It was pretty exciting. / It was utterly thrilling.
1 I didn't want to stay. / I couldn't wait to leave.
2 The weak plot completely ruined the film. / The film was let down by a weak plot.
3 The acting could have been better. / The acting couldn't have been worse.
4 I loved it from start to finish. / I enjoyed it all.
5 I'd recommend that you see this film. / Don't miss this film!
6 The characterisation was utter rubbish. / The characterisation wasn't very good.

8 Write a short account of each of the following, saying what you thought or felt and why. Explain your ideas to a partner. Do you have any similar likes or dislikes?

1 something you bought which turned out to be a disappointment
2 a place you visited which you really loved
3 a website you found useful or interesting
4 a really bad concert or play you went to

plot eventually comes to seem a bit tedious.

I don't mean that the film is completely terrible. The special effects are imaginative and convincing, and visually, the film is simply stunning. Although the cast are little-known actors, they deliver great performances. But, to my mind, the film lacks a heart.

People who've never read *Watchmen* might find more to enjoy than I did. But if you're a fan like me, I wouldn't recommend it. You'd be better off staying at home and rereading the novel instead!

Ready to write!

Your school newsletter is looking for film reviews with the following title: *The last film that I watched*. Write a review for the newsletter, saying what kind of film it is, what you liked or didn't like about it, and whether you would recommend it.

Write your review in **120-180** words in an appropriate style.

9 Read the task above and decide which film to write about. Tell your partner:

1 what the film was.
2 what you liked about it.
3 what you didn't like about it.
4 if you would recommend it to them.

10 Read the *Exam tip*, then write a paragraph plan for your review. In which paragraph will you need to include a recommendation?

Writing Part 2: a review

Exam tip

Try to make your review interesting!
► Give a short summary of your film, but don't describe every detail.
► Say what you liked or didn't like about it.
► Give reasons for your opinions.
► Use a variety of language to add interest, e.g. verbs, adjectives and adverbs.
► Give a recommendation at the end of your review.
► Remember to address all of the points in the task, and don't forget to include a title if you are asked for one!

Writing reference ▶ p. 174

---

11 Make notes about language to include in each paragraph. Think about expressions for opinions and recommendations, as well as verbs, adjectives and adverbs.

12 Write your review. When you have finished, look at the checklist on page 174. Check your work and make any corrections.

Unit 10

1 Complete the second sentence so that it has a similar meaning to the first sentence. Use between two and five words, including the word given.

1 'Well done for winning the award!', she told the director.   **CONGRATULATED**

   She _____ the award.

2 'Don't follow me here again!', the actress told the photographers.   **HER**

   The actress warned the photographers _____ _____ again.

3 She told him that she couldn't solve the murder in that book.   **WORK**

   She told him, 'I can't _____ _____ the murderer is in this book.'

4 'I'm sorry I wasn't on time for the film', he said.   **LATE**

   He apologised _____ the film.

5 I asked Elena if she'd discovered when the film started.   **FIND**

   I asked Elena, '_____ when the film starts?'

6 'I'll never leave you, I promise,' said the hero.   **WALK**

   The hero promised _____ _____ on her.

2 Choose the correct alternatives to complete the questions and answers.

Journalists (outside author's house)

1 'Ms Jones, **would you mind** / **mind you** if we asked a few questions?'

2 'Do you **believe** / **find** it easy to invent new plots?'

3 'Who's going to be the lead **character** / **hero** in your next novel?'

4 'How did you develop such an incredible eye **to** / **for** detail?'

5 'How did you **build** / **get** up such a big fan base so quickly?'

Author (inside house)

6 'Don't you **find** / **realise** how much I hate all these questions?'

7 'I won't **do** / **put** up with this harassment!'

8 'Go away, and mind your own **behaviour** / **business**!'

9 'If you don't leave soon, I'll end **out** / **up** calling the police.'

Units 1–10

3 Choose the correct alternatives to complete the text.

Criticising the critics!

Think **(1) about / for / on / with** all the people involved in the production of **(2) that / a / the / some** film. **(3) Who / Whom / Whose / Which** is the most important? The director, the actors? What about the critic?

Critics can help **(4) get / do / make / put** the difference between a film, show, or book **(5) to be / be / been / being** a success, or a total disaster. Some reviewers can be **(6) extremely / much / greatly / slightly** critical indeed. For instance, here's one comment on a first novel: "This is possibly the worst book ever **(7) publish / publishing / published / to publish**. If you **(8) must / could / need / may** buy it, for goodness' sake, **(9) won't read / don't read / didn't read / wouldn't have read** it! Watching paint dry is far more interesting." Unsurprisingly, critics are **(10) hardly / often / absolutely / regularly** fiercely hated. The author John Updike wrote a story called Bech Noir, **(11) where in / in which / which in / in where** the writer, Bech, decides to murder all the critics who have **(12) ever / yet / since / even** upset him! Important they may be, but it **(13) shows / displays / seems / looks** that critics are rarely loved!

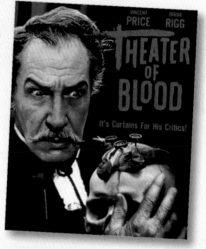

4 The *Bad TV* website wants to hear about the most boring / annoying / unfunny TV programmes you've ever seen. Write short comments, using the words in brackets. Feel free to be extremely critical!

0 (**take / seriously**)

   I can't take Eurovision seriously. The singers are usually absolutely awful, and the dancing is even worse!

1 (**made / mistake**)
2 (**switch off**)
3 (**fed up**)
4 (**found / out**)
5 (**sense / humour**)
6 (**embarrassing**)

11

UNIT TARGETS

Topic vocabulary: art and culture ● the senses ● music
Grammar: participle clauses ● inversion
Word building: comparative expressions ● collocations (4)
Writing: an informal email ● preparing for Part 1
Exam preparation: Reading Part 2 ● Use of English Parts 1 and 2 ● Listening Part 3 ● Speaking Part 2 ● Writing Part 1

Art and culture

1 How much do you know about the arts? Complete the table in pairs. Then try to think of **one** famous person from your country who matches each category.

	0	1	2	3	4	5	6	7
abstract noun	*composition*	art	drama		sculpture	design		
person	composer			photographer			architect	poet

2 🔊 11.1 Listen to three people talking about the arts and choose the correct answers, A, B or C.

Speaker	A	B	C
1 What is this woman's job?			
2 What kind of paintings does this artist prefer to paint?			
3 What kind of art does this professor like best?			

3 🔊 11.1 Match the expressions to the speakers. What do the pronouns in red refer to?

0 They way it was reported was a bit **over the top**.
Speaker Three. it = the lecture
1 ... which was a **turn-off** for me.
2 They're always surprised when I admit that it rather **passes me by**.
3 I'm quite fond of working on those **now and again**.
4 ... something I quickly **grew out of**!

4 In pairs, write definitions for the expressions in blue.
over the top = excessive, too much

Word boost ▶ Art and culture ▶ Workbook p. 64

Over to you!

5 Work in groups. An international arts magazine has asked people to suggest works of art to represent their country. Choose:

1 two songs or pieces of music.
2 two paintings or works of art.
3 two plays, novels or poems.

6 Present your ideas to the rest of the class. When everyone has finished, vote on the best item to include for each category.

 1 In pairs, discuss the paintings on the right.

1 Why might the artists have created these works?
2 Which do you like best? Why?

2 Work in pairs. Student A, you believe graffiti is art. Student B, you believe graffiti is vandalism. Make notes, using ideas in the list.

crime   boredom   destructive   modern   original
self-expression   selfish   talented

3 Debate your ideas. Is there anything you agree about? When you have finished, tell each other what you *really* think!

> **Useful expressions**
> *I completely disagree with you, because ...*
> *I see your point, but ...*
> *That might be true, but ...*
> *Have you considered the fact that ...*

Exam practice

4 In pairs, complete the sentences in the *Exam tip* with your own ideas. Can you add any more suggestions?

> **Exam tip**
> **Reading Part 2:** *the exam*
> 0 First, *read the whole text for gist.*
> 1 Read the text again and ...
> 2 Choose ...
> 3 Make sure that ...
> 4 When you have finished, check ...

5 You are going to read a magazine article about a graffiti artist called Banksy. Seven sentences have been removed from the article. Choose from the sentences **A–H** the one which fits each gap (**1–7**). There is one extra sentence which you do not need to use.

A This original approach to style and colour, coupled with his preference for often controversial topics, helped set Banksy apart from other artists.

B It lends an air of mystery to his work, and has aroused enormous media interest.

C However, Banksy defends the belief that his work is art rather than vandalism.

D Other people are thought to have made much more money from Banksy's work than the artist himself!

E But his efforts were not received enthusiastically by the local authorities.

F It depicts monkeys wearing placards with the slogan, 'Laugh now, but one day we'll be in charge.'

G Banksy is also keen to explore new art forms as well as settings, often using some surprising materials.

H It was on one of these occasions that he found himself hiding under a train carriage.

A 'Gualicho', Argentina

Outsider art

The British graffiti artist Banksy is making his mark ...

Banksy has become something of a celebrity in the art world. There are **whispered** rumours that Brad Pitt and Angelina Jolie once forked out an astonishing €200,000 for samples of his work. Recent exhibitions have been sell-out events, with fans queuing for hours for admittance. Not bad for an artist who conceals his identity – and is wanted by the police!

For Banksy, fame has been bittersweet, as he hasn't been able to celebrate his success in the usual way. In the UK and many other countries, graffiti is considered to be a criminal offence. Consequently, Banksy has been forced to keep his identity hidden. He's never attended any of his own art shows, nor allowed his face to be shown in photos or on TV or YouTube footage. However, there are some advantages to this secrecy, too. **1** In these days of mass exposure, having a celebrity who doesn't want to be seen is something of a rarity!

Banksy began his career as a graffiti artist in the

Vocabulary in context: *the senses*

6 Look at the words in **bold** in the text and match them to the different categories. How many more adjectives can you think of for each category?

1 colour *colourless*
2 touch
3 smell
4 sound
5 shape and lines

7 What does the adjective *bittersweet* mean in paragraph 2?

Word boost ▶ The senses ▶ Workbook p. 64

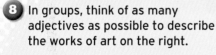

B 'Banksy', UK

1990s. Working with the DryBreadZ crew, he enlivened dull, **colourless** city streets with his designs. [**2**] They moved quickly to clean up Banksy's creations, sometimes while the paint was still **damp**!

Unsurprisingly, Banksy has spent a lot of time running away from the police. [**3**] Trying to ignore the **stinking** oil fumes and the **deafening** noise, he found himself staring up at a fuel tank. He later claimed that the number painted on the tank inspired him. It had been created using a stencil, or cut out shape. Banksy decided to borrow the idea for his own work so that he could paint faster, and escape more quickly!

And so Banksy's signature style was born. Graffiti murals are typically created with **bright** spray paints. In contrast, most of Banksy's works can be identified by their **sharp** outlines and a **monochrome** palette of greys, whites and blacks. [**4**]

Banksy has often been described as a thought-provoking artist. He tries to challenge his audience as well as charm them, as illustrated in one of his most famous pieces. [**5**] His work often expresses this somewhat mischievous sense of humour.

Today, Banksy's work is often allowed to remain on the streets. Ironically, some murals have been covered with **smooth**, **clear** plastic by concerned local councils, who are now keen to protect them from vandals! Theft is another big – and costly – problem. [**6**] In some cases, people have literally broken down walls in order to take away a Banksy original.

As his talents have developed, Banksy has moved ever further afield. In Paris, he memorably hung a copy of the Mona Lisa in the Louvre, repainted with a **round**, smiley acid yellow face! Unfortunately, the portrait was hurriedly removed. Obviously, Louvre officials were more alert than those in the British Museum, where a fake 'prehistoric' cave painting of a man pushing a shopping trolley was exhibited for several weeks! [**7**] For example, one LA art display featured a live elephant, with its **rough** skin painted to resemble expensive wallpaper! One thing is for certain – love him or hate him, Banksy continues to surprise ...

Over to you!

8 In groups, think of as many adjectives as possible to describe the works of art on the right.

9 Your teacher has asked you to choose **one** of the artworks as a poster to decorate your classroom. Decide which one you're going to choose and why.

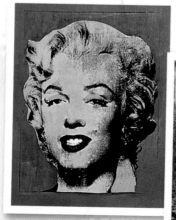

1 Read about artists behaving badly, ignoring the expressions in red. Why do you think the artists did these things?

A **Wanted** (As a result of being wanted) for murder, Caravaggio spent several years in exile.

B Władysław PodkowiÐski destroyed his own masterpiece **hanging** (which was hanging) in a gallery.

C **Having argued** (After he had argued) with Gauguin, Van Gogh famously cut off his own ear!

D Jackson Pollock died in a car crash **caused** (which was caused) by driving while drunk.

2 Match sentences A-D in Activity 1 to rules 1-3 below. For each one, decide *why* there is a present, past or present perfect participle.

Participle clauses

We sometimes use participle clauses to replace:
1 (**formal**) a reason or result clause (*because of*)
2 (**formal**) a time clause (*when, while*)
3 (**formal OR informal**) a relative clause when *who* or *which* is the subject of the verb.

We replace **active** verbs with a present or present perfect participle (*wanting, having wanted*).

We replace **passive** verbs with a past participle (*wanted*).

Language summary ▶ p. 166

3 Quickly read the article and find two unusual things about the artist Congo. Then rewrite the underlined clauses as participle clauses.

(o) referred to as 'the Cézanne of the apes'

Monkey business ...

An artist **(0)** <u>who was referred to as 'the Cézanne of the apes'</u> shot to fame in the 1950s. He first appeared on the TV show *Zoo Time*, **(1)** <u>which was presented by Desmond Morris.</u> **(2)** <u>After he had given Congo a brush,</u> Morris announced that he wanted to find out if chimpanzees could paint! The works **(3)** <u>which were painted by Congo</u> were very abstract in style, but some people felt they showed talent. **(4)** <u>When he received a painting as a present,</u> Picasso was so impressed he put it on his wall! In 2005, Congo's paintings were sold at Bonhams, an auction house **(5)** <u>that specialised in art.</u> **(6)** <u>As they sold for more than $25,000,</u> they fetched a higher price than works by Warhol and Renoir!

4 Look at the book cover from a museum called MOBA and read the visitors' comments. What's special about MOBA?

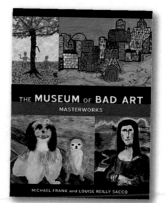

1 A Were these artworks burnt, I would not be sad!
  B If these artworks were burnt, I wouldn't be sad!
2 A I have seldom seen such terrible art.
  B Seldom have I seen such terrible art.
3 A You can only learn to appreciate good art by studying bad art like this.
  B Only by studying bad art like this can you learn to appreciate good art.

5 Read the rules. In 1-3 above, does sentence A or B express a stronger opinion?

Inversion

We can use inverted word order (auxiliary verb + subject) to add emphasis in formal English:
• after negative or restrictive expressions, e.g. *never, little, hardly, at no time, no sooner, rarely* or expressions with *only*.
• in conditional clauses with *were, had* or *should*, omitting *if* or *whether*.

Language summary ▶ p. 166

6 Rewrite 1-3, beginning with the words in **bold**. Discuss which sentences you agree with.

1 I have **never** seen worse paintings than those in Activity 4.
2 If I **were** an artist, I would refuse to let MOBA exhibit my paintings.
3 I would pay MOBA a visit if I **should** ever be in the area.

Over to you!

7 Complete the first lines of these four stories. Then swap answers with a partner and write the next **two** sentences to your partner's stories.

1 No sooner had she started to paint than ...
2 The woman shown in the picture...
3 Having finished the portrait ...
4 Had the artist known ...

Get ready for the exam

1 Read the *Exam tip*. In pairs, write down as many kinds of grammatical and lexical structures as you can think of that might be tested in Part 2.

pronouns, collocations

2 Complete the questions below, using the clues to help you. When you have finished, add four more questions. Use a range of language, and include at least one phrasal verb and one collocation.

Use of English Part 2: *the exam* **Exam tip**

1 Read the text first for gist.
2 Look at the whole of each gapped sentence as well as the words before and after a gap.
3 Think about grammatical structures and vocabulary.
4 Write one word for each gap – don't use contractions (*it's, don't*).

The arts: a questionnaire

1 Are you fascinated _____ art or do you find _____ a turn-off? Why? **(preposition, pronoun)**

2 _____ you ever _____ inspired by a poem or the lyrics of a song? How _____ it affect you? **(auxiliaries)**

3 When was _____ last time you visited _____ art gallery? Do you enjoy visiting galleries? **(articles)**

4 _____ you could own any famous painting _____ one would you choose and why? **(linker, pronoun)**

5 How easy do you think it is to _____ a living as _____ artist? Why? **(collocation, article)**

6 Which of these hobbies _____ you rather take _____ and why: photography, sculpture or drama? **(verb form, phrasal verb)**

3 Ask and answer the questions in Activity 2 and your own questions in pairs. Find at least **three** things that you and your partner have in common.

Exam boost ▶ Revision ▶ Workbook p. 67

Exam practice

4 Complete the exam task.

For questions **1–12**, read the text below and think of the word which best fits each gap. Use only **one** word in each gap. There is an example at the beginning **(0)**.

Write your answers **IN CAPITAL LETTERS**.

Shakespearean rap!

What have Shakespearean plays and rap **(0)** .GOT. in common? **(1)** .... first, they seem worlds apart. However, both use the popular language of the day and are best enjoyed in performance. And both deal **(2)** .... life's 'big issues' – **(3)** .... only love and friendship but also darker emotions **(4)** .... as jealousy, violence and prejudice. The rapper Tupac Shakur, **(5)** .... lyrics could be poetic as well as contentious, was known to love Shakespeare. He admired *Romeo and Juliet* **(6)** .... particular, comparing the Montagues and Capulets to twentieth-century street gangs. Similarly, the director Baz Luhrman **(7)** .... the decision to set his film version of Romeo and Juliet against the backdrop of a gang war, featuring shootings and car chases set to a rock and rap soundtrack.

Today, Shakespeare and rap are taught alongside each **(8)** .... in some US schools, as a way of making **(9)** .... dramatist appear more relevant to students. According **(10)** .... one teacher, "Just **(11)** .... rap artists, Shakespeare wrote for ordinary people, not the elite. Who knows, maybe **(12)** .... he'd been born in modern-day Brooklyn, he might have written rap songs instead of plays!"

Get ready: *music*

1 In pairs, talk about the photo. What's happening? What's the **worst** musical performance you have ever heard?

2 Discuss whether you find the following music a treat (☺) or a torture (☹)! Can you think of any more musical genres?

1 heavy metal   5 rap
2 jazz   6 classical
3 folk   7 disco
4 opera   8 punk

3 Add **two** more questions about music to the questionnaire below, using two of the expressions in the list.

> ballad catchy chart cover version
> duet instrumental solo soundtrack

MUSIC QUESTIONNAIRE

1 Can you play a musical **instrument** or sing **in tune**?

2 Do you prefer listening to **live** or **recorded** music?

3 Are you a **fan of** any bands or singers from your country? Have you seen any of them **on tour**?

4 When you go to a **concert** or music **festival**, do you prefer to be near the **stage** or at the back?

5 Do you ever **download tracks** from the internet? How often?

6 Which is usually more important to you: the **lyrics** or the **melody**?

4 Ask and answer questions 1–6 above and your own questions in pairs. Do you and your partner have similar tastes in music? Is there anything you completely disagree about?

Word boost ▶ Music ▶ Workbook p. 64

Exam practice

5 Read the *Exam tip* and put points A, B and C in the correct order. Can you think of any more useful tips for Part 3?

> **Listening Part 3:** *the exam* **Exam tip**
>
> A Listen carefully. The speakers won't use exactly the same words, so think about synonyms and paraphrases.
> B Listen again and check your answers. Give an answer for every speaker.
> C Read the rubric and statements A–F to get a general idea of the topic.

6 11.2 You will hear five different people talking about a music festival they have recently attended. For questions **1–5**, choose from the list (**A–F**) what each speaker says. Use the letters only once. There is one extra letter which you do not need to use.

Speaker 1 ☐   Speaker 2 ☐   Speaker 3 ☐
Speaker 4 ☐   Speaker 5 ☐

A The festival was quite expensive.
B The performers were disappointing.
C You have to book in advance to attend the festival.
D Crime was a problem at the festival.
E People stayed at the festival site overnight.
F Under-eighteen-year-olds are not allowed at the festival.

Over to you!

7 Work in groups and design your ideal festival. Agree on:

1 the location
2 the time of year
3 the music
4 other entertainment
5 the facilities.

8 Present your ideas to the class, then take a class vote on the best festival!

| Why might people want to listen to music in these situations? |

1 In pairs, compare the photos and discuss why you think people might want to listen to music in these situations.

2 🔊 11.3 Listen to Isabel and Peter do a Part 2 task, then answer the questions.

1 Who does the examiner interrupt? Why?
2 Who asks the examiner a question? Why?
3 In your opinion, do Isabelle and Peter do the task well or badly? Why?

3 🔊 11.3 Complete these phrases from the recording. Then listen and check.

0 B*oth* photos s *how* people listening to music.
1 They're listening to music f_____ very d_____ reasons.
2 S_____ the people in the second photo are a_____ listening to music for fun.
3 I listen to music a lot, a_____ it's probably **my f**_____ hobby!
4 **P**_____, **I f**_____ **that** music can help me to relax.

4 Complete the table with some of the expressions from Activity 3. Then add your own ideas.

Similarities	Differences	Personal opinions
Both photos show ...		

Exam practice

5 Complete the sentences in the *Exam tip* with *Do* or *Don't*.

> **Speaking Part 2: Exam tip**
> *the exam*
>
> 1 _____ look at your photos and read the question carefully.
> 2 _____ answer the question!
> 3 _____ waste time describing every detail in the photos.
> 4 _____ use comparative expressions to discuss the photos.
> 5 _____ stop speaking until the examiner tells you to.
> 6 _____ listen carefully to the other candidate or candidates. Remember, you will need to answer a question about their photos.

6 🔊 11.4 Work in groups of three. Student A, turn to page 150. Student B, turn to page 152. Student C, turn to page 154. Listen to the instructions and complete the task.

Comparative expressions

1 🔊 **11.5** Listen to part of a game on a radio quiz show called *What Am I?* Then work in pairs and guess what is being described in questions 1-4.

2 🔊 **11.5** Complete these sentences from the recording with *as* or *like*. Then listen again and check.

1 It seems _____ though we've reached the final round.
2 Tom Wilks also works _____ a teacher.
3 I feel cold _____ snow.
4 People usually eat me _____ a dessert.
5 When you have to be on time for something, _____ a meeting or an exam, you usually look at me.
6 This summer, _____ usual, I'll follow you everywhere.
7 I'll copy all your actions, _____ I always do.
8 When it looks _____ if it's getting dark, I'll disappear.

3 Read the rules and match A–F to the sentences above.

like, as, as if / though	
We use ...	
like	A to mean "for example / such as" B + *noun / pronoun* to talk about similarity
as OR (informal) *like*	C + *clause* to talk about similarity
as	D + *noun* to talk about someone or something's role or function E in fixed expressions, e.g. *as usual, as you know.*
as if / as though OR (informal) *like*	F + *clause* to say what a thing or situation seems like

Watch out!

Don't add *like* or *as* if it isn't necessary.

It tasted ~~like~~ delicious.

4 Complete the sentences with *like, as, as though, as if,* or nothing (Ø). More than one correct answer may be possible. Can you guess who or what's being described?

1 This material was first made _____ a luxury item in China. It feels _____ smooth and looks _____ shimmering water. However, it was originally made by caterpillars!
2 When this wooden, stringed instrument is played badly, it sounds _____ someone is hurting a cat! However, played by experts _____ Yehudi Menuhin, it sounds _____ extremely melodic.
3 Many people think this animal looks _____ ugly. However, its legs are enjoyed in France _____ a delicacy. Apparently, they taste _____ chicken!

Collocations (4): *verbs + nouns*

5 Read the article quickly. Why are smells important? Work in pairs and choose the correct alternatives to complete the article.

We tend to assume that sight and hearing are the two most important senses, and (**0**) **pay** / **take** less attention to smell, taste and touch. But studies have shown that all the senses can (**1**) **do** / **have** a powerful effect on the way we view the world. For instance, psychologists who've (**2**) **done** / **put** research into our sense of smell have (**3**) **made** / **seen** the discovery that it's closely connected to emotion. Scents like lemon have been shown to improve concentration (useful when you're (**4**) **getting** / **taking** an exam or hoping to (**5**) **catch** / **get** a new job), while lavender can help us to slow down and (**6**) **pay** / **take** better care of ourselves. Advertisers are increasingly (**7**) **having** / **taking** an interest in 'sense psychology', and (**8**) **making** / **taking** use of it to try to sell us products!

Over to you!

6 What smells, sounds or tastes remind you of a place, time or person? Tell your partner, giving details.

Word boost ▶ The senses ▶ Workbook p. 64

Get ready for the exam

1 In pairs, complete the sentences in the *Exam tip*. Can you add any more ideas?

Exam tip

Use of English Part 1:
the exam

1 You will be tested on a variety of language, which may include …
2 First, read …
3 Then look at …
4 Consider *all* four options, and think about …
5 Read your completed sentences. Do they …

2 With your partner, complete as much of the quiz as you can in **one minute**.

One Minute Memory Quiz!
Write three:
1 verbs that have a similar meaning to *think*
2 collocations with *make*
3 adjectives + prepositions
4 phrasal verbs that include the particle *up*
5 linkers to express contrast
6 compound adjectives
7 idioms.

3 Write three true and two false sentences about yourself using expressions from Activity 2. Can your partner guess which are true?

Exam boost ▶ Revision ▶ Workbook p. 65

Exam practice

4 Complete the exam task.

For questions **1–12**, read the text below and decide which answer (**A**, **B**, **C** or **D**) best fits each gap.

Touching the past

Have you ever **(0)** WONDERED what life was like 100, 1,000 or even 1,000,000 years ago? Historians can **(1)** .... us about the facts, but what if you could experience the past **(2)** .... you were really there? Although scientists haven't come **(3)** .... with any designs for a workable time machine yet, researchers at the universities of York and Warwick may have invented the next best thing. The 'Virtual Cocoon' will **(4)** .... the wearer to experience a wide **(5)** .... of pre-programmed sights and sensations. In theory, users could **(6)** .... out what it's like to travel into the past, or meet people who are no longer in **(7)** .... ! For instance, the cocoon could recreate the sights and smells of Da Vinci's workshop for art lovers, or the sounds of a Beatles concert for people **(8)** .... on 1960s music! The makers of the cocoon believe it to be so **(9)** .... they have labelled the technology 'real virtuality', as opposed to virtual reality. **(10)** ...., those eager to take **(11)** .... of this new invention will have to wait a little longer. As well as **(12)** .... the costs, scientists have to address the ethical implications of creating a 'fake' reality.

0	**A** wondered	**B** realised	**C** dreamed	**D** believed
1	**A** speak	**B** explain	**C** tell	**D** say
2	**A** such as	**B** in case	**C** just like	**D** as if
3	**A** down	**B** on	**C** up	**D** about
4	**A** give	**B** allow	**C** support	**D** let
5	**A** range	**B** set	**C** amount	**D** extent
6	**A** find	**B** look	**C** bring	**D** turn
7	**A** reality	**B** force	**C** existence	**D** fact
8	**A** interested	**B** keen	**C** passionate	**D** fond
9	**A** actual	**B** convincing	**C** likely	**D** possible
10	**A** However	**B** Moreover	**C** Though	**D** Despite
11	**A** use	**B** benefit	**C** help	**D** advantage
12	**A** carrying away	**B** weighing up	**C** putting out	**D** working for

Prepare

1 Look at the people photographed with an item that's special to them, and answer the questions.

1 Why do you think they chose these items?
2 Who would you most / least like to meet? Why?
3 If you had to choose one item to appear with you in a photo, what would you choose? Why?

Analyse the task

2 Read Rory's email and Isabel's reply. Why does Rory want Isabel to think of a 'special object'? What does she choose and why?

3 In Paper 2, you need to think about a number of things, not just accuracy! Which of these things did Isabel forget to consider? How could you improve her email?

1 addressing all of the notes
2 logical paragraphs
3 correct grammar, spelling and vocabulary
4 suitable register (informal or formal)
5 range of language

From:	Rory Martins
Date:	15th March
Subject:	Photography project

Hi there!

How's it going? It's been pretty busy here. I've just started an art class at school and it's absolutely brilliant! Are you interested in art? ——— *Yes, because ...*

Anyway, I was wondering if you could help me out with some homework. I'm doing a photography project called 'People and Personality' and I'd love to include you in it! Would it be OK if I took your photo sometime next week? ——— *Yes! Say when*

The photo needs to show people a bit about who you are. Can you think of any object we could include that's special to you? Remember Becky? Well, she's really into heavy metal, so she chose an electric guitar! ——— *Say what and why*

Let me know what you think, anyway. If you need to know anything else, just ask. ——— *Ask about ...*

Speak soon, hopefully!

Rory

From:	Isabel Losada
Date:	16th March
Subject:	RE: Photography project

Dear Rory, Great to hear from you! Yes, I'm quite interested in art, especially comic book artists, like Art Spiegelman. I like some abstract art too, but I don't know much about it. Your project sounds great, and of course I'd love to help out. Why don't you come round on Saturday morning? You could stay for lunch afterwards. I spent a lot of time thinking about a special object for the photo. It's hard to choose just one! In the end I decided on my dog, Berto. As you know, I love animals, and Berto's very special to me. Do you need me to wear any special clothes for the photo, or would jeans and a T-shirt be OK? Looking forward to seeing you soon! Take care, Isabel

Preparing for Part 1

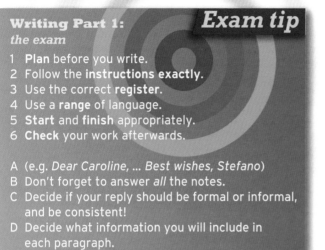

Writing Part 1:
the exam

1 **Plan** before you write.
2 Follow the **instructions exactly**.
3 Use the correct **register**.
4 Use a **range** of language.
5 **Start** and **finish** appropriately.
6 **Check** your work afterwards.

A (e.g. *Dear Caroline,* ... *Best wishes, Stefano*)
B Don't forget to answer *all* the notes.
C Decide if your reply should be formal or informal, and be consistent!
D Decide what information you will include in each paragraph.
E Don't copy too much from the source material.
F Look at the checklist on page 169 for ideas.

Writing reference ▶ p. 168

4 Look at the *Exam tip* on the left and the checklist on page 169.

1 Match 1-6 to A-F in the *Exam tip* box to make six tips.
2 What kind of task might you have to write in Part 1?
3 How many notes will you need to answer?
4 How can you decide whether you need to use formal or informal language?
5 What expressions can you think of for ending a) a formal, b) an informal letter or email?

5 Look at the exam task and follow the instructions below.

1 Read the exam task carefully, including the instructions and all the notes.
2 Make short notes about what you want to say (only spend a few minutes on this!).
3 Write your answer, using the tips in the *Exam tip* box.
4 When you've finished, check and correct your work.
5 After 40 minutes, stop!

Exam practice

You **must** answer this question. Write your answer in **120–150** words in an appropriate style.

Your English-speaking friend, Caroline, is coming to visit you next month. Read Caroline's email and the notes you have made. Then write an email to Caroline, using **all** your notes.

From:	Caroline Speakman
Date:	25th February
≡▾ Subject:	My visit!

Hi there,

How's it going? I'm really looking forward to my visit next month!

You asked me what I'd like to do, so here are a few ideas.

As you know, I'm studying art at university. Are there any interesting galleries, museums or buildings near you we could visit? —— *Yes, suggest ...*

Also, it would be good to listen to some music from your country – I've heard it's brilliant! Who's your favourite group or singer? —— *Give details*

You mentioned being interested in American culture. I'd love to bring you a present! Would you prefer a book, a CD or a DVD? —— *Ask for ...*

Finally, would you like to stay with me in the US over the summer? It would be great to return the favour! —— *No, because...*

See you soon!

Caroline

Unit 11

1 Complete the second sentence so that it has a similar meaning to the first sentence. Use between **two** and **five** words, including the word given.

1 Someone stole the instruments belonging to the band.
   OWNED
   Someone stole the instruments _____ the band.

2 Instead of listening to the teacher, he drew pictures in his notebook.
   ATTENTION
   Not _____ the teacher, he drew pictures in his notebook.

3 It was rare that he saw masterpieces like these.
   SUCH
   Seldom _____ masterpieces.

4 Someone photographed her moments after her arrival.
   ARRIVED
   Scarcely had _____ her photo.

5 The cathedral wasn't built for many years.
   LATER
   Only many _____ built.

2 Many famous people have had synaesthesia – they experience the senses differently. Write the correct form of the words in red, and complete the gaps with *like, as, as though, as if* or *nothing (Ø)*.

0 For the (**WRITE**) _writer_ Vladimir Nabokov, the letter *a* looked _like_ wood!

1 The (**POEM**) _____ Baudelaire thought that some images and scenes smelled _____ perfume.

2 For the *Radiohead* (**MUSIC**) _____ Thom Yorke, music seems _____ it's painted in different colours!

3 The (**ART**) _____ David Hockney believes that some art sounds _____ musical.

4 Pythagoras, known for his work _____ a (**PHILOSPHY**) _____ and (**MATHEMATICS**) _____ , believed that numbers had qualities, _____ dignity or honesty.

3 Complete the sentences. Then say whether they are true for you, giving details.

0 I think it's wrong to _download_ tracks from the internet without paying for them.

1 I don't _____ much attention to what's happening in the art world.

2 I always try to see my favourite bands when they go _____ tour.

3 Certain smells have a strong effect _____ me.

Units 1–11

4 Complete the text. Write one word in each gap.

Stradivarius

Many musicians and composers (**1**) _____ become famous. Rarely (**2**) _____ this true for instrument makers, however! Antonio Stradivari is one of (**3**) _____ exceptions. (**4**) _____ a living as an instrument maker in seventeenth century Italy, Stradivari designed violins which became as famous for their excellence (**5**) _____ for their mysteriousness. Even today, no one is entirely sure how they (**6**) _____ made! The violins are (**7**) _____ legendary that they have inspired their own folklore. The violinist Niccolo Paganini (1782–1840) played so well on a Stradivarius he was (**8**) _____ to have sold his soul to the devil – although that rumour was probably started (**9**) _____ a jealous rival! The violins have also appeared in many works of fiction, (**10**) _____ as the stories of Sherlock Holmes. Today, it's possible for a Stradivarius (**11**) _____ fetch over a million dollars at auction! We should feel sympathetic, then, (**12**) _____ the poor violinist who accidentally (**13**) _____ his Stradivarius behind in a taxi. Luckily, the taxi driver was very honest and returned the violin, (**14**) _____ was worth four million dollars. The grateful violinist treated not only the driver (**15**) _____ also his friends to a free concert – at the taxi stand!

STRADIVARIUS IN HIS WORKROOM.

5 Cross out the word in each group which does NOT belong with the prefix or suffix.

0 **un-** certain / employed / ~~logical~~

1 **ir-** reliable / rational / responsible

2 **dis-** believe / truthful / honest

3 artist / pessimist / psychiatrist **-ic**

4 cheer / talent / success **-ful**

5 invent / report / football **-er**

UNIT TARGETS

Topic vocabulary: work ● crime ● learning
Grammar: review of tenses and verb patterns
Word building: affixes ● phrasal verbs (6)
Writing: a formal letter ● preparing for Part 2
Exam preparation: Reading Part 3 ● Use of English
Parts 3 and 4 ● Listening Part 4 ● Speaking Parts 3
and 4 ● Writing Part 2

A

B

C

D

Work

1 🔊 **12.1** Choosing a career is difficult! In pairs, speculate about what jobs these people a) have now, b) had in the past. Listen and check. Were you surprised?

> **Useful language**
>
> *I'm not sure, but perhaps he / she ...*
> *He / She looks like a ... to me.*
> *I'm just guessing, but I think he / she might be ...*
> *He / She looks as though* + clause

2 Look at these advertisements. What job is being advertised in E–G?

E

> Nine-to-five position available in prestigious local hotel for individual with excellent communication skills and helpful manner. Competitive annual salary and good promotion prospects offered for someone who wants to make a career in hospitality.
> Please phone 01994 87615 for details.

F

> **Need an extra income?**
> Part-time weekend work available in a popular local bar. Successful applicants must be happy to work occasional overtime on busy nights. Good rate of pay starting at £6.00 p/h plus customer tips. Please apply to mike@wellsbar.com, attaching a CV.

G

> Enthusiastic and dynamic person required for a temporary summer job, showing visitors the sights of the city!
> Mon-Weds or Thurs-Sat shifts available.
> A uniform and full training will be provided.
> No qualifications or experience necessary. Please enquire at the Tourist Office.

3 Answer the questions. Say which words gave you the answer. Which job (E, F or G):

1 is not permanent?
2 requires you to work a full day?
3 may require you to work extra hours?
4 may help you to reach a higher position?
5 may pay you extra money for good service?

4 🔊 **12.2** Listen and match the people to the jobs in the advert. Compare your answers with a partner, explaining your decisions. Which job would *you* prefer to do? Why?

Word boost ▶ Work ▶ Workbook p. 70

Over to you!

5 Tell your partner what your dream job a) is now, b) was when you were at primary school. How have your ambitions changed?

1 Some types of jobs are more frequently represented in the media than others! Look at these stills from TV shows and discuss the questions in pairs.

   1 What kinds of jobs are shown?
   2 Why might audiences be interested in watching people doing these jobs?
   3 Do you think that television represents these jobs accurately? Why? / Why not?

2 Quickly read the article on page 139. What do the five people have in common? Whose job would you like to have the most / least? Why?

Exam practice

3 The sentences in the *Exam tip* are incomplete. Work in pairs and complete the sentences with your own ideas. Can you think of any more tips for Part 3?

> **Target Reading Part 3:**   *Exam tip*
> *the exam*
>
> 0 First, read *the text or texts quickly for gist.*
> 1 Then read the prompt sentences and _____
> 2 Next, search the text or texts _____
> 3 Think about _____
> 4 Make sure _____
> 5 If you have time, _____

4 You are going to read an article about five people who work in the field of crime. For questions 1-15, choose from the people (**A-E**). The people may be chosen more than once.

Which person mentions

being dishonest to others?	1 ☐
the negative media image of their profession?	2 ☐
that some aspects of their job resemble how it is shown on TV?	3 ☐
that there is some truth in criticisms of their profession?	4 ☐
the importance of having interests outside work?	5 ☐
wanting to have an unconventional career?	6 ☐
not always enjoying their work?	7 ☐ 8 ☐
how their work has benefitted someone?	9 ☐
not being keen to talk about their work?	10 ☐
attempting to persuade others to view their profession differently?	11 ☐
wishing their work could resemble its media image more closely?	12 ☐
not minding the repetitive element in their work?	13 ☐
not being focused on making money?	14 ☐
a moral issue in relation to their work?	15 ☐

Vocabulary in context: *crime*

5 Underline all the words related to crime in the article. Then find words that mean:

   1 people who might have committed a crime *(A)*
   2 person who saw an event *(B)*
   3 the state of being responsible for committing a crime *(B)*
   4 the field of observation and spying *(C)*
   5 the act of making someone suffer because they've done something bad *(D)*
   6 commit a crime again *(D)*
   7 name and personal details *(E)*
   8 person hurt by a crime *(E)*

6 In pairs, explain the difference between *steal* (D) and *rob* (E).

Word boost ▶ Crime ▶ Workbook p. 70

Over to you!

7 Discuss these questions with your partner.

   1 What crimes were mentioned in the text? Which do you think is the most / least serious? Why?
   2 Do you think prison is always the most suitable form of punishment for criminals? Why? / Why not?

A **Max Greenway (Police detective)**

Officers promoted to this position usually come well-prepared for the stress, but underestimate the tedium! Yes, it can be exciting when you're arresting suspects or engaged in high-speed car chases, but there's also a lot of paperwork. It's a struggle to stay motivated sometimes, especially when you're doing unpaid overtime. You've got to be in this job because you're committed, not for the glamour or the salary. I love my work, but I do make a point of taking a couple of weekends off now and again to watch the football or go fishing. You can't live and breathe this job 365 days a year – it isn't healthy.

B **Arlene O'Hanlon (Lawyer)**

Some people are convinced that lawyers are all dishonest and money-hungry, and nothing will change their minds. I know, I've tried! I'm not claiming that the profession's reputation is entirely undeserved, but we're not all cheating villains! Fortunately, shows like *Ally McBeal* and *The Practice* have portrayed law's more human side, even if neither are terribly realistic. What's true is that real-life courtrooms can be just as dramatic, with a witness breaking down in tears, or a defendant shouting at the judge. I find it hard to switch off when I'm working on a case, and I tend to be short of time for hobbies. I'm often asked how I can justify working for a client accused of murder or kidnap. To me, it's simple – regardless of their guilt or innocence, everyone deserves a fair trial.

C **Anonymous (Spy)**

Of course I have to keep a lot of secrets, even from friends or family, which can be hard sometimes. Frustratingly, I rarely get the chance to show off about my work, as I generally have to tell people I'm a bank manager! In the James Bond films, spies lead tremendously exciting lives. Much as I'd love that to be true, in reality the last thing a spy wants to do is stand out. Unlike Bond, I don't carry weapons and I don't work head-to-toe in designer gear – I couldn't afford

it even if I wanted to! I mainly investigate large-scale crimes, like international fraud or suspected terrorism, which can be very complex. Computer skills are a must for anyone in surveillance, as nowadays you spend a lot of time searching for evidence online. It's lucky that I'm quite a patient person as sometimes you have to cover the same ground over and over until you spot a clue. But it's a wonderful feeling when finally everything clicks into place.

D **Malcolm Burns (Prison officer)**

If there's been a drama that shows prison officers in a flattering light, I haven't seen it. In *Prison Break*, some of the guards are worse than the criminals! In reality, most officers are genuinely motivated by feeling they can make a difference, and prison is about more than punishment. My colleagues and I work hard to help prisoners develop skills so they don't reoffend. One former thief I worked with is now a very successful chef – earning good money instead of stealing it! It's stories like that that keep me going because, I'll admit, trying to keep order in a prison full of unhappy, locked-up inmates can sometimes feel less than rewarding.

E **Aisha Khan (Forensic scientist)**

Since *CSI* and *Bones*, applications to study forensics have rocketed, and now, annoyingly, I'm always being pestered by eager students with endless questions. Only a few years ago, the subject was deemed to be a bit unusual and 'out there', which I suppose was part of its original appeal for me, although I've learnt to value other aspects now. I spend much more time in the laboratory than the media would have everyone believe, but I wouldn't have it any other way. I find analysing details very rewarding, like piecing together a jigsaw puzzle. Whether I'm trying to work out who robbed a bank, or establishing the identity of a murder victim, no two days are ever the same.

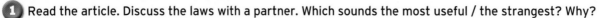

1 Read the article. Discuss the laws with a partner. Which sounds the most useful / the strangest? Why?

STRANGE LAWS

1 By the end of tomorrow, most men in the UK **will have committed** a crime. **Practising** with a bow and arrow for two hours a day is still a legal requirement for all adult males – although those who **break** this law are unlikely **to end up being** arrested!

2 It **was** once illegal for Mexicans **to take** their feet off the pedals while they **were cycling**.

3 In Toronto, Canada, bus drivers can **refuse to let** you **get** on board if you**'ve been eating** garlic. They**'d** obviously **been having** trouble with this problem before the law **was passed**!

4 A law in Atwoodville, USA, **prohibits** people from **playing** Scrabble while they**'re waiting** for a politician **to speak**. They'd better not **play** chess, either, as that**'s** also **forbidden**!

5 No one **will be chewing** gum in Singapore until the government **decides to overturn** this law: **to reduce** litter, the government **has banned** the sale of gum!

6 An old law **made** it an offence for Samoan men **to forget** their wife's birthday!

2 Look at the verb forms in blue. What tense is used in each? Why?

3 Complete the text with the correct form of the verbs. Do you agree with this law? Why? / Why not?

Some countries' laws may seem strange at first, but they (**0 invent**) *were invented* for good reasons.
The Singapore government (**1 make**) the sale of chewing gum illegal in 1992. Until then, the work of cleaning gum from streets and buildings (**2 cost**) the government over a million dollars a year. Since the ban (**3 introduce**), the problem of litter in Singapore (**4 decrease**).
Chewing gum is a big problem because it (**5 be not**) biodegradable. And the problem (**6 grow**). By the end of next year, it (**7 estimate**) that over twenty billion packs of gum (**8 sell**) worldwide. That's potentially a lot of litter! Perhaps it (**9 not be**) long before other countries introduce a chewing gum ban?

4 Look at the verb forms in red in Activity 1. Work in pairs and try to write rules for when we use these verb patterns.

	Verb pattern	Use	Examples
1	gerund (-ing)	*after a preposition*	*from playing*
2	infinitive without *to*		
3	infinitive with *to*		

5 Write the correct form of the verbs to complete the article. Which criminal do you think was the stupidest? Do you know any more stories like these?

*Could these (**0 be**) be the world's stupidest criminals?*

• Robbers ordered the owner of a pizza restaurant (**1 hand**) over his cash and a large pizza. They then let the manager (**2 go**). He called the police, who arrived in time (**3 arrest**) the gang. They had returned (**4 complain**) the pizza was burnt!

• Two inmates attempted (**5 get**) out of a police cell by (**6 crawl**) through ceiling pipes. Sadly, they didn't succeed in (**7 escape**) – after (**8 fall**) through the ceiling, they landed in the office of the police chief!

• A house burglar decided he would rather not (**9 leave**) the scene of the crime immediately. He decided (**10 turn**) on the TV. (**11 Watch**) TV obviously made him (**12 feel**) relaxed, because the owners returned (**13 find**) him asleep!

Language summary ▶ p. 167

Over to you!

6 Discuss the picture and questions in pairs. Compare your answers with another pair. What punishment is best for the man?

What do you think:
1 is happening in the picture?
2 happened before this scene?
3 will happen afterwards?

Get ready for the exam

1 Look at the crime and work cartoons below. Which do you find funniest? Why?

A "Miss Frimley, do I take sugar?"

B "CRIME DOES NOT PAY!.... UNLESS, OF COURSE, YOU'RE GOOD AT IT!"

C We really have to stop letting him watch the news.

D I SHOULDN'T HAVE TAKEN THIS JOB.

PIERO TONIN

2 Make sure you revise a range of structures and language. Rewrite the cartoon jokes below, using the clues to help you.

1 Mr Marsh asked Mrs Frimley ... sugar. (*reported question*)
2 Crime doesn't pay if ... at it. (*conditional*)
3 We really must stop allowing ... the news. (*verb pattern*)
4 If ... this job. (*regret*)

Exams boost ▶ Revision ▶ Workbook p. 73

Exam practice

Use of English Part 4: *Exam tip*
the exam
➤ This part tests grammar and vocabulary.
➤ Each question is worth **two** marks, so if you're not sure – guess!

3 The *Exam tip* is incomplete. In pairs, add three more useful tips for Part 4.

4 Complete the exam task.

For questions **1–8**, complete the second sentence so that it has a similar meaning to the first sentence, using the word given. **Do not change the word given**. You must use between **two** and **five** words, including the word given. Write **only** the missing words **IN CAPITAL LETTERS**.

0 On arriving at work, go straight to the manager's office.   **SOON**
   Go straight to the manager's office as *SOON AS YOU ARRIVE* at work.

1 They say he got the job because the company director is a friend of the family.   **SAID**
   He .... the job because the company director is a friend of the family.

2 He continued to work even though he wasn't getting paid.   **CARRIED**
   He .... even though he wasn't getting paid.

3 I regret not setting off earlier for the interview.   **WISH**
   I .... off earlier for the interview.

4 Salim was the best candidate we interviewed.   **BETTER**
   Salim was .... candidates we interviewed.

5 According to my brother, his employer was a very unpleasant woman.   **BEING**
   According to my brother, he was .... a very unpleasant woman.

6 Asking for a bigger salary was a mistake.   **SHOULD**
   I .... for a bigger salary.

7 I don't know why Lucy applied for the job.   **MADE**
   I don't know .... for the job.

8 She tried really hard to please her boss but she still didn't get the promotion.   **EFFORT**
   Despite really .... to please her boss, she still didn't get the promotion.

Get ready: *learning*

1 In pairs, choose the correct alternatives to complete these revision tips, then discuss your opinions of them.

Study tips

the good, the bad, and the strange!

1 Listening to rock music will help you to concentrate **for** / **on** your studies – and it will make revising **about** / **for** your exams less boring too!

2 Find it difficult to **remember** / **remind** things? In the weeks before you **take** / **make** your exams, try eating more fish!

3 Look **down** / **up** new words in a dictionary and write **down** / **up** the word, a definition and an example sentence in your notebook.

4 Always study on your **own** / **self**, so you aren't distracted **by** / **for** other people.

5 Wear orange – it will help you to **stay** / **hold** alert and keep **calm** / **quiet** under pressure!

6 Learn answers to questions by **heart** / **mind** and try to **repeat** / **retell** these in the exam.

2 12.3 Listen to an exams expert giving her opinion of the tips above. Does she agree with your ideas?

3 Work in groups. Agree on your **five** top tips for new exams students. Has everyone in your group followed these tips?

Word boost ▶ Learning ▶ Workbook p. 70

Exam practice

4 Put sentences A–D in the *Exam tip* in the most logical order.

Listening Part 4: *the exam* — **Exam tip**

A If you can't answer a question on the first listening, don't panic! Keep listening and try to answer the next one.
B Read the questions and options *before* you listen and underline any key words.
C Listen again and check your answers. This time, *always* choose an option, even if you aren't sure.
D Listen for synonyms and paraphrases.

5 12.4 You will hear a radio interview with a teacher, Mark Vickery, who spent a month training to be a music DJ, and his mentor, DJ Alice Electric. For questions 1–7, choose the best answer (**A**, **B** or **C**).

1 Whose idea was it initially for Mark to take part in *LifeSwap*?
 A his own
 B a colleague's
 C some students'

2 Alice was most worried about Mark's
 A personality.
 B knowledge of music.
 C appearance.

3 When he was performing as a DJ, Mark struggled because he
 A couldn't remember everything.
 B lacked musical talent.
 C was too tense.

4 Mark criticises dance music for being
 A rather repetitive.
 B unnecessarily loud.
 C very unimaginative.

5 What was Mark most nervous about in Ibiza?
 A seeing his students
 B looking silly
 C disappointing people

6 What do Mark's students like about his classes?
 A The lessons are not too difficult.
 B The students can discuss ideas.
 C The subject is fascinating.

7 What has Mark changed as a result of taking part in *LifeSwap*?
 A his fashion sense
 B his taste in music
 C his teaching style

Over to you!

6 Imagine you could try out someone else's job for a week. What would you choose? Why?

1 A local school is organising a careers day for students. In pairs, discuss how interesting the people above might be as speakers. Choose **two** people to invite to speak at the school.

2 🔊 **12.5** Listen to two students doing part of a Part 3 task and part of a Part 4 task.

1 Which two speakers do the students choose to invite to the careers day?
2 What Part 4 question do they answer?
3 How well do the speakers do the task? Do they a) answer the question? b) respond to each other? c) use a range of language?

3 🔊 **12.5** Work in groups. Listen again and tick (✓) the expressions you hear. Check your answers with the rest of the group.

Opinions	Agreeing and disagreeing
(Personally,) I (don't) think that …	I totally / completely agree / disagree.
It seems to me that … / I've got a feeling that …	That's a good point(, but …)
As far as I can tell, …	Absolutely (not). / Really?
In my opinion / view, … / To me, …	That makes sense. / I see what you mean.
I've always thought that ….	I suppose so (, but …)
I'm not sure.	Me too. / Me neither.
I hadn't thought of that.	I agree up to a point, but …

Moving a discussion on	Giving yourself time to think
Why don't / Shall we start with / by …	I haven't thought much about this before …
Shall we / Let's look at …	That's an interesting question …
What next?	I mean, … / You see, …
So, have we decided which …	Let me see / think …
Have we reached a conclusion?	Right, / Well, ….

Exam practice

4 Look at the sentences in the *Exam tip*. Do they refer to Part 3 (*3*), Part 4 (*4*) or both (*B*)?

5 Work in pairs and do the exam task on page 154.

Speaking Parts 3 and 4: *the exam* *Exam tip*

1 ____ Discuss every photo or picture and answer *both* questions!
2 ____ Respond to your partner's ideas and ask for their opinions.
3 ____ Negotiate with your partner to reach a final decision.
4 ____ Discuss your opinions with your partner and explain your ideas.
5 ____ Remember, there is no 'right' answer – you will get marks for the way you manage the discussion, not for your opinions.

Affixes: *review*

1 Read the article. Match the jobs to the pictures. Which job do you think is the worst? Why?

The worst jobs in history?

1 **Ploughman** (12ᵗʰ C). Person with great physical strength and endur**ance** required to work in the fields in all weathers. It's **un**likely you'll get proper**ly** paid but **in**adequate or care**less** work may result in starv**ation**.

2 **Food taster** (16ᵗʰ C). We're delight**ed** to adver**tise** a wonder**ful** role for food lov**ers**. The sole require**ment** is to taste the King's food. Some of this may be poison**ous**, so if you **dis**like taking risks, this job obvious**ly** isn't for you! Optim**ists** preferred.

3 **Spit turner** (16ᵗʰ C). Here's a great job opportun**ity** for teenagers (**non**-vegetarians only). You will cook meat on a scorch**ing** fire all day long. **Ir**respons**ible** cooks who black**en** the meat will not be paid.

4 **Hermit** (18ᵗʰ C). Are you **anti**social? Do you get **im**patient with other people or find them annoy**ing**? As a hermit, you'll spend your exist**ence** in isola**tion**, living by yourself in a cave. Not suit**able** for those who hate being alone!

A **B** **C** **D**

2 Work in pairs. Match the affixes in **bold** in the article to the categories below. Try to add one more example word for each category.

1 negative prefix   *un-,*
2 noun suffix – a thing
3 noun suffix – a person
4 adjective suffix
5 verb suffix
6 adverb suffix

3 Complete the sentences with the correct form of the stem words. Are these statements true for you? Why / Why not?

1 I would find it (**POSSIBLE**) to do any of the (**HISTORY**) jobs in the article, even for a week!

2 Having an (**ENJOY**) job is more important to me than being (**WEALTH**).

3 I think that people's choice of (**PROFESS**) tells you a lot about their (**PERSONAL**).

4 I work much more (**EFFECTIVE**) when I'm working (**DEPENDENT**), by myself, than as part of a team.

Phrasal verbs (6): *work*

4 Read these advertisements for unusual jobs. Which would you like to try the most? Why?

E Would you **jump at** the chance to play computer games for money? As a games tester you'll test new games and let us know if you **come up against** any problems. We'll then **sort out** any issues before the games reach the shops.

F Do you have a talent for **seeing through** people's deceptions and **catching** them **out** when they tell a lie? A private detective firm requires a new investigator to join our team.

G For a career that's out of this world, why not become an astronaut? The successful candidate will be good at **taking** lots of information **in** and **coping with** pressure. A head for heights is also essential!

H Wanted: a nature lover to **look after** a tropical island! You'll explore the island and record all the wildlife you **come across**. You'll report your experiences to a video diary, so you need to be good at **getting** your ideas **across**!

5 Match **six** of the phrasal verbs in bold in Activity 4 to the definitions below.

1 encounter (a difficulty)
2 make something understood
3 solve
4 learn and understand
5 work out the truth behind (something)
6 accept eagerly

Over to you!

6 Write a short description (50–100 words) of the worst job you can think of. Include at least four words with different affixes and two phrasal verbs.

7 Read other students' descriptions and try to match each job to a person. Has anyone described a job you would really like or really hate to try?

Word boost ▶ Workbook p. 87

Get ready for the exam

1 The *Exam tip* is incomplete. What things should you think about?

2 In pairs, complete sentences 1–6 with the correct form of the stem words.

A good boss should be:

1 _____, and care about his staff's problems.
   (SYMPATHY)

2 full of _____ when things go right!
   (APPRECIATE)

3 slow to _____ when things go wrong!
   (CRITICAL)

A bad boss is:

4 _____, and never thinks about other people.
   (CONSIDER)

5 cruel and _____ to his team.
   (PLEASE)

6 slow to pay any of his _____!
   (EMPLOY)

3 Write two more sentences to describe a good or a bad boss. Include gaps and stem words and ask another pair to complete them.

Exam boost ▶ Revision ▶ Workbook p. 71

Exam practice

4 Complete the exam task.

For questions **1–10**, read the text below. Use the word given in capitals at the end of some of the lines to form a word that fits in the gap **in the same line**. There is an example at the beginning **(0)**.

Write your answers **IN CAPITAL LETTERS**.

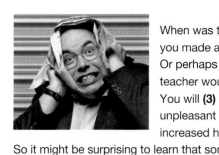

Stress!

When was the last time you felt really **(0)** _STRESSED_ ? Maybe you made a mistake at work and your boss was **(1)** .... Or perhaps you were late with your homework, and you knew your teacher would be **(2)** ....
STRESS
FURY

SYMPATHY

You will **(3)** .... remember that moment as a deeply unpleasant time. Symptoms of stress vary but may include an increased heart rate or feeling excessively **(4)** .... or tired.
PROBABLE

ANXIETY

So it might be surprising to learn that some stress may actually be good for us!

It seems that a short attack of stress such as that experienced before an exam or a job interview can actually improve **(5)** .... and memory. It has also been suggested that it can even be beneficial to our health – by temporarily **(6)** .... blood vessels and boosting heart and lung power, it effectively acts like a mini 'work out'!
CONCENTRATE
WIDE

But the **(7)** .... of time we experience stress is important. Long-term stress is *not* good for us, and without treatment can have very **(8)** .... consequences. If stress is making you depressed or ill, then try to change the **(9)** .... or seek help. Don't go on suffering in **(10)** .... !
LONG
HARM
SITUATE
SILENT

Prepare

1 In pairs, discuss how learning languages can be useful, thinking about the topics below. Do you think learning languages will be important to you in the future? Why? / Why not?

travel   hobbies   friends and family   work

Analyse the task

2 Read the task below and look at the photo. Would you like to do this type of job? Why? / Why not? Do you ever visit places like these?

You see this advertisement on an English language website.

GLOBAL CHAT

We are looking for people to work in our internet café for two months in the summer.
- Are you interested in computers?
- Do you have any useful experience?
- Is your level of English good?

Apply to the manager, Miss Wade, saying why you think you are suitable for the job.

Write your **letter of application** in **120-180** words in an appropriate style. Do not write any postal addresses.

3 In this task, will you need to write a formal or an informal letter? Which information helped you to decide?

4 Read Julia's letter, ignoring the missing words. What is the **main** topic of paragraphs A, B, C and D?

5 Julia's letter is a first draft. She has crossed out several mistakes! In pairs, choose suitable words or expressions to complete her letter.

A Dear Miss Wade,

I **(1)** in response to your advertisement for people to work in internet cafés. I would like to **(2)** for a position with Global Chat.

B I am very interested **(3)** computers, and I hope **(4)** information technology at university in the future. I have a good understanding of the internet as I regularly use it for research.

C Last summer I worked part-time in my uncle's restaurant **(5)** three months, where I learnt how to serve customers, deal with money and prepare simple meals. I believe **(6)** these skills could be useful in a new role with Global Chat.

D I **(7)** English for five years, and I **(8)** a First Certificate exam in English next month. I would welcome the opportunity to speak English as part of my work, as I would **(9)** to develop my skills further.

Please **(10)** hesitate to contact me if you have any questions. I look **(11)** to hearing from you.

Yours **(12)** ,

Julia Nowak

Preparing for Part 2

6 Complete the *Exam tip* with five of these numbers:

one two three four five six 120 150

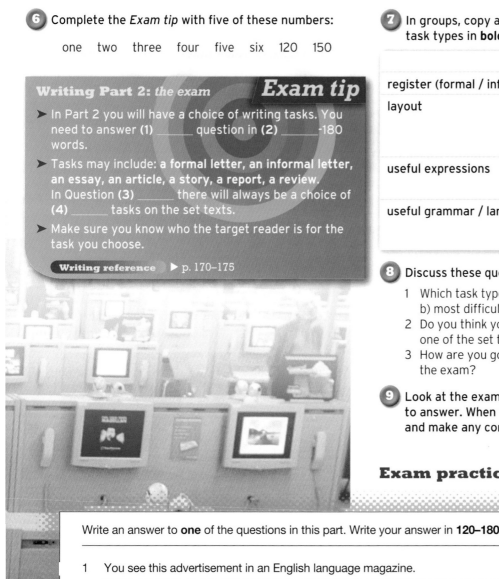

Writing Part 2: *the exam* — *Exam tip*

➤ In Part 2 you will have a choice of writing tasks. You need to answer **(1)** _____ question in **(2)** _____-180 words.

➤ Tasks may include: **a formal letter, an informal letter, an essay, an article, a story, a report, a review.** In Question **(3)** _____ there will always be a choice of **(4)** _____ tasks on the set texts.

➤ Make sure you know who the target reader is for the task you choose.

Writing reference ▶ p. 170–175

7 In groups, copy and complete the table for each of the task types in **bold** in the *Exam tip*.

	formal letter
register (formal / informal)	• *formal*
layout	• *formal letter style* • *a new paragraph for each new piece of information*
useful expressions	• *Dear Sir / Madam,* • *I am writing to ...*
useful grammar / language	• *indirect questions* • *polite expressions*

8 Discuss these questions in your groups.

1 Which task types do you usually find the a) easiest, b) most difficult? Why?
2 Do you think you are likely or unlikely to write about one of the set texts? Why?
3 How are you going to prepare for this paper before the exam?

9 Look at the exam tasks below and choose **one** question to answer. When you have finished, check your work and make any corrections.

Exam practice

Write an answer to **one** of the questions in this part. Write your answer in **120–180** words in an appropriate style.

1 You see this advertisement in an English language magazine.

> **THE ONE WORLD MUSIC SHOP IS LOOKING FOR SUMMER STAFF**
>
> • Do you enjoy different kinds of music?
> • Do you speak English?
> • Do you have any useful experience or skills?
>
> *Apply to the manager, Mr Burton, saying why you think you are suitable for a job in our international music shop.*

Write your **letter of application**. Do not write any postal addresses.

2 You have decided to enter a short story competition advertised on a website. The story must **begin** with the following words:

Tim's first day at work did not start well.

Write your **story**.

3 You have had a class discussion on work. Your teacher has now asked you to write an essay, giving your opinion on the following statement:

Some jobs are more important than others.

Write your **essay**.

Units 1-12

1 People do some strange things at interviews! Complete these real life stories from interviewers with the correct form of the verbs.

0 A candidate once (**bring**) _brought_ her mum to an interview, saying 'My Mum (**understand**) _understands_ me best!'

1 A bald candidate suddenly (**leave**) _____ the interview room. When he (**return**) _____, he (**wear**) _____ a wig!

2 Even though it was a very serious interview, the candidate (**keep**) _____ (**laugh**) _____.

3 A candidate said, 'I (**know**) _____ this is off the subject, but (**you / marry**) _____ me?'

4 A man asked, '(**you / work**) _____ here this time next year? Only I would like (**have**) _____ your job.'

5 One candidate (**announce**) _____ she (**not had**) _____ lunch and proceeded (**eat**) _____ a takeaway!

6 An applicant stated, 'Sometimes I (**feel**) _____ like (**smash**) _____ things.'

7 A woman explained, 'I didn't have time (**take**) _____ all my exams because I (**kidnap**) _____ by criminals.'

8 While the interviewers (**ask**) _____ her questions, the candidate (**switch**) _____ on her MP3 player!

2 For questions 1-12, read the text below and decide which answer (**A, B, C or D**) best fits each gap.

Could you be the next 'Q'?

The media often glamorises certain professions, giving the (0) _impression_ that the world of work is full of action and excitement. On screen, spies greatly outnumber accountants, and (1) .... anyone spends any time at the office! However, sometimes it seems that life can imitate art.

In the films, James Bond always (2) .... a visit to the eccentric inventor 'Q' whenever he wants to take (3) .... of the latest technology. Q's numerous inventions included an exploding alarm clock and an underwater craft designed to (4) .... a crocodile!

Now it seems that the fictional (5) .... of Q may soon have a real-life equivalent! The British intelligence agency, also called MI5, are looking (6) .... someone with world-class expertise in the fields of science and technology to take on a (7) .... as their chief scientific advisor. Anyone who wants to be (8) .... for the post will need to demonstrate a talent for (9) .... up with innovative ideas. The successful candidate will be expected to develop futuristic technology to help (10) .... the country against threats from terrorism and other (11) .... crime. However, it seems highly (12) .... that he or she will ever be called upon to modify a sports car like that owned by 007!

	A	B	C	D
0	impact	effect	(C) impression	response
1	infrequently	hardly	practically	rarely
2	does	gives	goes	pays
3	profit	advantage	benefit	use
4	resemble	seem	imagine	pretend
5	performance	character	personality	actor
6	for	at	into	on
7	career	work	role	task
8	recognized	considered	regarded	appreciated
9	bringing	giving	coming	putting
10	save	support	rescue	protect
11	strong	great	serious	heavy
12	impossible	uncertain	incredible	unlikely

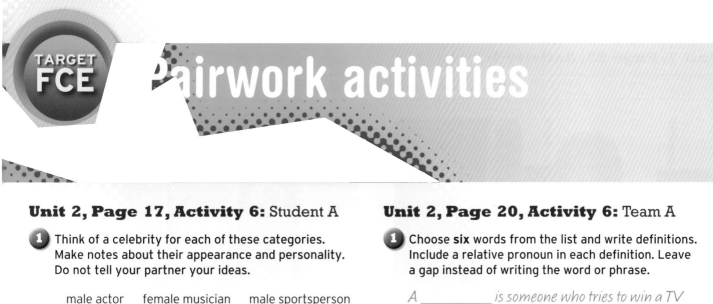

Unit 2, Page 17, Activity 6: Student A

1 Think of a celebrity for each of these categories. Make notes about their appearance and personality. Do not tell your partner your ideas.

> male actor   female musician   male sportsperson

2 Describe each celebrity to your partner *without giving their name*. Describe these things in order, and keep a record of your partner's score.

- **appearance** (a correct guess at this stage = 15 points)
- **personality** (a correct guess = 10 points)
- **career** (a correct guess = 5 points)

3 Listen to your partner describe three celebrities and try to guess who they are. The more quickly you guess the right answer, the more points you will get!

Unit 2, Page 20, Activity 6: Team A

1 Choose **six** words from the list and write definitions. Include a relative pronoun in each definition. Leave a gap instead of writing the word or phrase.

> *A _____ is someone who tries to win a TV contest. (Answer: contestant)*

> autobiography   arrogant   celebrity
> contestant   forehead   heroic   plump
> selfish   sensible   stunning

2 Take it in turns to read your definitions to Team B. Each team has twenty seconds to guess the correct answer. The team with the most correct answers wins.

Unit 2, Page 23, Activity 4: Student A

What might be difficult about doing these jobs?

Unit 2, Page 27, Activity 5

Answers

1 Johnny Depp (*American actor who played Captain Jack Sparrow in the Pirates of the Caribbean films*)

2 Pelé (*Brazilian football player, considered to be one of the world's greatest*)

3 Steven Spielberg (*American film director whose films include ET and Schindler's List*)

4 Shakira (*the highest-selling Columbian singer of all time*)

5 Matt Groening (*American cartoonist who created The Simpsons and Futurama*)

6 Nicole Kidman (*Australian actress whose films include Moulin Rouge! and The Golden Compass*)

Unit 7, Page 83, Activity 4: Student A

Why is a computer important to these people?

Unit 10, Page 116, Activity 7: Student A

1 You are a **journalist**. Ask the celebrity five questions. Try to make them as interesting as possible!

Your fans will probably be quite shocked by this news. What message would you like to give them?

2 You are in the audience of a TV show, *Celebrity Gossip*. Listen to the presenter talking about your interview and interrupt if you think he / she is not reporting your interview accurately! Do you agree with the presenter's final opinion?

Unit 11, Page 131, Activity 6: Student A

Why is music important to these groups of people?

Unit 3, Page 36, Activity 1

Answers

1 Sahara 2 flea 3 Amazon 4 football

Unit 4, Page 46, Activity 1

Answers

1 spider 2 kangaroo 3 butterfly 4 panda
5 ostrich 6 anaconda 7 rabbit 8 cockroach

Unit 4, Page 48, Activity 5

Answers

A POLLUTION; DROUGHT; EXTINCTION B Still only 6!
C V. **Explanation:** The letters are in alphabetical order, but some letters are missing! Between A and B there is no gap, between B and D there is a gap of 1 letter, between D and G there are 2 letters, then 3 letters between G and K, 4 letters between K and P, and finally 5 letters between P and V.
D (breed; die); H (catch; hide); T (hunt; track)
Did you get them all right? Well done - you might be geniuses!

Unit 2, Page 17, Activity 6: Student B

1 Think of a celebrity for each of these categories. Make notes about their appearance and personality. Do not tell your partner your ideas.

  female sportsperson   male musician   actress

2 Listen to your partner describe three celebrities and try to guess who they are. The more quickly you guess the right answer, the more points you will get!

3 Describe each celebrity to your partner *without giving their name*. Describe these things in order, and keep a record of your partner's score.

  • **appearance** (a correct guess at this stage = 15 points)
  • **personality** (a correct guess = 10 points)
  • **career** (a correct guess = 5 points)

Unit 2, Page 20, Activity 6: Team B

1 Choose **six** words from the list and write definitions. Include a relative pronoun in each definition. Leave a gap instead of writing the word or phrase!

A _____ person is someone who is very well-known. (Answer: famous)

  argument   chin   dyed   famous
  glamorous   marriage   mischievous
  reality show   skinny   sympathetic

2 Take it in turns to read your definitions to Team A. Each team has twenty seconds to guess the correct answer. The team with the most correct answers wins.

Unit 2, Page 23, Activity 4: Student B

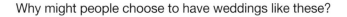

Why might people choose to have weddings like these?

Unit 4, Page 47, Activity 4: Student B

What might people enjoy about looking at these animals?

Unit 7, Page 83, Activity 4: Student B

Why is it difficult to use a mobile phone in these situations?

Unit 10, Page 116, Activity 7: Student B

1 You are the **celebrity**. Answer the journalist's questions. Try to be as interesting as possible!

That's not true! What really happened is this ...

2 You are in the audience of a TV show, *Celebrity Gossip*. Listen to the presenter talking about your interview and interrupt if you think he / she is not reporting your interview accurately! Do you agree with the presenter's final opinion?

Unit 10, Page 118, Activity 1

What kind of 'thinker' are you?

Some scientists believe that the right and left sides of your brain process information in different ways. As most people tend to use one side of the brain slightly more than the other, this may mean that your personality is shaped by your brain type!

Did you answer:
• **Mostly As?** You are probably a right-brain thinker. Right-brain people tend to be emotional thinkers. They spend more time dreaming and imagining than left-brain thinkers. As students, they tend to prefer more imaginative, open tasks. They are equally as intelligent and thoughtful as left-brained thinkers, but they tend to be happier to take risks and try out new language.
• **Mostly Bs?** You are probably a left-brain thinker. Left-brain people tend to be logical thinkers. They spend more time studying and analysing than right-brain thinkers. As students, they usually prefer well-organised, structured tasks. They are equally as intelligent and creative as right-brained thinkers, but they are more likely to check their work and think about accuracy.

Unit 11, Page 131, Activity 6: Student B

What are the people enjoying about these concerts?

Unit 7, Page 78, Activity 5

1 Look at the avatars on page 79. Imagine you are going to design an avatar for yourself! Draw or write a short description of your avatar. Do *not* write your name!

2 Work in groups. Take it in turns to describe your avatar, explaining why you have chosen it. When everyone has finished speaking, discuss as a group how attractive or interesting each avatar is. Then decide which one is the most unusual and why.

Useful language

I've based this on ...
This is meant to look (a bit) like ...
This represents ...

3 Find another group *(B)* and swap your drawings and written descriptions. In your group *(A)*, look carefully at the information you've been given. Can you match each avatar to a person in group B?

Unit 9, Page 101, Activity 6: *Student A*

1 Complete all the squares in the box. Yellow challenges are for you, and blue challenges are for your partner. Remember to time your partner carefully!

2 Finished? If you have tied (= got the same score), try this challenge: *Write as many phrasal verbs (e.g. end up, set out, etc.) as you can in thirty seconds.* You must be able to give the meaning if challenged! The person with the greatest number wins.

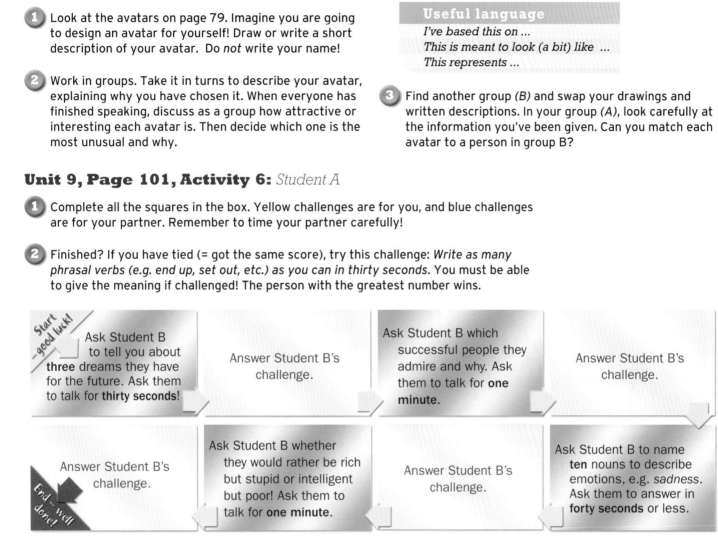

Start – good luck!

Ask Student B to tell you about **three** dreams they have for the future. Ask them to talk for **thirty seconds**!

Answer Student B's challenge.

Ask Student B which successful people they admire and why. Ask them to talk for **one minute**.

Answer Student B's challenge.

Answer Student B's challenge.

Ask Student B whether they would rather be rich but stupid or intelligent but poor! Ask them to talk for **one minute**.

Answer Student B's challenge.

Ask Student B to name **ten** nouns to describe emotions, e.g. *sadness*. Ask them to answer in **forty seconds** or less.

End – well done!

Unit 8, Page 92, Activity 7

1 Discuss the following questions about each photo. Use modals of deduction.

1 What do you think is happening?
2 Why do you think this is happening? (What happened before?)
3 What do you think will happen next?

Unit 10, Page 116, Activity 7: Student C

 You are a **TV presenter**. Listen to a journalist interviewing the celebrity from Activity 6. Make notes about what they say.

2 Report back on what both people said for your show, *Celebrity Gossip*. Remember, you need to be accurate: the journalist and the celebrity will both be in the audience! At the end, give your own personal opinion of the celebrity.

The journalist asked Ela if she had been shocked by the news.

Unit 11, Page 131, Activity 6: Student C

What is difficult about performing in these situations?

Unit 12, Page 143, Activity 5

1 Discuss these Part 3 questions. Talk for **three minutes**.
- Why are these jobs important?   • Which job would be the most interesting to do?

2 Discuss three of the Part 4 questions on the right. Talk for **four** minutes. When you have finished, discuss how well you think you did the task with your partner. Are there any areas you think you could improve on before the exam?

1 Do you enjoy watching sporting events like these? Why? / Why not?
2 Why do you think so many people want to become professional footballers?
3 What kind of things should people think about when they're choosing a career?
4 Why do some people have to wear uniforms at work?
5 Do you prefer working on your own or as part of a team? Why?

Unit 8, Page 95, Activity 5

- How can these things make people feel happier if they are feeling sad?
- Which two of these things would be the most effective?

Unit 9, Page 101, Activity 6: *Student B*

1 Complete all the squares in the box. Yellow challenges are for you, and blue challenges are for your partner. Remember to time your partner carefully!

2 Finished? If you have tied (= got the same score), try this challenge: *Write as many phrasal verbs (e.g. end up, set out, etc.) as you can in thirty seconds*. You must be able to give the meaning if challenged! The person with the greatest number wins.

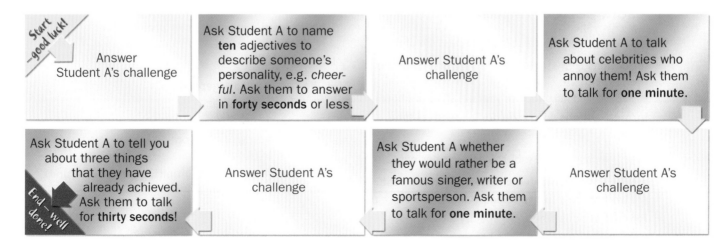

Unit 1

Present tense review

We use the present simple ...

- for regular or repeated actions.
  - *I play tennis every Tuesday.*
- for situations that don't change.
  - *I live in London.*

We use the present continuous ...

- for actions in progress now.
  - *He's playing tennis at the moment.*
- for temporary situations.
  - *I'm living with my aunt for a few months.*

We use the present perfect ...

- for past actions where we don't specify a time.
  - *I've met her a few times.*
- for past actions with a present result.
  - *Oh, no! I've forgotten my passport!*
- for actions that started in the past and continue in the present.
  - *I've lived here for three years.*

We use the present perfect continuous ...

- to emphasise that an action which started in the past is still continuing.
  - *I've been working all day. (I'm still working)*

Remember ...

- we don't use the present continuous with stative verbs (*hate, have got, hear, know, like, love, remember, understand*, etc).
  - *I don't like this soup. (NOT I'm not liking this soup.)*

Present perfect vs past simple

We use the present perfect (not the past simple) ...

- for actions that started in the past and continue in the present.
  - *I've worked here for two years. (I still work here)*
- for past actions where we don't specify a time.
  - *I've seen that film.*

We use the past simple (not the present perfect) ...

- for actions that started and finished in the past.
  - *I worked there two years ago. (I don't work there now)*
- for past actions where we specify a time.
  - *I saw that film last week.*

Adjective suffixes

-able	enjoy**able** reli**able** accept**able**
-al	music**al** natur**al** environment**al**
-ent	excell**ent** differ**ent** depend**ent**
-ful	hope**ful** pain**ful** use**ful**
-ic	artist**ic** scientif**ic**
-ish	child**ish** fool**ish** self**ish**
-ive	act**ive** creat**ive** attract**ive**
-less	hope**less** pain**less** use**less**
-ous	glamor**ous** danger**ous** fam**ous**
-y	sport**y** health**y** luck**y**

We can add suffixes to nouns and verbs to form adjectives. Note that sometimes there are other spelling changes.

- *glamour → glamorous*
- *rely → reliable*
- *science → scientific*

Verbs + infinitive / gerund

Verbs + to infinitive

decide hope expect learn manage promise refuse want would like

Verbs + gerund

can't stand deny enjoy finish give up hate keep look forward to suggest

Verbs + gerund or to infinitive

begin continue like love prefer start

Note ...

- We can use *like* + gerund.
  - *I like dancing. (I enjoy it)*
- We can also use *like* + *to* infinitive.
  - *I like to do my homework on Friday evenings. (I prefer to do this)*
- We use *would like* + *to* infinitive (but not gerund).
  - *I would like to dance.*

Unit 2

Relative clauses

Which relative pronoun we use depends on whether it is used in a defining or non-defining relative clause, on what the pronoun describes, and whether it is the subject or object of the clause.

	defining relative clause		non-defining relative clause
	subject	**object**	
thing	which / that	which / that / -	which
person	who / that	who / that / -	who

We can also use *where* for places, *when* for times and *whose* for possession.
- *The village where I grew up is tiny.*
- *Do you remember when we first met?*
- *That's the man whose sister plays the trombone.*

Defining relative clauses give more information about a person or thing, and make it clear (or *define*) which one we are talking about.
- *The man who lives next door to me is very nice.*
- *The film which / that we saw was really good.*

In defining relative clauses, we can omit the relative pronoun when it is the object of the clause, but not when it is the subject of the clause.
- *The man (who) I met is very nice.*
  (I met **the man** = object).
- *The man who lives there is very nice.*
  (**The man** lives there = subject)

Non-defining relative clauses give extra information. We use commas to separate them from the rest of the sentence.
- *Simon, who lives in London, is a doctor.*
- *The film, which was made in 2001, is really good.*

In non-defining relative clauses, we can't omit the relative pronoun, and we use *which*, not *that*, for things.
- *The house, which / that is very big, is near the station.*

In formal English we use whom instead of who as the object of a defining relative clause.
- *The man whom I met is very nice.*

In formal English, we put a preposition before *which* or *whom*. In informal English, we put the preposition at the end of the clause.
- *The doctor to whom I spoke was very kind.* (formal)
- *The doctor I spoke to was very kind.* (informal)

Compound adjectives

kind- cold- hard-	-hearted
fair- dark- black-	-haired
blue- brown- dark-	-eyed
thick-	-skinned
well- smartly- scruffily-	-dressed
narrow- broad- open-	-minded

We can form compound adjectives by joining two other words together.
- *She's got dark hair.* → *She's dark-haired.*
- *He dresses well.* → *He's well-dressed.*
- *a girl with blue eyes* → *a blue-eyed girl*

Phrasal verbs (1): *relationships*

Verb	Particle
get	on
go	out
fall	out
split	up
make	up
get	back together
settle	down
bring	up

We form phrasal verbs with a verb + particle.
- *They get on very well.*
- *Tom and Sara have fallen out.*

Some phrasal verbs can be followed by another particle or preposition.
- *I get on well with my brother.*
- *John wants to settle down with Lucy.*
- *John and Lucy want to settle down together.*

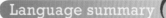

Unit 3

Narrative tenses

We use the past simple, past continuous, past perfect and past perfect continuous in narratives.

We use the past simple for the main actions or events.
- John **got** up at seven o'clock. He **had** breakfast and **left** the house.

We use the past continuous …

– for actions that continued while the main events happened.
  - The sun **was shining** when he got up.

– for events which were interrupted by the main events.
  - The phone rang while he **was having** a shower.

We use the past perfect …

– for background events or facts, which happened before the story started.
  - Sara lived in London. She **had moved** there when she was sixteen.

– to refer back to events that happened earlier.
  - He went to the station, but the train **had left**. (it left before he arrived)

We use the past perfect continuous for actions that continued for some time before a main action or event.
- I **had been waiting** for over an hour when the bus finally came.

Comparatives and superlatives

We can use adjectives and adverbs in these structures to compare things.

just / exactly				
nearly / almost / not quite	as	adjective / adverb	as
twice / three times				

a bit / a little / slightly	comparative	than
much / a lot / far		

easily / by far	superlative

We can use (just/exactly) as … as to say that two things are the same.
- My brother is as tall as me.
- Going by train is just as expensive as flying.

To talk about a small difference, we can use …

– a bit/a little/slightly + comparative.
  - This chair is slightly more comfortable than the old one.
  - She can run a bit faster than me.

– almost/nearly/not quite as … as.
  - Our car is almost as old as yours. (your car is slightly newer)

To talk about a big difference, we can use …

– much / a lot / far + comparative.
  - The second exam was much more difficult than the first one.

– twice/three times as … as.
  - This hotel is twice as expensive as the other one.

– easily / by far + superlative.
  - It's by far the best film I've ever seen.

Verb patterns (2): *gerund / infinitive with a change in meaning*

Some verbs can be followed by either a gerund or infinitive, but with a change in meaning.

Verb + gerund

I stopped talking to her. (I was talking, then I stopped)

I won't forget meeting him. (I met him and I won't forget)

I remember posting the letter. (I posted it and I remember)

I tried skiing last year. (I did it)

He went on laughing. (he continued)

Verb + *to* infinitive

I stopped to talk to her. (I stopped, then I talked)

I forgot to meet him. (I forgot, so I didn't meet him)

I must remember to post the letter. (I must remember and post it)

I tried to ski, but I couldn't. (I didn't manage to do it)

He went on to become a famous singer. (he later became one)

Unit 4

Future forms

We use several different forms to talk about the future.

We use *will* ...

- for general predictions.
  - *I think you will enjoy this film.*
- for decisions you make as you are speaking.
  - *Sit down. I'll make you a cup of tea.*
- for promises.
  - *Don't worry, I'll be careful.*

We use *be going to* ...

- for plans.
  - *I'm going to buy a new car next month.*
- for predictions based on evidence.
  - *Look at those clouds – it's going to rain!*

We use *may / might / could* when we don't feel certain about the future.

- *I might go to university, but I don't know yet.*

We use the present continuous for fixed future arrangements.

- *I'm having lunch with Tom tomorrow.*

We use the present simple for schedules and timetables.

- *The next train leaves at 11.50.*

We use the future continuous for an action in progress at a particular time in the future.

- *At seven o'clock tomorrow I'll be flying to New York.*

We use the future perfect for an action that will be completed by a particular time in the future.

- *By next July I'll have left school.* (I will leave school before July)

We use the future perfect continuous for an action that will continue up until a particular time in the future.

- *By July, I will have been studying English for five years.*

With stative verbs, we use the future perfect simple for this meaning.

- *By next February, I will have known Sarah for ten years.*

Determiners: *countable and uncountable nouns*

Some determiners can be used with countable or uncountable nouns, and some can be used with both.

+ countable noun	+ uncountable noun	+ countable or uncountable noun
a/an a few / few each every many	a little / little a large amount much	all a lot any enough no none some the

Note that *all of* and *some of* are followed by a plural verb, but *none of* is followed by a singular verb.

- *All of the tourists have cameras.*
- *None of the tourists has a camera.*

Note that *a little* and *a few* have a positive meaning, but *little* and *few* have a negative meaning.

- *I've invited a few friends round.*
- *She's got very few friends.* (almost none)
- *I can lend you a little money.*
- *They've got very little money.* (almost none)

Phrasal verbs (2): *solving problems*

We use these phrasal verbs to talk about solving problems.

- *carry on* (continue)
- *come across something* (find something by chance)
- *come back* (return)
- *fill something in* (complete something that is missing)
- *find something out* (discover information)
- *look after something* (take care of something)
- *look into something* (investigate something)
- *sort something out* (deal with a problem)
- *work something out* (find a solution)

Unit 5

Conditionals 0-3

	If clause	Main clause
zero conditional	If I drink coffee,	I feel ill.
first conditional	If it's sunny tomorrow,	we'll go to the beach.
second conditional	If I had lots of money,	I'd travel all over the world.
third conditional	If I'd worked harder last year,	I would have passed my exams.

We use the zero conditional to talk about general truths, or things that always happen.

We form the zero conditional using:
If + present simple, present simple
   • *If he gets tired, he just falls asleep.*

We use the first conditional to talk about a possible event in the future.

We form the first conditional using:
If + present simple, *will* + infinitive
   • *If I see Tim, I'll invite him to the party.*

We use the second conditional to talk about an imaginary situation.

We form the second conditional using:
If + past simple, *would* + infinitive
   • *If I spoke Chinese, I'd go and live in China.* (but I don't speak Chinese)

We use the third conditional to talk about events in the past which did not happen.

We form the third conditional using:
If + past perfect, *would have* + past participle
   • *If you'd told me about the party, I would have come.* (but you didn't tell me, so I didn't come)

With all conditionals, the *if* clause or main clause can come first. If the main clause comes first, we don't put a comma between the two clauses.
   • *We won't go to the beach if it rains.*
   • *If it rains, we won't go to the beach.*

Compound nouns

We can form compound nouns by joining two or more words together.
   • *A crossing for pedestrians* ➜ *a pedestrian crossing*
   • *Fumes from traffic* ➜ *traffic fumes*
   • *A restaurant serving fast food* ➜ *a fast-food restaurant.*

Some compound nouns are written as one word.
   • *nightlife, pushchair, skyscraper*

Some compound nouns are written with a hyphen.
   • *father-in-law, x-ray, t-shirt*

Collocations (1): *prepositions + nouns*

Preposition	Nouns
at	(at) all (at) the beginning
by	(by) bus
for	(for) a change (for) a while
in	(in) trouble
on	(on) foot (on) the way (on) time
out of	(out) of breath (out) of shape

Some prepositions combine with nouns to form expressions.
   • *We went by bus.*
   • *Let's sit down for a while.*
   • *You'll be in trouble if you do that!*

Unit 6

Modal verbs (1): *obligation, necessity and advice*

We use *should* and *ought to* to give advice.
- *You should get more sleep.*

We use *should / shouldn't have* to say that something someone did in the past was a bad idea.
- *I'm sorry, I shouldn't have borrowed your phone without asking.*

We use *have to, need to* or *must* to talk about something that is necessary, or something we are obliged to do.
- *Hurry up – we have to leave now.*
- *You must carry your passport with you at all times.*

We use *mustn't* to talk about something that is forbidden.
- *You mustn't tell anyone about this.*

We use *needn't* and *don't have to* to talk about something that is not necessary.
- *You needn't buy your ticket in advance – you can buy it on the day.*

Notice the difference in meaning between *didn't need to* and *needn't have*.
- *It was raining, so I didn't need to water the garden.* (it wasn't necessary and I didn't do it)
- *It rained the following day, so I needn't have watered the garden.* (I watered it, but it wasn't necessary)

Modal verbs (1): *ability*

We use *can / can't* to talk about ability in the present.
- *I can swim.*

We use *could / couldn't* to talk about general ability in the past.
- *I couldn't swim when I was three.*

We use *be able to* to talk about ability in any tense.
- *Next year we will be able to visit you.*

We use *was / were able to* and *managed to* to talk about an ability on one occasion in the past.
- *The window was open, so I was able to escape.*

Adverbs

We use adverbs of manner to describe how an action happens. They usually go before or after the verb.
- *She walked slowly to the door.*

We use adverbs of comment to give our own opinion about something. They usually go at the beginning of a sentence.
- *Amazingly, no one was hurt.* (I think this is amazing)

We use adverbs of degree to modify an adjective or another adverb. They go before the adjective or adverb.
- *He's really clever.*

We use adverbs of frequency to say how often something happens. They go after the verb *be* or before other verbs.
- *He's never late.*
- *He never arrives late.*

We use adverbs of time to say when something happens. They usually go after the verb and object.
- *I'll phone you tomorrow.*

Phrasal verbs (3): *health*

We can use these phrasal verbs to talk about health.
- *cut down on something* (eat less of something)
- *cut something out* (stop eating something)
- *eat out* (eat in a restaurant)
- *give something up* (stop doing or eating something)
- *stick to something* (keep doing something)
- *take something up* (start doing something)
- *work out* (do exercises in a gym)

Unit 7

The passive

	Active	**Passive**
Present simple	*They grow apples in England.*	*Apples are grown in England.*
Present continuous	*They are building a new stadium.*	*A new stadium is being built.*
Past simple	*Someone stole my car.*	*My car was stolen.*
Past continuous	*Workmen were fixing the road when the car crashed.*	*The road was being fixed when the car crashed.*
Present perfect	*No one has found the money.*	*The money hasn't been found.*
Will	*Someone will find a cure for this disease.*	*A cure for this disease will be found.*
Modals	*They must finish the job.*	*The job must be finished.*

We use the passive ...

– to change the emphasis of a sentence. Compare:
  • *My uncle grows apples in his garden.* (active – emphasis on *my uncle*)
  • *Apples are grown in the garden.* (passive – emphasis on *apples*)
– when the person doing the action of the verb is not known, not important or obvious.
  • *My car was stolen last night.* (I don't know who stole it)
  • *Cars are made in this factory.* (it's not important who makes them)
  • *She was fired for stealing from clients.* (it's obvious that it was her boss who fired her)

We can use *by* + agent in a passive sentence to say who does the action.
  • *This painting was painted by Rembrandt.*

Only transitive verbs (verbs which take a direct object) can have a passive form. Intransitive verbs like *arrive, come, die, happen, rain, sleep* do not have a direct object to become the subject of the passive sentence.

Negative prefixes

dis-	**dis**obedient **dis**approve **dis**agree
il-	**il**logical **il**legal **il**legally
im-	**im**mature **im**moral **im**possible
in-	**in**accurate **in**convenient **in**dependent
ir-	**ir**responsible **ir**regular **ir**reversible
un-	**un**reliable **un**happy **un**employment

We add negative prefixes to adjectives, adverbs, verbs and nouns to form words with an opposite meaning.
  • *I disagree with you.* (I don't agree)
  • *He's unemployed.* (he's not employed)

Collocations (2): *verbs + prepositions*

Verb	**Preposition**
believe	*in something*
be dedicated	*to something*
depend	*on something*
discourage someone	*from doing something*
experiment	*on animals*
help	*with something*
know	*about something*
laugh	*at something*
study	*for an exam*
succeed	*in doing something*
suspect someone	*of something*
think	*about something*

Some verbs are followed by collocating prepositions.
  • *My parents discouraged me from getting a job.*
  • *We succeeded in finishing the job.*

Unit 8

Modal verbs (2): *deduction*

We use *may, might* and *could* when we are not sure if something is true.
- *He might be a student.*
- *She could be ill.*

Notice the difference between the negative forms.
- *They might / may not know about this.* (it's possible that they don't know)
- *Don't be silly – it couldn't have been a lion!* (it's not possible that it was)

We use *must* when we are sure that something is true.
- *He must earn plenty of money to buy a car like that.*
- *The train must have been delayed.*

We use *can't* when we are sure that something is not true.
- *You can't be serious!*
- *You can't have finished already!*

Responses

We use these expressions to congratulate someone and say we are pleased for them.
- *Congratulations!*
- *Good for you!*
- *Well done!*

We use these expressions when someone tells you something very surprising.
- *I don't believe it!*
- *You must be joking!*
- *You can't be serious!*

We use these expressions to sympathise with someone when they are disappointed.
- *What a shame!*
- *Never mind.*
- *Oh dear!*

We use these expressions to say 'yes' when someone asks us something.
- *That's fine by me.*
- *Of course.*
- *No problem.*

Phrasal verbs (4): *behaviour*

Separable	
calm someone down	(make them feel more relaxed)
cheer someone up	(make them feel less sad)
let someone down	(disappoint them)
make something up	(invent it)
tire someone out	(make them feel tired)

Inseparable	
fit in with someone	(be accepted by or comfortable with them)
look down on someone	(feel you're better than them)
rely on someone	(depend on them)
rush into something	(act quickly, without thinking)
stand up for something	(defend it)

Phrasal verbs that take an object can be separable or inseparable.

With separable phrasal verbs ...
- the object can come before or after the particle when it is a noun.
  - *I didn't make up this story / make this story up!*
- the object must come between the verb and particle when it is a pronoun.
  - *I didn't make it up!*
  - *I don't want to let you down.*

With inseparable phrasal verbs, the object always comes after the particle.
- *You should stand up for your rights.*
- *Don't rush into it.*

Unit 9

Wishes and regrets

We use *I wish / If only* + past simple to express a wish about a present situation or state.

- *I wish I had more money!*
- *If only I had a good job!*

We use *I wish / If only* + *would* to express a wish about something that we want to happen now. We often use this structure for criticisms.

- *I wish the sun would come out.*
- *I wish he would do more to help!* (a criticism)

We use *I wish / If only* + *could* to express a wish that is very unlikely to come true.

- *If only I could spend all my time travelling!*

To express a regret about the past, we can use ...

- − *I wish / If only* + past perfect.
  - *I wish I had worked harder for my exams!* (I didn't work hard and I regret it)
- − *I regret* + gerund.
  - *I really regret leaving school at 16.*

We can use *shouldn't* + *have* + past participle to express a regret or criticism about the past.

- *I shouldn't have shouted at him.* (I regret this)
- *You shouldn't have stayed so late.* (a criticism)

Mixed conditionals

If clause	Main clause
If I'd accepted that job,	*I would be rich today.*
If I was a better singer,	*I would have won that competition.*

We can sometimes mix different conditional forms.

- − We can use *If* + past perfect + *would* + infinitive to talk about how an unreal event in the past would affect the present.
  - *If I'd accepted that job, I would be rich now.* (I didn't accept the job, so I'm not rich now)
- − We can use *If* + past simple + *would have* + past participle to talk about how an unreal present situation would have affected the past.
  - *If I was a better singer, I would have won that competition.* (I'm not a very good singer, so I didn't win the competition)

Words with similar meanings

These groups of words have similar meanings.

- *You **succeed** in your job. / You **achieve** something difficult. / You **realize** your dream. / You **score** a goal.*
- *You visit an **exhibition** of paintings. / You watch a **performance** by an actor. / You watch a **display** of juggling. / You watch a funny comedy **act**.*
- *You play a football **match**. / You take part in a poetry **contest**. / You run in a **race**. / You play a **game** of chess.*
- ***Spectators** watch a sports event. / **Onlookers** watch something happening in the street. / An **audience** watches a play or film. / **Viewers** watch a TV show.*
- *You **earn** money. / You **profit** from a good deal. / You **win** a game or competition. / You **gain** knowledge or experience.*

Collocations (3): *adjectives + prepositions*

Adjective	Preposition
brilliant	*at something*
concerned	*about something*
considerate	*to someone*
experienced	*in something*
fascinated	*by something*
guilty	*of something*
interested	*in something*
keen	*on something*
obsessed	*with something*
passionate	*about something*
responsible	*for something*

Some adjectives are followed by collocating prepositions.

- *Are you interested in sport?*
- *We're very concerned about the environment.*

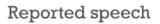

Unit 10

Reported speech

Direct speech	Reported speech
present simple	past simple
present continuous	past continuous
past simple	past perfect
past continuous	past perfect continuous
present perfect	past perfect
past perfect	no change
can	*could*
will	*would*
would, could, should, must	no change

In reported speech, the verb usually moves back one tense.
- *'I'm hungry!'* → *He said he was hungry.*

The tense does not have to change if what the person says is still true now.
- *'I live in Leeds.'* → *She said she lives in Leeds.*

There is no change in reported speech to the past perfect, *would, could, should* and *must*.
- *'I hadn't finished.'* → *He said he hadn't finished.*
- *'That would be great!'* → *She said that would be great.*

Reported questions

Direct question	Reported question
'Where's the exit?'	*She asked where the exit was.*
'Where did you put the key?'	*He asked where I had put the key.*
'Are you cold?'	*She asked if / whether I was cold.*

In reported questions, we …

- move the verb back one tense, as in reported speech.
- change the word order to the word order of an affirmative sentence.
- don't use auxiliaries *do* or *did*.
- use *if* or *whether* in yes / no questions.

Expressions with *mind*

We use *mind* in these expressions.

- *Do you mind!* (that's annoying)
- *Don't mind me.* (pay no attention to me)
- *I don't mind.* (it's not important to me)
- *I've changed my mind.* (I've changed my decision)
- *Make up your mind.* (make a decision)
- *Mind out!* (be careful)
- *Mind your own business.* (this doesn't concern you)
- *My mind went blank.* (I couldn't remember anything)
- *Never mind.* (it's not important)
- *That's a weight off my mind!* (I'm not worried now)
- *What's on your mind?* (what are you thinking about?)
- *Would you mind …?* (used to make a request)
- *You're out of your mind!* (you're mad)

Phrasal verbs (5): *life's dramas*

We use these phrasal verbs to talk about life's dramas.

- *build something up* (improve it) (separable)
- *call something off* (cancel it) (separable)
- *end up* (finally be) (no object)
- *get over something* (recover from it) (inseparable)
- *get through something* (complete it) (inseparable)
- *own up* (admit something) (no object)
- *put up with something* (tolerate it) (inseparable)
- *turn someone down* (refuse or reject them) (separable)
- *turn out to be something* (be found to be) (inseparable)
- *walk out* (leave your husband or wife) (no object)

Unit 11

Participle clauses

We can use participle clauses to replace other clauses, especially in formal English.

- We use an *-ing* participle clause to replace a clause with an active verb.
  - *The man waiting at the bus stop was my uncle.* (the man who was waiting ...)
  - *Having read the newspaper, I put it in the bin.* (after I had read ...)
  - *Having seen the film already, I didn't go to the cinema.* (because I had seen ...)

- We use an *-ed* participle clause to replace a clause with a passive verb.
  - *The paintings damaged in the fire will be replaced.* (the paintings which were damaged ...)

Inversion

When we use certain words or expressions at the beginning of a sentence, we invert the subject and auxiliary verb. These structures are used in formal English, to add emphasis.

We can use inversion after some negative or restrictive expressions.

- *I have never seen such a beautiful painting.*
  ➜ *Never have I seen such a beautiful painting.*
- *We had no sooner arrived, than it was time to leave.*
  ➜ *No sooner had we arrived, than it was time to leave.*

When we invert a sentence without an auxiliary verb, we add one.

- *He rarely goes out.* ➜ *Rarely does he go out.*
- *I only met him once.* ➜ *Only once did I meet him.*

We can also use inversion after *were*, *had* or *should* in conditional clauses.

- *If I were rich, I'd fly all over the world.*
  ➜ *Were I rich, I'd fly all over the world.*
- *If you had worked harder, you would have passed your exams.*
  ➜ *Had you worked harder, you would have passed your exams.*

Comparative expressions

We use *like* + noun / pronoun to say what something is similar to.
- *It looks like a horse.*
- *It tastes like chicken.*

Note that we don't use *like* before an adjective.
- *It looks lovely.* (NOT *It looks like lovely.*)

We can also use *like* to give an example.
- *Singers like Madonna are very popular here.*

We use *as* to talk about someone's role or something's function.
- *He works as a teacher.*
- *You can use it as a spare bed.*

We also use *as* in some fixed expressions.
- *Tom was late, as usual.*

We can use *as* + clause to say that something is similar. We can also use *like* + clause in informal English.
- *I left for work at eight, as / like I always do.*

We use *as if / though* + clause to say how a situation seems. We can also use *like* in informal English.
- *It looks as if it's going to rain.*
- *She looks like she's upset.*

Collocations (4): *verbs + nouns*

Verb	Noun
do	*research*
get	*a job*
have	*fun*
make	*a discovery*
make	*use of something*
pay	*attention*
take	*an exam*
take	*care of something*

Some verbs and nouns go together as collocations.
- *I need to get a job.*
- *When do you take your exams?*

Unit 12

Review of tenses

Tense	Example
Present simple	*I play tennis every day.*
Present continuous	*He's playing tennis now.*
Past simple	*I had lunch at one o'clock.*
Past continuous	*I was having lunch when the phone rang.*
Present perfect	*I've seen that film.* *He's just left.* *I've lived here for three years.*
Present perfect continuous	*I've been working all morning.*
Past perfect	*When we got to the cinema, the film had already started.*
Past perfect continuous	*When I got there, the others had been waiting for an hour.*
Will	*Doctors will be able to cure this disease one day.* *I'll help you!*
Future continuous	*Next week I'll be lying on a beach.*
Future perfect	*By next week I'll have finished my exams.*

Review of verb patterns

We use a gerund …
- after some verbs.
  - *Do you enjoy travelling?*
- as the subject of a sentence.
  - *Playing tennis is fun!*
- after prepositions.
  - *He was arrested for stealing some money.*

We use an infinitive with *to* …
- after some verbs.
  - *I want to do well.*
- after adjectives.
  - *The film is likely to be popular.*
- to express purpose.
  - *I went home to rest.*

We use an infinitive without *to* …
- after modal verbs.
  - *You must come with us!*
- after the verbs *make* and *let*.
  - *He let me borrow his bike.*
- after some expressions.
  - *We had better wait here.*

Affixes: *review*

Type of affix	Examples
noun suffix	perform**ance** introduc**tion** agree**ment** happi**ness**
adjective suffix	enjoy**able** care**ful** pain**less** spor**ty**
verb suffix	advert**ise**
adverb suffix	careful**ly** quick**ly**
negative prefix	**un**happy **in**accurate **im**possible **dis**agree

We use affixes to form new words from word stems.
- agree → agreement, agreeable, disagree

Sometimes there are other spelling changes.
- happy → happiness, unhappy, happily

Phrasal verbs (6): *work*

We use these phrasal verbs to talk about work.
- *catch someone out* (show they are lying) (separable)
- *come across something* (find it by chance) (inseparable)
- *come up against something* (face something difficult) (inseparable)
- *cope with something* (deal with it) (inseparable)
- *get something across* (communicate it) (separable)
- *jump at something* (accept it eagerly) (inseparable)
- *look after something* (take care of it) (inseparable)
- *see through something* (see that it is untrue) (inseparable)
- *sort something out* (solve it) (separable)
- *take something in* (learn or understand it) (separable)

Writing reference

Part 1 – An email or letter

In Part 1, which is compulsory, you will read some input material (such as a letter, email, etc.) with notes or prompts. You will need to write a letter or email of between **120** and **150** words, addressing all of these notes or prompts.

Sample task

You have received an email from your English-speaking friend, Daisy, discussing a music festival which you will be attending together. Read Daisy's email and the notes you have made. Then write an email to Daisy, using **all** your notes.

To:	José
Date:	19th June
Subject:	music festival

Hi,

Thanks for getting back to me so quickly! I'm really glad you can make it to the music festival. Hope you're looking forward to it as much as I am!

Yes!

I checked out the festival website last night. It looks like there are going to be loads of bands – pop, rock, R&B, all sorts. What kind of music are you into?

Explain

Don't forget to bring your tent and a sleeping bag for the campsite! Do you think we should take a camping stove for cooking, or shall we just buy food there? I don't mind either way ...

Say which and why

I forgot to ask you earlier, but do you want to stay over at my place on Friday night? Then we could go to the festival together on Saturday. Let me know, anyway!

No, because ...

Speak soon,

Daisy

Write your **email**. You must use grammatically correct sentences with accurate spelling and punctuation in a style appropriate for the situation.

Model answer

To:	Daisy
Date:	19th June
Subject:	music festival

Hi Daisy,

use chatty, colloquial language in an informal email or letter

I'm **really excited** about the festival **too**! It **sounds like** it's going to be **loads of fun**.

start a new paragraph for each main idea

I love listening to all kinds of music, but I'm mainly into pop and disco – music that makes you feel like dancing! I can't stand goth music. It's too depressing!

Thanks for the reminder about the camping gear. Don't worry, I won't forget to bring my stuff! I haven't got a camping stove, and anyway I'm terrible at cooking, so shall we just buy our food on site?

use informal punctuation, including contractions (I'm) and exclamation marks (!) – but not too many!

Thanks for the invite to stay. **Unfortunately, it's my brother's birthday on Friday, and I don't want to miss it!** Let's meet up at the festival on Saturday. If we both take our mobiles, it should be easy enough to find each other.

develop your ideas – give reasons or examples

I can't wait!

See you soon,

José

use suitable opening and closing expressions

Target Writing Part 1: checklist

Make sure you:
- ☑ address *all* of the points.
- ☑ use the correct register (formal or informal).
- ☑ use a variety of language in the appropriate register.
- ☑ divide your letter or email into paragraphs.
- ☑ link your ideas – remember you're writing a letter / email, not a list!
- ☑ use the correct number of words.
- ☑ check your work for accuracy.

Useful informal language

For formal letters / emails see page 175.

Opening expressions
Dear Daisy,
Hi Daisy, / Hi there,
Great to hear from you!
How are things (with you)?
How's it going?
I'm sorry I haven't written for ages, but ...

Giving news
Did I tell you that ...?
By the way, ...
Guess what?

Responding to invitations & requests
Thanks for the invite. I'd love to ...
Sorry, but I can't ... because ...
That sounds like a great idea.
Of course! No problem.

Asking questions
Could you tell me (more) about ...
I'd love to know more about ...
Would you like to ...?
I wanted to ask you, do you ...?
Let me know if you ...

Making suggestions
Why don't you / we ...?
What / How about ...?
If I were you, I'd ...
Let's ... / Perhaps we could ...

Closing expressions
Anyway, that's all for now.
I have to go now, because ...
Speak / Write soon.
See you soon.
Can't wait to see you / catch up!
Bye for now,
Take care, / All the best,
Love, / Lots of love,

Part 2 – An article

Sample task

> You have seen this advertisement on an international travel website.
> Write your **article** in **120-180** words in an appropriate style.

Model answer

get readers' attention right from the start!

Marrakech: the best city in the world!

My absolute favourite city in the world has to be Marrakech, in Morocco. It has beautiful architecture, great shops and restaurants, and lots to do and see. **What's not to like?**

ask questions to engage your readers

The old town (Medina) is full of picturesque historic buildings and mysterious passageways, while the town square is packed day and night with colourful stalls and lively performance acts. And as if this wasn't enough, the Atlas Mountains are less than an hour away, offering spectacular views that will **take your breath away.**

I grew up just outside Marrakech and I quickly fell in love with it. **For me,** the city has a blend of traditional charm and modern excitement that is completely unique. It seems that many other people feel the same way – Marrakech is now a major tourist destination!

Marrakech may not be as big and loud as New York, or as chic as Milan, but to its many fans it's twice as fascinating, and always full of surprises! **If you haven't seen it, you must come soon. You'll never forget it!**

be personal!

end with an interesting last sentence

Target Writing Part 2:
article checklist

Make sure you:
- ☑ include an interesting, catchy title.
- ☑ use a lively, chatty, semi-formal style.
- ☑ speak directly to your readers – don't sound too formal!
- ☑ give your own opinion.
- ☑ include descriptions, examples and stories to support your ideas.
- ☑ use colourful language, such as phrasal verbs, collocations and idioms.
- ☑ make sure that you answer all the points in the question.
- ☑ use the correct number of words.
- ☑ check your work for accuracy.

a few idiomatic expressions can make your article sound more interesting

Useful language

Addressing the reader
Have you ever ...?
You absolutely must ...
Can you imagine ...
I'm sure you'll agree ...
I must tell you about ...
You wouldn't believe ...

Giving a personal response
For me, ... / To me, ...
Personally, I think / find / believe ...
It seems to me ...
In my view, ...
One thing I love / remember ...
I'll never forget ...

Giving a strong opinion
It's absolutely + *stunning /
terrible* **(strong adjective).**
It took my breath away.
I will never forget it.
There's nothing in the world like it.

Adding and developing ideas
For a start ...
Secondly, / Thirdly, / Finally, ...
And then there's the fact that ...
On top of that, ...
Apart from that, ...
I must also mention ...
As if this wasn't enough, ...

Giving examples
..., such as ...
..., particularly ...
..., like ...

Part 2 – A story

Sample task

> You have decided to enter a short story competition in an international magazine.
> The story must **begin** with the following words:
> *When Ella checked the alarm clock, she saw that it was midnight.*
> Write your **story** in **120-180** words in an appropriate style.

Model answer

use past continuous for background information

use a range of descriptive language

*use a range of expressions to show **when** things happened*

When Ella checked the alarm clock, she saw that it was midnight. Her parents **were spending** the night away and wouldn't be due back until the morning. So what on earth was making that dreadful noise in the kitchen?

Ella suddenly felt wide awake as she imagined all the worst possible explanations. What if somebody had broken in? What if she was in danger? Well, there was nothing else for it. She would have to go and investigate.

Shivering with cold and fright, Ella crept downstairs. The noise seemed to get louder and louder, and Ella thought she'd never been so scared **before in her life. Eventually**, she reached the kitchen. Hardly daring to look, she bravely pushed open the door – and saw her cat, Charlie, trying to get some food scraps out of the bin!

Ella immediately felt relieved, embarrassed and cross with Charlie all at the same time. **After she'd cleaned up the mess** Charlie had made, she went back to bed. She decided not to tell her parents what had happened. **She knew they would only laugh!**

*use the past perfect for events which happened **before** the main events in the story*

have a clear ending – don't just stop writing!

Target Writing Part 2: *story checklist*

Make sure you:
- ☑ begin or end your story with the sentence you are given.
- ☑ give your story a clear beginning and end.
- ☑ describe atmosphere and feelings, not just events.
- ☑ create interest by using adjectives and adverbs.
- ☑ use a range of narrative tenses, not just the past simple.
- ☑ use time expressions and sequencing words to organise your story.
- ☑ use the correct number of words.
- ☑ check your work for accuracy.

Useful language

Narrative tenses
- past continuous for setting the scene
  The sun was shining ...
- past simple for main events
  We set off early.
- past perfect for events that happened before the main action
  After he'd left, I felt ...

Time and sequencing expressions
At first ... / In the beginning, ...
Firstly, / Next, / Then, ...
Soon / Shortly after ...
As / While / When ...
Meanwhile, / While that was happening, ...
Gradually, / Slowly, ...
Suddenly, / Just then, ...
Immediately, / Straight away, ...
Afterwards, / After that, ...
Eventually, / In the end, / Finally, ...

Describing reasons and results
because ... / as ... / since ...
so that ... / (in order) to ...
Because of ... / As a result of ...

Describing feelings and responses
... was so + *adjective* that ...
... was such a + *adjective* + *noun* that ...
...had never felt / been so + *adjective* + before in all my life.
I couldn't believe my eyes / ears when ...
It was a terrible shock / wonderful surprise.

Part 2 – An essay

Sample task

> You have had a class discussion on computers. Your teacher has now asked you to write an essay, giving your opinion on the following statement.
>
> *Young people spend too much time using computers.*
>
> Write your **essay** in **120-180** words in an appropriate style.

Model answer

use formal expressions

use longer sentences and connect ideas with linkers

put arguments for and against a statement in separate paragraphs

Nowadays, computer technology is an important part of everyday life for many people, especially teenagers. **However, some experts are concerned that spending too much time using computers might be dangerous.**

On the one hand, a few young people seem to become addicted to computers. They would rather play games or chat online than do anything else, which can affect their studies and social skills. Understandably, these cases are treated with great concern by teachers and parents.

On the other hand, the number of users who become addicted in this way is very small. Many young people enjoy using computers alongside other hobbies, such as sport or socialising. What is more, studies have shown that regular computer use actually has many benefits.

use examples to support your ideas

For example, it can help to develop problem-solving abilities as well as technical expertise.

do not forget to sum up your own opinion at the end!

On balance, I believe that the majority of teenagers use computers responsibly. Moreover, as computers are now essential equipment in many homes, schools and workplaces, I feel it is important that young people are encouraged to understand and enjoy this technology.

Target Writing Part 2: *essay checklist*
Make sure you:
- ☑ stay on topic - do not include irrelevant information.
- ☑ use a new paragraph for each main issue.
- ☑ begin with an introduction to the topic.
- ☑ end with a conclusion summarising your views.
- ☑ use formal language.
- ☑ add ideas with linkers of addition (e.g. *furthermore*).
- ☑ contrast ideas with linkers of contrast (e.g. *despite*).
- ☑ use the correct number of words.
- ☑ check your work for accuracy.

Useful language

Giving other people's opinions
Studies have shown that ...
It has been suggested / claimed / argued that ...
Some people are of the opinion that ...
According to ...
It is generally agreed that ...

Expressing your opinion
In my opinion, ...
I firmly / strongly believe that ...
It seems clear to me that ...
While I agree that ... , I disagree that ...

Linkers of contrast
On the one hand, ... On the other hand, ...
However, ...
Although ...
In spite of / Despite + *noun / gerund*
In spite of / Despite the fact that + *clause*

Linkers of addition
In addition, ...
Moreover, ...
Furthermore, ...
What is more, ...

Giving examples
For example, / instance, ...
..., such as ...

Reaching a conclusion
Overall, / On balance, ...
On the whole, ...
To sum up, / conclude, ...
In conclusion, ...

Part 2 – A report

Sample task

> A group of students from the USA are going to visit your town or city next month as part of an exchange visit. Their teacher has asked you to write a report about shopping in your town / city, including the following information:
> - local specialities which the students could buy as souvenirs
> - the best places for teenagers to go shopping
> - cheap cafés or restaurants where the students could eat.
>
> Write your **report** in **120-180** words in an appropriate style.

Model answer

Shopping in Kraków
simple headings can help you to organise your ideas

Introduction
we often use passive structures in formal writing

This report considers shopping in Kraków. **The local specialities are described, and suggestions are given** on the best places for teenagers to go shopping and buy food.

Local specialities

Kraków is especially famous for amber jewellery, as well as many traditional crafts. The local gingerbread biscuits would also make an inexpensive as well as attractive gift.

do not use a lot of descriptive language; be clear and factual

Places for teenagers to shop

There is a very wide choice of shopping in Kraków. However, teenagers might particularly enjoy the following:

- **Galeria Krakowska, which is an upmarket shopping mall in the city centre**
- **Hala Targowa, which is a big outdoor market where many unusual gifts are sold.**

Affordable cafés and restaurants

If students want to eat in a cheap, good-quality café or restaurant, I would strongly recommend that they avoid the main tourist centre and visit the suburbs. Alternatively, they can buy cheap snacks from many market stalls.

Conclusion

In my opinion, Kraków is a superb shopping destination. If students follow my recommendations they will enjoy an excellent trip without too much expense.

you can use numbers or bullets to highlight key points

you can summarise any recommendations in a conclusion

Target Writing Part 2: *report checklist*

Make sure you:
- ☑ think about who your reader is and what they want to know.
- ☑ begin with an introduction explaining the purpose of the report.
- ☑ address all of the points in the instructions.
- ☑ organise your ideas clearly, with headings if appropriate.
- ☑ include a personal recommendation if you are asked for one.
- ☑ use a variety of formal expressions and structures.
- ☑ use the correct number of words.
- ☑ check your work for accuracy.

Useful language

Introducing your report

This report is intended to show / discuss / outline ...
The aim / purpose of this report is to ...
In this report I will ...

Listing ideas

I would suggest the following:
... might like to consider the following:
The following are highly recommended:

1 ...	• ...
2 ... OR	• ...
3 ...	• ...

Suggesting additional ideas

Another option would be to ...
I would also suggest ...
Another point to consider is that ...
Alternatively, ...
Moreover, / Furthermore, ...
Apart from this / In addition to this, ...

Making recommendations

I would strongly / highly recommend ...
My first / second recommendation would be to ...
It would be (highly) advisable to ...
If my recommendations are followed, then ...
The best solution / ideas would seem to be ...

Part 2 – A review

Sample task

An international arts website is looking for reviews of novels for a new section called 'A Reader Writes'. You have decided to write a review of a novel you've recently read for this section. Describe the novel and say what you think about it. Would you recommend this novel to other people?

Write your **review** in **120-180** words in an appropriate style.

Model answer

make your review more interesting with personal comments

highlight key features - don't give too much detail

use adverbs and extreme adjectives for emphasis

you can add negative comments too!

I really enjoyed the film version of *The Bourne Identity* starring Matt Damon, but I thought the original novel by Robert Ludlum was even better. This book is so well-written, I didn't want to finish it!

The plot is gripping right from the start. When we first meet the lead character, Jason Bourne, he is being rescued from the sea. His identity is a mystery to everyone, including himself! Over the course of the novel we gradually find out who Bourne is, and follow him through a series of exciting adventures.

As well as a highly original plot line, the novel includes a number of fascinating characters, especially the villains! I only have one negative comment: in my view, the novel is strong on action but weaker on description. However, this is a small criticism of an otherwise excellent book.

I would highly recommend *The Bourne Identity* to anyone who enjoys action or crime stories. However, if you prefer more descriptive or romantic novels, then you should give it a miss. Personally, I can't wait to start reading the sequel!

explain your recommendation

Target Writing Part 2: review checklist

Make sure you:

- ☑ choose a book, film, restaurant, etc. that you know well!
- ☑ give basic details in the first paragraph.
- ☑ use different paragraphs for each main idea.
- ☑ finish with a positive or negative recommendation.
- ☑ give your opinions and reasons for them.
- ☑ use a lively, catchy style that will interest the reader.
- ☑ use a range of adjectives and adverbs.
- ☑ use the correct number of words.
- ☑ check your work for accuracy.

Useful language

Comparing and contrasting

... is even better than ...
... is (not) nearly as good as ...
... is twice as good as ...
... is the best I have ever seen / read / been to.
In comparison with ...
One of the strongest / weakest things about ...
In contrast, ... / On the other hand, ...

Describing a book / film / TV programme

... is set in ...
The main character is ...
It tells the story of ...
The plot / dialogue / acting / characterisation is ...

Giving an opinion

The only criticism I would make is that ...
What I really loved about ... is ...
To me, ... seemed ...
... was ... from start to finish.

+ exceptional / good value / gripping / lively / memorable / perfect / realistic / stunning / superb / well-written / -acted / -cooked etc.

− disappointing / dreadful / dull / inadequate / poor / predictable / sub-standard / unconvincing / unimaginative / uninteresting

Making a recommendation

I would highly / strongly recommend ...
I certainly wouldn't recommend ...
I strongly advise you (not) to ...
Everyone should see / do / read this ... immediately!
... is not to be missed!
You should give ... a miss!
Don't bother reading / seeing / going ...

Part 2 – A formal letter

Sample task

You have seen this advertisement in an English language magazine.

Write your **letter** of application in **120-180** words. Do not write any postal addresses.

EXPLORERS WANTED!

We are looking for people from different countries to join us on a two-week walking expedition in the rainforest in Africa. We will be raising money for a wildlife charity.

* Are you interested in animals and nature?
* Are you fit and happy to walk for long distances?
* Do you have a good level of English?

Please apply to our expedition leader, Mr Cabila, saying why you think you should be selected to join the expedition.

Model answer

always include a name if you are given one

Dear **Mr Cabila**,

use paragraphs to organise your letter

I am writing in response to your advertisement for people to participate in a walking expedition.

I would be very interested in joining this expedition as **I have always been** passionate about wildlife. **I am currently studying** environmental science at university and I hope to have a career in conservation after I graduate.

use a range of tenses and structures – not just the present simple

In my free time, I enjoy going for long walks in the countryside, and I also do cross-country running with a university sports club. I would describe my level of fitness as excellent, and I would relish the challenge of trekking through jungle conditions.

In addition to these skills, I have been studying English for many years and I hope to take my First Certificate exam in June.

*if you are applying for a job, say **why** you should be considered*

I enjoy working with other people, and I would describe myself as outgoing and sociable. For these reasons, I think I would make an excellent member of your team.

If you require any further information, please do not hesitate to contact me. I look forward to hearing from you.

indirect structures can sound more polite

Yours sincerely,

Tomo Micor

Target Writing Part 2:
formal letter checklist

Make sure you:

- ☑ use suitable opening and closing expressions.
- ☑ begin by saying why you are writing.
- ☑ address all of the points in the instructions.
- ☑ use short paragraphs for each new topic.
- ☑ use formal structures, expressions and linkers.
- ☑ end by saying what you would like to happen next (e.g. *I look forward to hearing from you*).
- ☑ use the correct number of words.
- ☑ check your work for accuracy.

Useful language

Opening and closing expressions

Dear Mr / Mrs / Miss + Name, ...
... Yours sincerely,
Dear Sir / Madam / Sir or Madam, ...
... Yours faithfully,

Giving a reason for writing

I am writing in response to your advertisement ...
I am writing to apply for / complain about / enquire about ...

Applying for a job

I have always been interested in ...
I have a lot of experience in / of ...
I consider myself to be / would describe myself as ...
I would like the opportunity to ...

Complaining

I am not satisfied with ...
... was (highly) unsatisfactory.
I am unhappy with the service I received.
I would like to request a refund.

Requesting information

I would be very grateful if you could ...
Would it be possible for you to ...?
Please could you tell me more about / send me further information about ...

Ending your letter

I look forward to hearing from you.
Thank you in advance for your help.
Thank you for considering my application.

Richmond Publishing
58 St Aldates
Oxford
OX1 1ST

ISBN: 978-84-668-0260-4

Printed by Orymu, S.A.
D.L. M-8787-2010

Publisher: Deborah Tricker
Development Editor: Imogen Wyllie
Proofreader: Soo Hamilton
Design and Layout: Lorna Heaslip, Giles Davies
Cover Design: Richmond Publishing
Photo Research: Magdalena Mayo
Audio Production: Motivation Sound Studios

Publisher acknowledgements:
The publishers would like to thank the following for their valuable participation in the review process and pilot project, which have made *Target FCE* possible.

Nilz Bustamante & colleagues (Colegio Tabancura, Chile), Richard Chapman (University of Ferrrara, Italy), Caroline Cooke (British Council Madrid, Spain), Karen Dyer (Spain), Cathy Ellis (UK), Karen Geiger (Liceo Cevolani / Liceo Ariosto, Italy), Agnieska Gugnacka-Cook (ELC Łódz´, Poland), Gabby Maguire (International House Barcelona, Spain), Mario Oliva (Instituto Chileno Británico de Cultura de Valparaíso, Chile), Jackie Partington (International House Buenos Aires, Argentina), María Elena Pignataro (Argentina), Patrick Rafferty (Mexico), Laura Renart (ISP Dr Sáenz, Universad Virtual de Quilmes, Argentina), Anila Scott-Monkhouse (Università degli Studi di Parma, Italy), Graham Tippett (Universidad Politécnica de San Luis Potosí, Mexico), Agnieszka Tyszkiewicz-Zora (ELC Łódz´, Poland), Elizabeth Wootton (International House Barcelona, Spain)

The publishers would also like to thank all those who have given their kind permission to reproduce or adapt material for this book.

Photographs:
J. Escandell.com; J. Jaime; J. V. Resino; M. Moreno; S. Enríquez; A. G. E. FOTOSTOCK; ACI AGENCIA DE FOTOGRAFÍA; CORDON PRESS/The Granger Collection, New York; EFE/SIPA-PRESS/J. Sommers, SOTHEBY'S; GETTY IMAGES SALES SPAIN/Chris Jackson, Bill Holden, Neale Clark, Maremagnum, Peter Richardson, Raymond Patrick, Steve Casimiro, Mitchell Funk, Bob Thomas; HIGHRES PRESS STOCK/AbleStock.com; ISTOCKPHOTO; MUSEUM ICONOGRAFÍA/J. Martin; SEIS X SEIS; Rex Features/Humberto Carreno, Tim Moran; Electronic Arts Inc.; MATTON-BILD; SERIDEC PHOTOIMAGENES CD; ARCHIVO SANTILLANA; BFI; PA PHOTOS; T. Morton, Vice Magazine; T. de Marco; R. Battafarano; Talkback Thames/SYCO TV; T. Hryckowian; www.cartoonstock.com; EverQuest II is a registered trademark of Sony Online Entertainment LLC in the U.S. and/or other countries. ©1999-2009 Sony Online Entertainment LLC. Used with permission from Sony Online Entertainment LLC. All rights reserved.

Texts:
p7 Extract from *The Life and Times of the Thunderbolt Kid* by Bill Bryson, published by Black Swan. Reprinted by permission of The Random House Group Ltd.
p16 *Our best friends?* Statistics used with the permission of Euromonitor International.
p43 *Throwing our future away?* Statistics on the European Space Agency reproduced with permission of swissinfo.ch (www.swissinfo.org)
p69 *Home gym?* Extract from Housework burns calories used with permission of the author, Venice Kichura.
p79 *Only a game?* Based on information from the article *It's Official, Games can make you Smarter...* reproduced with permission of UsabilityNews.
p85 ENIAC statistic reprinted with permission of The Linux Information Project (LINFO) www.linfo.org
p89 *Heartbreak Hotel* Words and music by Mae Boren Axton and Tommy Durden and Elvis Presley © 1956, reproduced by permission of EMI Harmonies Ltd, London W8 5SW
p89 *Lay all your love on me* Words and music by Benny Andersson and Björn Ulvaeus © 1980, Bocu Music Ltd, London W1H 2QF; used by permission
p89 *Three Little Birds* Words & Music by Bob Marley. © Copyright 1977 Blue Mountain Music Limited. All Rights Reserved. International Copyright Secured. Used by permission of Music Sales Limited.
p91 *The secret of happiness The Happy Planet Index* was developed by nef (the new economics foundation) www.neweconomics.org
p100 *Scream Therapy* Reprinted with permission of Thorpe Park
p129 *Shakespearean Rap* Based on information from the article Hip Hop Education 101 published by Vibe Lifestyle Network LLC at VIBE.com

Illustrations:
Krister Flodin, Scott Garrett, Sarah Goodreau, Phil Hackett, Katie Mac, Peter Mac, Judy Stevens